WHY AMERICA NEEDS TO REPENT

For the Kingdom of God is at Hand

DWANE MASSENBURG

WESTBOW
PRESS®
A DIVISION OF THOMAS NELSON
& ZONDERVAN

Copyright © 2022 Dwane Massenburg.

All rights reserved. No part of this book may be used or reproduced by any means, graphic, electronic, or mechanical, including photocopying, recording, taping or by any information storage retrieval system without the written permission of the author except in the case of brief quotations embodied in critical articles and reviews.

This book is a work of non-fiction. Unless otherwise noted, the author and the publisher make no explicit guarantees as to the accuracy of the information contained in this book.

WestBow Press books may be ordered through booksellers or by contacting:

WestBow Press
A Division of Thomas Nelson & Zondervan
1663 Liberty Drive
Bloomington, IN 47403
www.westbowpress.com
844-714-3454

Because of the dynamic nature of the Internet, any web addresses or links contained in this book may have changed since publication and may no longer be valid. The views expressed in this work are solely those of the author and do not necessarily reflect the views of the publisher, and the publisher hereby disclaims any responsibility for them.

Unless marked otherwise, all Scripture quotations are taken from the New King James Version®. Copyright © 1982 by Thomas Nelson. Used by permission. All rights reserved.

Scripture quotations marked KJV are taken from the King James Version.

ISBN: 978-1-6642-5431-2 (sc)
ISBN: 978-1-6642-5432-9 (hc)
ISBN: 978-1-6642-5433-6 (e)

Library of Congress Control Number: 2022901904

Print information available on the last page.

WestBow Press rev. date: 02/02/2022

Reader's Prayer: Beginning

> Dear Lord,
>
> Your Bible is my main source of information. I pray that as I read this book about repentance that I weigh it against what I have been taught in Your word via reading, study, the preached word, and Your Holy Spirit. I thank you for the opportunity to take an honest reflective look at what You have said, what I have received, and how I have responded.
>
> Amen.

About the Author

Pastor Dwane Massenburg has a degree in Mechanical Engineering from Georgia Tech. He has a master of divinity degree from Virginia Union University's Samuel Dewitt Proctor School of Theology. Blessed to be married to his high school sweetheart and wonderful wife for over forty years, they have three wonderful grown children. Two of their children are married with great spouses. The two married children have blessed him with seven beautiful and energetic grandchildren.

The author was introduced to God in a small Baptist church in southeast Virginia. After being born again while attending Georgia Tech, he has held just about every position there is to hold in the Baptist church. The positions include being a choir member, deacon, trustee, youth minister, treasurer, Young Entrepreneurs Club founder, Sunday school superintendent, Marriage Ministry chairperson, associate pastor, and a senior pastor for two congregations.

Pastor Massenburg was ordained as a deacon at Saint James Baptist Church in Waynesboro, Virginia. The powerful Reverend Doctor Wesley K. McLaughlin in Petersburg, Virginia, licensed and ordained him to preach. The two congregations where God called him to be senior pastor were Oak Grove Baptist Church in Kenbridge, Virginia, and Trinity Baptist Church in Danville, Virginia. He has visited malls and walked the streets in several cities, praying and evangelizing. He has been a guest speaker in several states across the country.

Currently Pastor Massenburg is pastoring Christians United Congregation, (www.christiansunitedcongregation.org). It is a ministry designed to get all Christians to work together, regardless of which congregation they belong to. For daily prayers of strength, hope, encouragement, love and teaching email your request to: 1warriorministry@gmail.com.

Have the conversation. This book can be used for Bible Study. To get the details about an assisted Zoom or unassisted Bible Study for your family or congregation send your email request to: 1warriorministry@gmail.com. An associated workbook is available.

Contents

Chapter 1	America	1
Chapter 2	I Repent for Not Caring Enough to Read the Whole Bible for Myself	23
Chapter 3	I Repent for Being Covetous	31
Chapter 4	I Repent for Not Practicing True Love	41
Chapter 5	I Repent for Not Watching	51
Chapter 6	I Repent for Sometimes Acting Like There Are Alternatives to God	59
Chapter 7	I Repent for Not Asking	69
Chapter 8	I Repent for Not Acknowledging the Fruits of the Spirit Within Me	79
Chapter 9	I Repent for Being So Selfish that I Forget the Plight of the Poor	89
Chapter 10	I Repent for Using God Like a Vending Machine	99
Chapter 11	I Repent for Misusing and Abusing My Fellow Man and Fellow Woman	109
Chapter 12	I Repent for Allowing Racism to Continue in My Presence	119
Chapter 13	I Repent for Accepting Promiscuity and Adultery in Our Society	137
Chapter 14	I Repent for Failing to Call Sin, Sin	155
Chapter 15	I Repent for Lying	165
Chapter 16	I Repent for Accepting the LGBTQ Lifestyle as a God-Approved Way of Life	173
Chapter 17	I Repent for Not Speaking Up about Sin and Evil	185
Chapter 18	I Repent for Clergy: Pastor, Bishop, Priest, Prophet, Evangelist, and Elder Abuse	193

Chapter 19	I Repent for Ignoring What Nature Teaches Us	203
Chapter 20	I Repent for Not Parenting	211
Chapter 21	I Repent for Worldliness—Falling for the Hype	219
Chapter 22	I Repent for Not Really Knowing What Jesus Did for Me	229
Chapter 23	I Repent for Trying to Win at All Cost	237
Chapter 24	I Repent for Trying to Find Answers in All the Wrong Places	245
Chapter 25	I Repent for Giving Lip Service to My Belief, Work, and Faith in God	255
Chapter 26	I Repent for Believing I Serve a One-Dimensional God	265
Chapter 27	I Repent for Not Setting the Atmosphere	275
Chapter 28	I Repent for Arguing and Debating	283
Chapter 29	I Repent for Not Giving Strong Support for the Disadvantaged and Persecuted	291
Chapter 30	I Repent for Not Thanking and Appreciating God for My Trials and Tribulations	301
Chapter 31	I Repent for Child Abuse and Neglect	309
Chapter 32	I Repent for Not Saying No	317
Chapter 33	I Repent for Not Believing in the Power of God	325
Chapter 34	I Repent for Drinking, Drugging, and Getting High	333
Chapter 35	I Repent for Not Honoring Marriage	341
Chapter 36	I Repent for Not Honoring the Sabbath Day	349
Chapter 37	I Repent for Wanting to Be Rich and Famous at All Cost	357
Chapter 38	I Repent for Not Giving Like I Should	365
Chapter 39	I Repent for Not Forgiving Properly	373
Chapter 40	I Repent for Celebrating Sex Appeal, Sexuality, and Sexiness Outside of Marriage	381
Chapter 41	I Repent for Not Believing in the Power of Prayer	389
Chapter 42	Conclusion: I Repent Because God Said So	397

Thanks/Acknowledgments

First, thank God for all He has done in my life to allow me to write this book. Looking back, I appreciate every activity, workplace, situation, congregation, friend, and enemy God has allowed me to meet, participate in, or endure. I do not believe there is one part of the fabric that could be torn away that would still allow me to arrive where God has brought me. To God be the glory.

Second, I must thank my wife, Sophia Massenburg, who has endured with me since high school. We were twenty-one when we got married. Neither she nor I, nor our marriage, has been perfect, though some have said we look that way from the outside. She has been as close to perfect as a wife can be. I love her with all my heart. Her gift in life has been to allow me to follow God. Our life has been a great journey. There have been a few great hills and a few deep valleys. I thank her for sticking with me. We have both had to sacrifice for me to deliver this work from God. We both have had to live through the journey that allowed the Holy Spirit to reveal this work to me. Together we are doing all that we can for the kingdom of God. Thank you, darling, for letting the Lord lead you to be a great wife. Also, thank you for your editing assistance.

Third, I must acknowledge my parents, Herbert and Virginia Massenburg. My father was a powerful, strong, hardworking best friend of mine. He took the time to take me fishing and hunting. He was the sole breadwinner for our household. My mother was a homemaker and the spiritual leader of the family. We went to church as a family, but it was my mother who made sure I participated in plays and the church choir. She also took me to afternoon church services, which assured I would be listening to more sermons. Therefore, I must give her credit for allowing the love of God to grow in me. My father is deceased now, but I must give both of my parents credit for being superparents.

Next, I would like to thank my pastor, Reverend Dr. Wesley K. McLaughlin. Pastor McLaughlin (Pastor Mac), has pastored Mount Olivet Baptist Church, in Petersburg, Virginia, for over thirty-five years. He has done a marvelous job. He is an awesome expositor of the word of God. People come from all over to hear him preach. God used Pastor Mac to encourage me. His preaching work ethic has inspired me. Pastor Mac licensed and ordained me (along with over fifty other ministers), to be a preacher of the gospel of Jesus Christ. Thanks for all you have done in my life.

Thank you, Reverend Jacquelyn Jones for your editing assistance and for helping to develop the Bible study workbook for this work. You are a great worker in the kingdom of God.

Finally, I would like to thank all those encouragers who have witnessed my life unfold, including those who are members of Christians United and the other churches I have been blessed to pastor. Many of you have continued to uplift me along the way. You know who you are. I cannot name names, but I want you to know that I love you and appreciate you, my Christian brothers and sisters.

Preface

There are many different religions in the world. Some of the religions allow for belief in more than one god (polytheistic), versus Christianity, which is monotheistic. Atheists and agnostics today form a large group of nonreligious believers in America. Everyone in the world has the right to make up their own mind. This book is based on Christianity. There are a few other things you should know about the book in your hands before proceeding.

Never Compare

People who don't read this preface are going to read maybe two or three lessons in this book and put it down. They will say to themselves, "Who does this author think that he is?" This author must think he is "Mr. Perfect." However, let me say to the world, loud and clear, when Jesus died on the cross, my sins were a part of what put Him on that cross. My sins played a part in the mocking, and scourging, and being spat on, and the nail(s) in His left hand, and the nail(s) in His right hand, and the nail(s) in His feet. I am very far from perfect, and the closer I have gotten to my Lord, the more I realize what Isaiah meant when he said:

> But we are all as an unclean thing, and all our righteousnesses are as filthy rags; and we all do fade as a leaf; and our iniquities, like the wind, have taken us away. (Isaiah 64:6 KJV)

So please read on, my brothers and sisters. This book captures "just a few" of the many of our shortcomings before Almighty God. I am included. I was learning as I was putting these chapters together. Learn from Him. Never compare yourself to somebody else. Jesus Christ is the only person we should ever compare ourselves to. Everyone else will fall short and disappoint you. We are all individuals before God. Make this book personal. That is the way it was meant to be.

The Bible Is the Standard

Everyone has a standard or foundation from which they make decisions and navigate through this life. Some people in the world prefer inches and yards to measure length, while others prefer the metric system, which uses decimeters and meters to measure the same length. To be clear, this book is based on Jesus Christ as Lord and Savior. This book is written based on Christian beliefs. It is based on the Five Solae of the Protestant Reformation. Jesus Christ is *Solus Christus* (salvation is by faith in Christ alone). The Christian Bible is *Sola Scriptura* (Christian scriptures are the sole source of authority for Christian faith and practice). Christian justification for salvation is *Sola fide* (Christians are justified by faith alone). Christians earn salvation by *Sola gratia*, (Christian salvation comes by divine grace). This book is written for *Soli Deo Gloria*, (Glory to God alone).[1]

The Entire Bible Is Significant and Will Be Used—Old and New Testament

The God of Abraham, Isaac, and Jacob is referenced thirty-three times from Genesis to Acts. Often, some people want to separate the Bible and say this does not apply or that does not apply because that was Old Testament. Acts 3:13 ties Jesus Christ to God the Father of the Old Testament, who is the God of Abraham, Isaac, and Jacob.

> The God of Abraham, and of Isaac, and of Jacob, the God of our fathers, hath glorified his Son Jesus; whom

ye delivered up, and denied him in the presence of Pilate, when he was determined to let him go. (Acts 3:13 KJV)

Jesus Christ Himself references the Old Testament many times. A few examples are when He was taken into the wilderness after He was baptized by John (Matthew 3), during His sermon on the Mount (Matthew 5–7), and when He threw the money changers out of the temple in Jerusalem (Mark 11:15–17). Some want to dismiss things in the Old testament. Whenever the Bible is read, the reader should pray for the correct understanding and the correct interpretation of what is read. The entire Bible is worthy.

This Book Is Very Conservative

We are all a product of the generation and cultures we are living in. Most generation "Z" (born 1995 to 2015) young people have no clue what it was like to have to go to a particular location to make a phone call. On the other hand, the "Greatest Generation," (born between 1910 and 1924), were very aware of how to pinch pennies because they lived through the repercussions of the Great Depression and fought during World War II. While writing this book I was praying all the time and fasting much of the time. I was praying that God would allow me to write this book based on how the translation was initially inspired by God. The inspired messages from God then had to go through spoken word translations, different cultures, different genres, and finally written word translations that result in the Bibles we have today. Words have different meanings based on the generation in which they are spoken. Obviously, cultures affect our interpretation of a translated word. Jesus walked the earth and lived during a time when fishing and shepherding were major professions. Therefore, this book is going to seem very conservative, compared to most of today's American standards. My belief is that, through all the generations, culture changes, and translations, it is still quite plausible that the same God who created galaxies, black holes, planets, rivers, elephants, eagles, spiders, mosquitos, and this flesh of mine could also orchestrate who and what made it through history to wind up in my Bible in the twenty-first century. I believe my great God knew exactly what words he wanted to come to me. Some psychologists, historians, or other organizations may disagree. However, the Bible is the only authority for this book.

There are some things in here your bishop, pastor, or clergy has wanted to say boldly, but they did not dare do it for fear of hurting delicate feelings. Then the person with hurt feelings would run off with half the congregation, (brothers, sisters, aunties, and cousins of the disgruntled), after badmouthing the pastor. The pastor has not wanted to split the church, even though the truth needed to be told. So here it is. God sent it just for you.

Who Should Read This Book?

People who just got baptized last week should read this book. People who are fasting should read this book. People who have been "on the battlefield" for a long time should read this book. Perhaps God wants to address a particular area in your life that He wants to set straight before He can allow you to move to a higher level. People who are practicing Lent should read this book. Perhaps there is something in here that you should give up for Lent. People who just want to have a closer relationship with God should read this book.

People who do not know God and are skeptical about Jesus and the Bible can read this book to understand certain topics, but truthfully, I always recommend anyone who does not know much at all about God and the Bible should stick to reading the Bible first before reading different authors' opinions about what the Bible says. A sincere effort has been made to use the words of the Bible itself to reach conclusions in this book.

How Should One Read This Book?

Most authors want their books to be so enticing that people start reading them and cannot put them down. The intrigue is so great, and the suspense is so enticing that you feel as though you cannot wait to get to the end, to see what happens. However, this is a different type of book. The Bible is offered as literature at many schools. That is both good and bad. It is good for at least providing exposure to God's word. However, it is bad if it is not explained by the instructor that the Bible was written to be read as more than literature. It was written to be read as the inspired word of God. The Bible was written to introduce and provide vivid details about a God who loves humanity so dearly that He wants us to have a small understanding of who He is. You will see that in this book I will constantly quote scripture. While reading this book I hope you continuously take the time to refer to some of these scriptures in the Bible, for yourself. This is designed to be a thought-provoking book. It is designed for the reader to dwell on each chapter one by one, to seek God for your own thoughts about it, to pray about it, to repent if you need to, and then to proceed to the next chapter. Go as fast or as slow as you need to. Everyone in this world has fallen short of what God desires of us. The following text from Paul to the Romans points this out.

> Therefore by the deeds of the law there shall no flesh be justified in his sight: for by the law is the knowledge of sin. But now the righteousness of God without the law is manifested, being witnessed by the law and the prophets; Even the righteousness of God which is by faith of Jesus Christ unto all and upon all them that believe: for there is no difference: For all have sinned, and come short of the glory of God. (Romans 3:20–23 KJV)

Some chapters may be easy for you to move through. Some chapters should cause a lot of introspection if you are being true to yourself and to God, as you read. So, however you wound up taking the time to read these words, could this be another time when God is reaching out to you? Read this book with care. It may cause you to make a change in your life.

This book may cause you to pull away from God, in avoidance or, get closer to God, in humility (as it did for the author as I was writing). Don't just accept what is written in this book; sounds like heresy for an author to say, but I welcome it. Decide for yourself and deal with God on your own terms. I would love for this book to be read, perhaps one chapter per day or week. That way it can be absorbed. Dwell on it, question it, pray about it, and seek His face. Tear these topics apart. Pray and fast and ask God to reveal the truth about each topic to you. Consider Jesus. Consider His love, and how everything in the Bible is God reaching out to His creation, saying, "I am trying to explain who I am, how you got here, and how much I love you." Follow your love. When your love is in parallel with God's love, you will always be led to the right answer, which will lead you to the right direction. Let the Holy Spirit guide you. I pray God's will is done in your life. When used along with the workbook, you will have an opportunity to consider each lesson in terms of, "What do I personally need to change?"

Illustrations

The illustrations in this book are not meant to insult or belittle anyone's intelligence. They are for clarity, appreciating that there are different types of learners. The goal is for everyone reading this book to have a decision to make with God, not a decision about what was meant by the author.

Introduction

While pastoring Trinity Baptist in Danville, Virginia, during March one year, God inspired me to do "Thirty-One Days of Repentance." Each day in March that year, I was on the radio and social media, sharing thirty-one different thirty-second commercial topics the Holy Spirit laid on my heart that we as Christians need to take a closer and more serious look at if we are truly trying to follow the word of God. So often, we "church folk" like to find particular issues that fit our beliefs so we can pounce on someone else so they can get it right. We use a highlighter to mark these texts in our Bibles because they are important to us. I call these "Highlighter Christians." Basically, we pick and choose other people's faults while ignoring our own. What about when God is pointing His finger directly at us, though? Are we willing to have something pointed out to us in the Bible and make a change in our own lives? If the truth be known, there are enough topics in the Bible to make us all remain humble. We have all sinned and not lived up to what God wants us to be. I believe that no one in America can read this book and not be confronted with a decision to change, to get closer to God. Please consider this book to be just one letter in the English alphabet or one leaf on a tree. We need to do so much to enhance our relationship with God. This book will begin the conversation.

Our American Western culture is very far away from the
Christian lifestyle and behavior God has commanded in the Bible.
We are as far as night is from day.
We are as far as East is from West.

God and Humanity

Let's go back in time. Imagine we are living in year 31 (or whenever Jesus was just starting His ministry), in the city of Jerusalem. Dirt houses, camels, and desert sand are the norm. There are no sports, movies, soap operas, or game shows to watch on television. In fact, there is no such thing as a television. Life is lived without paved roads, vehicles, electricity, sewing machines, printed books, inside plumbing, books, telephones, radios, computers, dentists, doctors' offices, or hospitals. Go back to a time when there was no 911 emergency number, or fireman, or airplanes. Much of the history we are aware of has not even entered anyone's mind. Now, imagine that Jesus Christ is giving His Sermon on the Mount (Matthew 5–7), and He was already correcting many of the thoughts and habits of the people of the day. You heard "this," but I say "that." Humanity was already off track in their beliefs about major fundamental aspects of life.

Now fast-forward to our American culture today. The hustle and bustle of our daily lives—getting here and there to this appointment and that appointment—is mind-boggling. Making sure we see a certain thing on television broadcast from hundreds of miles away is a priority. Stopping by the store or fast-food restaurant to pick up dinner while making a cell phone call to an aunt living two states away seems normal. Life is very different than it was in the year 31.

Now compare the two paragraphs. Technology has changed, but we are still primarily the same human beings that could have lived three centuries ago. The earth is still basically the same. Yes, technology, communication, and the speed of travel have changed, but our relationship and relativity to God and the universe have not changed. Looking through the eyes of God, it is easy to see how far we are from what He intended. This book goes back and looks at how God's word would apply if it were delivered at the Sermon on the Mount today, on the steps of the Lincoln Monument. How would He make it clear that we are not doing what the Bible says we should be doing? Throughout the Bible is a common theme—repent. What does that mean? Be more specific, God. What do we need to repent for? That is the question this book answers. This book is designed to start the conversation on several specific topics that, according to the Bible, we need to change in our culture.

God and America

The United States of America has grown into a great and powerful country, especially prominent since the twentieth century began. Industrialization and two world wars positioned America to be a force throughout the world. Now, in the twenty-first century, even though the world is changing quickly, America is still thought of by many around the world as the most powerful economically and militarily. However, if American "might" has been our strength, it may also be a part of our spiritual weakness. Biblically, throughout history, there is a pattern of people being blessed by God and then forgetting about God.

Blessed by God	Forgot about God
Adam and Eve in the Garden of Eden	They chose to disobey God and listened to Satan through a serpent (Genesis 2–3).
Hebrews	They decided being led by God was not good enough, so they wanted a king like other nations (1 Samuel 8).
Northern and Southern Kingdoms after Solomon's death	They disobeyed God, and both kingdoms were taken into captivity (2 Kings 15–25).
Followers of Jesus	Many turned away after Jesus confronted them with being the Son of God (Matthew 6:65–68).

What will history say about the United States of America fifty years from now? What will they say three hundred years from now? Will the infighting caused by sin take us down? What kind of America will be left for your children? Is America too big and powerful to ever fail? How can we expect to be blessed if we continue to turn our backs on God? Will the spiritual history books say "America forgot about God?"

Nothing Starts until You Repent

Nothing starts until you repent. Doing things in order matters. Like eating a plain hot dog and then eating a spoonful of mustard. You did not have a hot dog "with" mustard. You had a hot dog "and" mustard. A hot dog with mustard is heavenly, the band plays, the birds sing, and everything is right in the world. On the other hand, a hot dog "and" mustard eaten separately is not complete and could be considered "yucky," as my four-year-old granddaughter says. Of course, repentance is much more serious than mustard on a hot dog, and this example is not meant to trivialize it. This example is only proposed to point out that some things need to happen in order. There are some things that should be done first, and then second, and so on. In other words, apply the mustard first, then eat the hot dog. Likewise, in God's world repentance comes first. Repent to God first, then grow your relationship with Him. One must accept that a breech has been made in our relationship with God. God demonstrates this example by sending John the Baptist to preach repentance prior to Jesus showing up on the scene.

Repent For What?

> Therefore say to the house of Israel, thus says the Lord God: "Repent, turn away from your idols, and turn your faces away from all your abominations. For anyone of the house of Israel, or of the strangers who dwell in Israel, who separates himself from Me and sets up his idols in his heart, and puts before him what causes him to stumble into iniquity, then comes to a prophet to inquire of him concerning Me, I the Lord will answer him by Myself. I will set My face against that man and make him a sign and a proverb, and I will cut him off from the midst of My people. Then you shall know that I am the Lord." (Ezekiel 14:6–8 NKJV)

> But if a wicked man turns from all his sins which he has committed, keeps all My statutes, and does what is lawful and right, he shall surely live; he shall not die. None of the transgressions which he has committed shall

be remembered against him; because of the righteousness which he has done, he shall live. (Ezekiel 18:21–22 NKJV)

In those days John the Baptist came preaching in the wilderness of Judea, and saying, "Repent, for the kingdom of heaven is at hand!" (Matthew 3:1–2 NKJV)

From that time Jesus began to preach and to say, "Repent, for the kingdom of heaven is at hand." (Matthew 4:17 NKJV)

There were present at that season some who told Him about the Galileans whose blood Pilate had mingled with their sacrifices. And Jesus answered and said to them, "Do you suppose that these Galileans were worse sinners than all other Galileans, because they suffered such things? I tell you, no; but unless you repent you will all likewise perish." Or those eighteen on whom the tower in Siloam fell and killed them, do you think that they were worse sinners than all other men who dwelt in Jerusalem? I tell you, no; but unless you repent you will all likewise perish." (Luke 13:1–5 NKJV)

Jesus answered and said to them, "Those who are well have no need of a physician, but those who are sick. I have not come to call the righteous, but sinners, to repentance." (Luke 5:31–32 NKJV)

Then Peter said to them, "Repent, and let every one of you be baptized in the name of Jesus Christ for the remission of sins; and you shall receive the gift of the Holy Spirit. For the promise is to you and to your children, and to all who are afar off, as many as the Lord our God will call." (Acts 2:38–39 NKJV)

Repent therefore and be converted, that your sins may be blotted out, so that times of refreshing may come from the presence of the Lord. (Acts 3:19 NKJV)

> And a servant of the Lord must not quarrel but be gentle all, able to teach, patient, in humility correcting those who are in opposition, if God perhaps will grant them repentance, so that they may know the truth, and that they may come to their senses and escape the snare of the devil, having been taken captive by him to do his will. (2 Timothy 2:24–26 NKJV)

Why does America need to repent and come back to God? We need to repent because the wording of our most precious government documents reveal that God was in the hearts of our Founding Fathers. We need to repent because we work better together with God, and understanding the love of God is the absolute best way to get us to do that. We need to repent because nothing else will work.

I told my children when they became young adults that the difference in their situations now versus when they were toddlers is like when we took them to the beach when they were young. When they were young, I would monitor, watch, and not allow them to go out too far into the waves. I knew how powerful the waves could be on their small bodies. That was my job as their parent. Now, however, as adults, when they go to the ocean, even if I am on the trip with them, they may go out into the waves too far for my arms to reach. Only God can save them now.

Similarly, America is beyond the best ideas of any person. America cannot save itself from most tragedies happening in our society by more laws, training, policies, procedures, or feel-good emotional experiences. We are way too far from how God intended for us to live in peace and harmony with everything around us. Those things are only Band-Aids to the root cause of what is happening. Sin is the real root cause. Not loving Jesus and our fellow humans is the problem. We are way too far out in the ocean to try anything else. Anything we try other than God is prolonging the agony and wasting time.

Chapter 1

AMERICA

America needs to repent for the kingdom of God is at hand. This is a bold statement to make when we consider ourselves to be the most powerful nation on earth. The portion of the earth we call America is somewhat hard to define. It depends on one's perspective. What we do know is that Christianity is the largest religion in America. So how do we grapple with America being a predominately Christian nation in the twenty-first century? We are many years from when Jesus walked the earth as a man. Are Christians allowed to be different now? Has God changed His mind about what it means to be a Christian? These questions deserve answers. We will consider America on the world stage. We will consider what repentance means and various reasons why America should repent. Several biblical examples of repentance are shared.

America

Exactly what is America? What is this country we call home? We call ourselves the USA, the "land of the free and home of the brave." When we say America, are we discussing the nearly 1.9 billion acres of landmass that make up the country? Is America only a conglomerate of fifty states and a few territories? Is it just a collection of the almost 330 million people who populate the land? In our generation, most Americans believe that our country is a world leader—the greatest country on earth. We currently believe that we are the most dominant political, military, and economic force on the planet. This country with a flag sometimes referred to as "Old Glory" has many aspects by which one could seek to define what is meant when someone says, "America."

For the purposes of this book, America refers to all citizens of the country who are old enough to know right from wrong based on biblical teachings. Also, for the purposes of this book, America refers to all Christians, or non-Christians if they are considering a belief in Jesus Christ, regardless of their denomination, convention, or orthodoxy. All who believe that Jesus Christ is the Son of God regardless of race or ethnicity are included.

- **Christians in America**

"Christianity is the most prevalent religion in America," according to a Pew Research study. In 2014, a survey was done that said 70.6 percent of Americans called themselves Christians.[2]

- **America to God**

> Behold, the nations are as a drop of a bucket, and are counted as the small dust of the balance: behold, he taketh up the isles as a very little thing. And Lebanon is not sufficient to burn, nor the beasts thereof sufficient for a burnt offering. All nations before him are as nothing; and they are counted to him less than nothing, and vanity. (Isaiah 40:15–17 KJV)

The Bible compares heaven to where God runs His kingdom. It says a planet the size of Earth is simply big enough for Him to rest His feet. That would make one nation very small and insignificant indeed. Per God's laws, America is not a perfect place to live. The perfect place has not existed since Adam and Eve were in the Garden of Eden. America, therefore, needs to swallow its pride and humble itself before God.

Repentance

- **Religion and Religious Activity Versus Christianity**

Take a snapshot of America today—a picture of how we are living, communicating, working, worshipping, and relaxing. Would the snapshot be a worthy example of how Christians should live according to the Bible? What if we took the snapshot fifty years ago? One hundred years ago? Two hundred years ago? The truth is that no snapshot available of any civilization, culture, nation, or people at any time would be an accurate example of how Christians should live. Humanity has failed when it comes to living sin free and loving one another. The only standard to live by is the example of Jesus Christ and the Bible. Therefore, every human being on the planet needs to repent.

Religion and religious activity do not make us worthy of salvation. They also do not mean that a person is beyond repentance. No one is perfect in God's eyes.

- **Repent Definition:** *Metanoeo*

Repentance is something that happens in the heart. People can fake repentance. They can act like things are different. They can act like they want to go in a different direction. However, true repentance happens on the inside.

> Therefore also now, saith the LORD, turn ye even to me with all your heart, and with fasting, and with weeping, and with mourning: And rend your heart, and not your garments, and turn unto the LORD your God: for he is gracious and merciful, slow to anger, and of great kindness, and repenteth him of the evil. (Joel 2:12–13 KJV)

The word in Old Testament Hebrew is *nacham*[3] meaning to sigh, to breathe strongly, to be sorry (in a favorable sense), to pity, to comfort. Nacham is translated as "to repent" forty-one times and "to comfort" fifty-seven times in the Old Testament. "To repent" means to make a strong turning to a new course of action. The word *repent* throughout most of the Old Testament refers to God having pity on humanity and deciding on a new course of action when or if we relent from our sinful ways.[4]

The New Testament Greek word for *repent* is the word referred to in this book.

> The word in Greek is "*metanoeo*,"[5] and means to perceive afterward. *(Meta*, "after," implying "change," *noeo*, "to perceive"; *nous*, "the mind, the seat of moral reflection"). The three steps found in metanoeo are 1. New knowledge, 2. Regret for the previous course, displeasure with self, 3. a change of action, (more than emotional). Metanoeo refers to a change of choice.[6]

We Americans need to consider our collective behavior and see if it is leading to our desired results. Like any great parent, God has only told us to do and behave in ways that are good for us. We need to perceive after looking back at our results and see if we are doing things God's way.

- **Repent why? God Is Serious**

Most Bible scholars, theologians, and churchgoers have a favorite scripture or text in the Bible. Some may also have two, three, or several scriptures that they cling to for support and encouragement. This comes in lieu of constantly reading and rereading the Bible while trying to glean every ounce of wisdom, knowledge, and spirituality from every word in the entire book. There are some parts of the Bible that some people want to ignore. The following text may be one of those texts.

> Enquire, I pray thee, of the LORD for us; for Nebuchadrezzar king of Babylon maketh war against us; if so be that the LORD will deal with us according to all his wondrous works, that he may go up from us. Then said Jeremiah unto them, Thus shall ye say to Zedekiah: Thus saith the LORD God of Israel; Behold, I will turn back the weapons of war that are in your hands, wherewith ye fight against

the king of Babylon, and against the Chaldeans, which besiege you without the walls, and I will assemble them into the midst of this city. And I myself will fight against you with an outstretched hand and with a strong arm, even in anger, and in fury, and in great wrath. And I will smite the inhabitants of this city, both man and beast: they shall die of a great pestilence. And afterward, saith the Lord, I will deliver Zedekiah king of Judah, and his servants, and the people, and such as are left in this city from the pestilence, from the sword, and from the famine, into the hand of Nebuchadrezzar king of Babylon, and into the hand of their enemies, and into the hand of those that seek their life: and he shall smite them with the edge of the sword; he shall not spare them, neither have pity, nor have mercy. And unto this people thou shalt say, Thus saith the Lord; Behold, I set before you the way of life, and the way of death. He that abideth in this city shall die by the sword, and by the famine, and by the pestilence: but he that goeth out, and falleth to the Chaldeans that besiege you, he shall live, and his life shall be unto him for a prey. For I have set my face against this city for evil, and not for good, saith the Lord: it shall be given into the hand of the king of Babylon, and he shall burn it with fire. (Jeremiah 21:2–10 KJV)

Jeremiah was a prophet of God, but his message was stern and forthright. He let King Zedekiah know that he and the nation of Judah were about to go down in a big way. Anybody left was going to be taken captive and shown no mercy. That was a horrible but historically true message. In the fifth verse of Jeremiah, it is said that God Himself will be against Judah. That is very sad, but they refused to turn back to God and live accordingly. God does not play. He is long-suffering and kind, like any good parent, but He is not playing with nations that continuously refuse to listen. Verse 8 is a summary of this entire text. The choice is ours. Life or death is totally in our hands. We can choose now, or we will have to choose later, but we shall surely choose.

- **Repent why? Relatively Speaking**

Taking the preceding section into account, it is believed that without repentance, America's sinful behavior will doom the country to failure. Without God, this country will self-implode like many of the other nations, empires, and kingdoms that have risen to power and then fallen over time. America is not the first dominant world leader.

Different empires have been dominant throughout world history.[7]

Empire	Approximate Years of Dominance
Egyptians	900
Assyrians	550
Persians	350
Greeks	400
Romans	700
Mongolians	250
England	250
France	150
Russia	TBD
United States	TBD
China	TBD

Russia, China, and the United States are only recent dominant countries in the history of the world. How long will they last? How long will they be dominant? America did not really become a standout on the world stage until perhaps after World War I. That would mean America as a world power has only been on the scene for a just over one hundred years. The country has existed longer than that, but as a world power, we are very young. Too much pride can make anyone think they are more than they are. America is a great country but relative to other dominant world empires throughout history, these numbers say we are just one of many. America is a blessed land, but we have not outgrown God. America is a blessed land, but we truly need God on our side.

> Except the LORD build the house, they labour in vain that build it: except the LORD keep the city, the watchman waketh but in vain. It is vain for you to rise up early, to sit up late, to eat the bread of sorrows: for so he giveth his beloved sleep. (Psalm 127:1–2 KJV)

This text says that America, (which was founded by many godly principles), still needs God. God has built and blessed our country. It is vain for us to sit around now, as if we alone can protect and preserve it without God. That is why the verse says the work of the watchman is vain. Without God, America will fall, just like every other empire that has influenced the world. No matter how much worry, loss of sleep, programs, policies, and procedures we try to come up with; without God on our side, America is vulnerable.

- **Repent why? Israel and America**

The nation of Israel is special to God. That is the nation God chose to help reveal Himself to humanity. We can see the depths of God's love, His patience, His tolerance, and His chastisement by studying how God has treated Israel.

> For thou art an holy people unto the LORD thy God: the LORD thy God hath chosen thee to be a special people unto himself, above all people that are upon the face of the earth. The LORD did not set his love upon you, nor choose you, because ye were more in number than any people; for ye were the fewest of all people: But because the LORD loved you, and because he would keep the oath which he had sworn unto your fathers, hath the LORD brought you out with a mighty hand, and redeemed you out of the house of bondmen, from the hand of Pharaoh king of Egypt. Know therefore that the LORD thy God, he is God, the faithful God, which keepeth covenant and mercy with them that love him and keep his commandments to a thousand generations. (Deuteronomy 7:6–9 KJV)

God loves Israel, but He also allowed them to go into bondage because they would not listen. The question for us is, if God would allow His chosen nation to go into bondage, what does that mean for America? We should not test God's patience.

- **Repent why? Love**

America has been very good to my immediate family. My parents were blessed in this country to find their way with only high school educations. My father retired from the army and retired two other times. He was a hard worker, bought land, and lived a happy, prosperous life. My mother worked odd jobs from time to time but was mostly a wonderful housewife who reared two children. My only sister is a successful retired school teacher who raised two beautiful daughters. My wife and I have three children and currently seven grandchildren. My three children are gainfully employed now and have never been without a means to take care of themselves.

Yes, God has been good to us. As a Christian, that is why more than anything, America needs to repent. I want my children and grandchildren to be able to continue to enjoy the same type of fulfilling, blessed life that I have been able to enjoy. I want them to be able to enjoy nice things, have peace and fulfillment, and have an opportunity to get to know God as I have. I want them to have this opportunity because I love them. I want them to feel the joy God has allowed me to have in my heart. For that to happen, all Americans have to find a balance and peace that allows us all to live together peacefully. Brothers learning to love brothers and sisters learning to love sisters is the only way all the riches of this life can be experienced. Furthermore, the only way this kind of love can be ubiquitous in the land is for all of us to know and understand the definition of love via Jesus Christ.

- **Repent why? Driven by our American Culture**

Who decides most of the styles of clothes the average person wears today? Is it you or the fashion designers? Who decides what you are going to see in any movie or television show? Is it you or the producer? Who decides how many sex scenes are in the commercials you watched last week? Is it you or the advertising agencies? It is eminent that Christians repent and begin to speak up about what is going on in our society because we are being bullied into acceptance of many things by a few people who may have un-Christian morals.

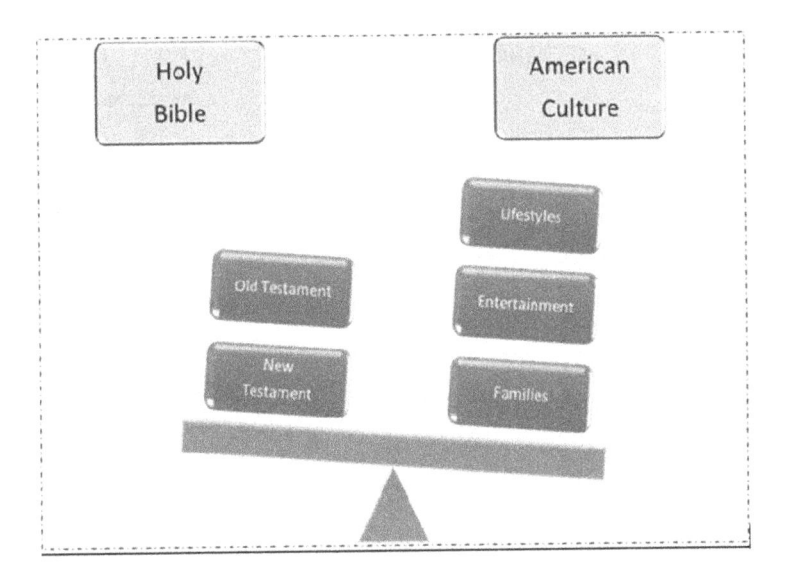

[Diagram: A balance scale weighing "Holy Bible" (with Old Testament, New Testament) against "American Culture" (with Lifestyles, Entertainment, Families), tipped toward the American Culture side.]

- **Repent why? Christianity Solves Real Issues for Society**

There is a tremendous difference between those that say they are Christians and those that are really trying to be more like Christ every day. Truthfully, as seen throughout our society, there are good doctors, and there are bad doctors. There are good construction workers, and there are lousy construction workers. There are great teachers, good teachers, and some pretty bad teachers. Likewise, within Christianity, there are those that profess to believe in the written word and there are those that are trying to live the precepts of the written word, trying to love their neighbor, trying to do the right thing and trying hard to refrain from a whole host of sins.

The truth is that if everyone in America was behaving as Christ and as the Bible instructs, then we would have no need for social services, and the police force could be spending their time helping firemen get stray cats out of trees. Our task as Christians is to disciple more Christians so America can be a better, more peaceful, and loving place.

Hemorrhaging results of the sins of our society

Manifestation of the Sin	"Some" of the Biblical Sin(s) that lead to it
Opioid epidemic	envy, inventers of evil things, without natural affection, covetousness
Gangs	murder, hatred, wrath, envy, boasters
Divorce	lovers of self, wrath, strife, reveling, pride, covenant breakers, adultery
Mass shootings	hatred, murder, without natural affection
Child abuse	lovers of pleasure, without natural affection, unmerciful
Sex trafficking	lovers of pleasure, lasciviousness, covetousness
Wars and rumors of wars	pride, malignity, envying, murder
Robbery	covetousness, envy
Random drive-by urban shootings	boasters, unmerciful, murder, strife
Murder/suicides	malignity, wrath, hatred
Selling sex/ sex appeal/ sexiness	lovers of selves, covetousness, lovers of the creature more than the creator
Corruption	without understanding, unmerciful, pride, covetousness
Drug cartels	covetousness, without natural affection
Terrorism	inventers of evil things, haters of god, wickedness
Suicide bombings	wrath, hatred, malignity, without natural affection

Sexual harassment	lovers of selves, adultery, fornication,
Bullying, racism, misogyny, elitism	pride, unholy, headstrong, boasters, murder, hatred, unholy, haughty, envy, unloving, brutal, slanderers, outbursts of wrath, boasters, malignity
Homosexuality	lust, lasciviousness, form of godliness but denying the power thereof, men leaving the natural use of the woman, burned in their lust for one another, men with men
Elitism	pride, boasters, whisperers, idolatry
Promiscuity	disobedient to parents, fornication, lasciviousness
Sacred house of worship shootings	haters of god, murder, wrath, maliciousness

See "other sins" section in chapter 17: I Repent for Not Speaking Up About Sin And Evil.

All the sins shown on the right side of this table are directly from the Bible (KJV).

- **Repent why? The Bible Versus Legality**

Some things may be legally and practically okay, but they are surely morally wrong. Our Supreme Court has become the god of our land. Whatever they rule is what we are told to do. The precarious reality about that is that can decide one way at one time and another way at another time. In other words, our Supreme Court has proven to be wishy-washy. For instance, in the past, slavery was legal. No one in America went to jail for owning slaves. However, it breaks the moral law of loving your neighbor as yourself. Some may say why did Jesus allow slavery to persist while He was here. We would have to ask ourselves why He allowed prostitution, robbery, and lying to continue, also. What we do know is that the Bible is consistent about loving one another and treating each other nicely.

Abortion is also one of these issues that cannot be reasoned adequately using our legal system. On the surface, should any human being have a right to say what happens with their own body? Under any other circumstance we would say absolutely, yes. No one would try to force someone to exercise, unless they signed up for it or joined the military. No one forces people to eat a certain way unless they have signed up and agreed to be on a special diet. No one says it is illegal to go skydiving because every individual has choice. Unfortunately, for the sake of clarity, things change when a baby is discovered in the womb. Now, the answer we seek in our culture is to understand when that sperm and egg become a human. Legally, using the laws of man, this will forever remain debatable.

However, morally, based on what we see in Jeremiah 1:5, the Bible points out that God knew Jeremiah before he was born. If God knew him, then the person Jeremiah would become was already decided. His personality was already evident to God. It was known that he would be a prophet before he was even conceived. He was already ordained for it. Therefore, God says that humans are alive prior to conception. The purpose is not to settle this discussion in this one paragraph. The purpose here is to point out the difference between a moral law and a legality. Courtrooms cannot legislate morality. That should be the job of the church and hence our need to repent, get busy sharing the gospel, and start treating each other with love.

> Owe no man any thing, but to love one another: for he that loveth another hath fulfilled the law. For this, Thou shalt not commit adultery, Thou shalt not kill, Thou shalt not steal, Thou shalt not bear false witness, Thou shalt not covet; and if there be any other commandment, it is briefly comprehended in this saying, namely, Thou shalt love thy neighbour as thyself. Love worketh no ill to his neighbour: therefore love is the fulfilling of the law. And

that, knowing the time, that now it is high time to awake
out of sleep: for now is our salvation nearer than when we
believed. (Romans 13:8–11 KJV)

Love, love, love, love is the message here. Love every person just as you love yourself. We want the best for ourselves. We want peace for ourselves. We want to feel loved. We want to be healthy. We want to be treated fairly. We want a chance. So does every other person that God knows or has ordained for a purpose in this life. We need to repent and learn to grant every other person the exact same things we want for ourselves.

- **Repent why? We Have Grace**

Sometimes it seems that people hear what they want to hear. This is also true sometimes with many Christians. People hear gladly that Jesus died for our sins. They hear that we are saved by His grace. Upon further study, they would realize that does not mean we have a free pass to keep on sinning.

> What shall we say then? Shall we continue in sin, that grace may abound? God forbid. How shall we, that are dead to sin, live any longer therein? (Romans 6:1–2 KJV)

As individuals, we need to repent. Likewise, our behavior as individuals carries over to our combined behavior as a nation. We do not have the right to say, "God will have grace on us and continue to bless us regardless of our actions." We are instructed to relinquish sin in our behavior.

> For if we have been planted together in the likeness of his death, we shall be also in the likeness of his resurrection: Knowing this, that our old man is crucified with him, that the body of sin might be destroyed, that henceforth we should not serve sin. For he that is dead is freed from sin. (Romans 6:5–7 KJV)

Here, Paul teaches that we are not bound by the sin of our flesh, and we should do away with it. God's grace is not an excuse as an individual or as a nation. The Bible is clear in the punishment for nations that are outside of the grace of God.

America is the Best There is and That is Enough.

The truth is that no one is good enough to be good in the eyes of God the Father. Jesus Christ Himself would not allow others to call Him good. Instead, in Mark 10:18 He questioned it. This is so important for us to understand as Christians. Many times, we hear people talk about how someone is a good person, a good man, a good woman, or a good friend. Many times, clergy say this about the deceased at funerals as if their words will usher the person through the pearly gates. Yes, many have done some good things, but to label the person as good negates all the bad that was done. It is not taking ownership of the bad. The truth is that many of us are good sometimes and bad sometimes. We cannot just mention the good. Likewise, America has done some good things for the world, but if we call ourselves Christians, we must be honest and say that we have done some bad things also, as has every other country. And more than that, if America was so good spiritually and morally, our fruit should show it all the time. Fruit does not change in midseason.

> Bring forth therefore fruits meet for repentance: And think not to say within yourselves, We have Abraham to our father: for I say unto you, that God is able of these stones to raise up children unto Abraham. And now also the axe is laid unto the root of the trees: therefore every tree which bringeth not forth good fruit is hewn down, and cast into the fire. (Matthew 3:8–10 KJV)

God is letting His chosen people know that unless they are bearing the right fruit, then do not try to claim it as their pedigree that makes them qualified and deserving to be saved. He tells them that even though they are the root of His relationship with humanity, they will be cut down because they are not bearing fruit.

> Whereupon, O king Agrippa, I was not disobedient unto the heavenly vision: But shewed first unto them of Damascus, and at Jerusalem, and throughout all the coasts of Judaea, and then to the Gentiles, that they should repent and turn to God, and do works meet for repentance. (Acts 26:19–20 KJV)

Apostle Paul is using himself as an example here. He is letting King Agrippa know that after he was converted, his life had totally changed. He says here that his fruit is showing that he really repented. Our fruit should be as consistent. Our nation should show the same.

> For ye were sometimes darkness, but now are ye light in the Lord: walk as children of light: (For the fruit of the Spirit is in all goodness and righteousness and truth proving what is acceptable unto the Lord. And have no fellowship with the unfruitful works of darkness, but rather reprove them. For it is a shame even to speak of those things which are done of them in secret. (Ephesians 5:8–12 KJV)

Here again, apostle Paul is letting the church at Ephesus know that if they are walking with God, there is no room for bragging about past escapades and sins. Many Americans would agree that our country was once known as a Christian nation. We should be known by doing the right thing by God and the people of God if that is still the case.

Repentance Examples

- **Two Brothers**

> But what think ye? A certain man had two sons; and he came to the first, and said, Son, go work to day in my vineyard. He answered and said, I will not: but afterward he repented, and went. And he came to the second, and said likewise. And he answered and said, I go, sir: and

went not. Whether of them twain did the will of his father? They say unto him, The first. Jesus saith unto them, Verily I say unto you, That the publicans and the harlots go into the kingdom of God before you. (Matthew 21:28–31 KJV)

This parable from Jesus makes it obvious that it is not what you say but what you do that makes the difference with God. He tells the crowd that those who do repent and do what thus says the Lord will make it into the kingdom God. The son in verse 29 repented from his response to his father and instead honored him by fulfilling his request.

- **Prodigal Son**

    And when he came to himself, he said, How many hired servants of my father's have bread enough and to spare, and I perish with hunger! I will arise and go to my father, and will say unto him, Father, I have sinned against heaven, and before thee, And am no more worthy to be called thy son: make me as one of thy hired servants. (Luke 15:17–19 KJV)

This parable demonstrates that a person does not have to be born good to please God. The thing that matters most is that when the Holy Spirit does confront a person with things that need to change, they accept whatever has been done incorrectly and turn away from it. The prodigal son admitted his mistake and turned in the opposite direction. His destitute situation led him to repentance, but sometimes that is what we need.

- **Nineveh**

    And the word of the LORD came unto Jonah the second time, saying, Arise, go unto Nineveh, that great city, and preach unto it the preaching that I bid thee. So Jonah arose, and went unto Nineveh, according to the word of the LORD. Now Nineveh was an exceeding great city of three days' journey. And Jonah began to enter into the city a day's journey, and he cried, and said, Yet forty days, and Nineveh shall be overthrown. So the people of Nineveh believed God, and proclaimed a fast, and put on sackcloth, from the greatest of them even to the least of them. For word came unto the king of Nineveh, and he arose from his throne, and he laid his robe from him, and covered him with sackcloth, and sat in ashes. (Jonah 3:1–6 KJV)

Nineveh is a good example for America. This text describes a fast that was started by the people throughout the entire city. That is exactly where repentance needs to start in America. It needs to start with the Christians in America that take God seriously. The sackcloth was often used by the Jews to represent a humble spirit before God. It was used as a sign of repentance and during times of mourning. The interesting thing about this time in Nineveh is that it appears all classes of people were involved. Imagine if politicians, movie stars, professional athletes, rich, poor, and middle class all took the same posture before God, in America. It would have great power in the direction of our country over the next one hundred years. From the top down, everyone repented and changed course. It would be wonderful if our president and other political leaders would truly bow before God and focus on making laws and policies that were truly righteous legislation for everyone. This same chapter records in verse 10 that when God saw their actions, He did not deliver the devastation intended for them. That is the beauty of repentance. God can completely remove evil from our world.

- **Manasseh**

And the LORD spake to Manasseh, and to his people: but they would not hearken. Wherefore the LORD brought upon them the captains of the host of the king of Assyria, which took Manasseh among the thorns, and bound him with fetters, and carried him to Babylon. And when he was in affliction, he besought the LORD his God, and humbled himself greatly before the God of his fathers, And prayed

> unto him: and he was intreated of him, and heard his supplication, and brought him again to Jerusalem into his kingdom. Then Manasseh knew that the LORD he was God. (2 Chronicles 33:10–13 KJV)

God is constantly trying to reach humanity. He is like any parent that allows some leeway and then must reign in their children for being hardheaded. Manasseh did evil before God. He was young when he took over Jerusalem. He built altars to other gods, used witchcraft, and even used his children for other types of worship. In America, we are worshipping many things that have nothing to do with God. Much of this will be discussed in the following chapters.

Manasseh, however, finally gets the message. He disregarded much of the work his father, Hezekiah, had done for God, but when he found himself in a bad situation, he changed. Too often it takes hard times to change us. America would be wise to not have to go this far before deciding to repent before God. That is because hard times can come in many forms. We have no idea what it could be. For Manasseh, it was affliction brought on by a foreign country.

- **Simon**

> But there was a certain man, called Simon, which beforetime in the same city used sorcery, and bewitched the people of Samaria, giving out that himself was some great one: To whom they all gave heed, from the least to the greatest, saying, This man is the great power of God. And to him they had regard, because that of long time he had bewitched them with sorceries. But when they believed Philip preaching the things concerning the kingdom of God, and the name of Jesus Christ, they were baptized, both men and women. Then Simon himself believed also: and when he was baptized, he continued with Philip, and wondered, beholding the miracles and signs which were done. (Acts 8:9–13 KJV)

The good news here is that no one must become perfect before they repent. Simon had deceived people for years. He had been lying and claiming he was somebody he was not. Fortunately, no one can get so far away from God that He will not accept you when you repent and turn back to Him. America is included.

Hearing the true preached word is what changed the life of Simon. He heard it, he believed, and his perspective on life changed. Some people have heard about God, but they may not have ever wholeheartedly opened their heart to consider if it could be true. A preached word will do it.

- **Saul/Apostle Paul**

  And Saul, yet breathing out threatenings and slaughter against the disciples of the Lord, went unto the high priest, And desired of him letters to Damascus to the synagogues, that if he found any of this way, whether they were men or women, he might bring them bound unto Jerusalem. And as he journeyed, he came near Damascus: and suddenly there shined round about him a light from heaven: And he fell to the earth, and heard a voice saying unto him, Saul, Saul, why persecutest thou me? And he said, Who art thou, Lord? And the Lord said, I am Jesus whom thou persecutest: it is hard for thee to kick against the pricks. And he trembling and astonished said, Lord, what wilt thou have me to do? And the Lord said unto him, Arise, and go into the city, and it shall be told thee what thou must do. (Acts 9:1–6 KJV)

There is no better example of repentance in the Bible than apostle Paul. He was putting early Christians into jail and murdering them. Paul says he did what he did in ignorance and unbelief, (1 Timothy 13). Yet, after meeting Jesus on the Damascus road, there is no evidence of him doing anything but making a full 180-degree turn toward following God. He did an about-face. The result of his repentance allowed him to become the most prolific writer in the New Testament. There is no limit to the good that could be done in America, if we repent.

America's Attitude

If the United States of America were a person, what kind of person would she be known as? We praise how we come together in times of crisis, but on the other hand, we have laws, practices, policies, and procedures in place that are unfair to some of God's children every day. We talk about the importance of family during the holidays, yet we have an entertainment industry that constantly produces dysfunctional, broken, and unhappy family material. We cannot blame Hollywood for this. Obviously, they are producing it because the public is buying it. We claim that we are "one nation under God," but our conversation, politics, and talk radio is very rude and often one-sided. Our delivery is very intolerant, cut throat, and increasingly nasty, especially during campaigns. We have many church buildings on every corner all over America, yet many congregations are only interested in self-sufficiency and do not thrive on coming out of their four walls and holistically helping people in need, right down the street. So, are we truly a loving, caring, family-oriented society? Our actions seem to demonstrate that we cannot make up our mind. Perhaps, when it comes to morals, America would be known as "wishy-washy," or uncertain.

Unfortunately for America, God has not changed His mind. Just because we have new technology, it does not mean God is somehow different. From Genesis to Revelation, God speaks in His word about humanity being disobedient and falling short of His commands. On a generic basis, this is still true. Below are some verses God shares with His beloved nation from Jeremiah.

> Thine own wickedness shall correct thee, and thy backslidings shall reprove thee: know therefore and see that it is an evil thing and bitter, that thou hast forsaken the LORD thy God, and that my fear is not in thee, saith the Lord GOD of hosts. For of old time I have broken thy yoke, and burst thy bands; and thou saidst, I will not

transgress; when upon every high hill and under every green tree thou wanderest, playing the harlot. Yet I had planted thee a noble vine, wholly a right seed: how then art thou turned into the degenerate plant of a strange vine unto me? For though thou wash thee with nitre, and take thee much soap, yet thine iniquity is marked before me, saith the Lord God. How canst thou say, I am not polluted, I have not gone after Baalim? see thy way in the valley, know what thou hast done: thou art a swift dromedary traversing her ways. (Jeremiah 2:19–23 KJV)

This is quite a sad text. Verse 19 tells the audience Jeremiah is addressing that their own behavior is going to be the very thing that will correct them. Their hypocrisy is mentioned to them in verse 20 by discussing the difference between what they say versus what they do. Their conversation and fake actions of repentance were not real, and God knew it. Verse 23 tells them to own up to their behavior and what they have done.

America should own up to the behavior we portray. We claim some things are important to us at certain times, but our daily actions are not showing it. That is exactly why Jeremiah was talking to the people of Jerusalem and trying to convince them to turn back to God. Right now, it appears America may be responding the same way. That would make the attitude of America be one of defiance or arrogance. That is something we should reconsider.

Moving Forward

"We the people of the United States of America, in order to form a more perfect union,"[8]

is a wonderful beginning to our American Constitution. And, while we revel that we practice the separation of church and state, I propose that the ideal of a more perfect union can never be complete without putting the love of Jesus Christ into practice. I unashamedly propose that without the kind of true love that Jesus Christ demonstrated, the sinful pains of our society will continue to grow and surface time and time again.

Each chapter in this book is a lesson that is very specific about something that is ubiquitous in our American culture in one way or another. While we cannot hit one light switch and change our entire culture all at one time, we can begin the change as we entertain each chapter honestly and individually, one person at a time.

Chapter 2

I REPENT FOR NOT CARING ENOUGH TO READ THE WHOLE BIBLE FOR MYSELF

Think about the one or two things you might consider yourself to be very proficient in. How much time have you spent in your life learning, studying, practicing, or participating in that particular thing? How many hours? How much frustration and aggravation have you gone through to learn what it took to be good at that thing? It may take three hours to watch a ball game, two hours to watch a tennis match, one and one-half hours to watch a short movie, one and one-half hours to watch a soccer match with your child, two hours working in the kitchen to make a new recipe, thirty minutes to wash a car, forty-five minutes to work a difficult crossword puzzle, and two to three hours sitting on a friend's couch just visiting for an afternoon. Time or money spent on something is the easiest way to tell if it is really important to a person.

So, how much time and money are we spending studying and enhancing our own personal relationship with God by reading and studying His word? It is a personal decision because even making the decision to go to a weekly Bible study requires a personal commitment. The group may talk and teach, but we must choose as an individual to pay attention and practice active listening. When it comes to reading the Bible, we often say we do not have time. Why is it important to read the Bible anyway?

Dwane Massenburg

Personal Decision

The reason you can read this book is the result of a personal decision to read the Bible. This seems like an appropriate place to share a personal testimony since this chapter is about caring. Certainly, anyone reading this book would like to know that the author cared enough to read and know the Bible personally and not just through hearsay.

I received my undergraduate degree in mechanical engineering from Georgia Tech in Atlanta, Georgia. Tech was on a quarter system at the time, instead of semesters. I started at Tech during the summer quarter, about two weeks after I finished high school. My sister was in her senior year at Virginia State University, in Petersburg, Virginia, and I had witnessed her participating in what was called a co-op program. That was a program in which you went to school one semester and worked in your profession the next semester. The co-op program seemed exciting to me and played a part in why I chose to attend Georgia Tech. I remember feeling very honored to be accepted because I knew it was a prestigious school for engineering. The co-op program would make it a five-year degree program until graduation instead of four.

After four quarters at Tech and three quarters working for Lynchburg Foundry in Lynchburg, Virginia, I was able to find another company that worked with Georgia Tech that would allow me to stay closer to home, save money, and be closer to my then fiancé in Richmond, Virginia. So, during the spring quarter of my sophomore year, I found myself working for Reynolds Metals, in Richmond, Virginia. Reynolds Metals, which has now been sold, was known for Reynolds Wrap, which is used in most kitchens throughout America. It was during this quarter in Richmond that I was also first introduced to a multilevel marketing business that promoted positive thinking and having a positive attitude. I bought into the whole notion right away. My fiancé, now wife, Sophia, and I went to several conferences and held several in-home sales events as we became enthralled in the company environment. My father had done several different successful business ventures in his life, so this multilevel marketing business seemed to fit right in with my personality to work hard and do "extra," if possible. I could certainly do it part time and be an engineer during the day.

Everything was wonderful that quarter, but it was eventually over, and I had to go back to Georgia Tech for the summer quarter. I was a sophomore on campus and signed up to take fifteen hours of classes. One of the classes was my first public speaking class. I was glad to be taking something that was easy amid my fourth quarter of calculus. The public speaking professor had the class set up so that classmates would critique each other in writing, every time we gave a speech. We were given subjects or topics for most of the speeches, but for one speech he allowed us to choose whatever we wanted to talk about. Leaning on my new-found experience from the previous work quarter, I prepared a speech entitled "Self-Image and Attitude." I quoted popular books at the time, like *Think and Grow Rich* and, *You Are What You Think You Are*. I thought it was a fantastic speech that would surely get me an A.

However, one of my classmates was not thrilled at all. He wrote on my critique simply, "You will be disappointed." I did not put too much thought into what he meant when I first saw it. A few weeks later though, I accidently ran into him in the campus bookstore at the student center. We began a casual conversation, and he began to share with me what I had said in my speech to the class. Having grown up with my parents taking me to church all my life, his words hit me like ice-cold water being poured on your back. He shared with me how my speech essentially said that I was the master of my entire universe. He shared with me that I had said everything that was going to happen in my life depended entirely on me. I was stopped in my tracks, because I already knew enough as a Christian to know that was not true. How had I let these words come out of my mouth? What did I really believe? Was I sure about how I was thinking? How could I be so off base? I knew I believed in God, so how could this have happened?

This was a major turning point in my life. After being raised in the church and feeling like I was a pretty good Christian, I now had to find out for myself. It was early in the quarter, so without telling my parents, I dropped all my classes except the public speaking class and an aerobics class. In other words, I was not going to have to spend a lot of time studying for the rest of the quarter. It was during this time that, for the first time in my life, I decided I had to find out what was in the Bible for myself. For the next approximately eight weeks, I was able to read about a third of the Bible. This was the beginning of my journey. That morning in the bookstore was my real born-again experience. That is when I decided that I did not want to take God's word for granted anymore. That is when I decided that I wanted a deeper understanding and not just the opinion of someone else. I did not want their interpretation. I wanted my own interpretation. I cared enough to make the decision to find out for myself.

Your experience does not have to be as dramatic as mine, but everyone should have some type of realization that the Word is the most important thing God has blessed us to have in our generation. Take advantage of the Word that you have an opportunity to read. Make the choice.

> And if it seem evil unto you to serve the LORD, choose you this day whom ye will serve; whether the gods which your fathers served that were on the other side of the flood, or the gods of the Amorites, in whose land ye dwell: but as for me and my house, we will serve the LORD. And the people answered and said, God forbid that we should forsake the LORD, to serve other gods; For the LORD our God, he it is that brought us up and our fathers out of the land of Egypt, from the house of bondage, and which did those great signs in our sight, and preserved us in all the way wherein we went, and among all the people through whom we passed: And the LORD drave out from before us all the people, even the Amorites which dwelt in the land: therefore will we also serve the LORD; for he is our God. And Joshua said unto the people, Ye cannot serve the LORD: for he is an holy God; he is a jealous God; he will not forgive your transgressions nor your sins. If ye forsake the LORD, and serve strange gods, then he will turn and do you hurt, and consume you, after that he hath done

you good. And the people said unto Joshua, Nay; but we
will serve the LORD. And Joshua said unto the people, Ye
are witnesses against yourselves that ye have chosen you
the LORD, to serve him. And they said, We are witnesses.
(Joshua 24:15–22 KJV)

In this text, Joshua confronts his people with an option to make a choice. Verse 15 tells them that just following God because your parents did it is not good enough to make the choice. Likewise, verse 15 also says that serving the Lord just because everyone else around you is doing it, is not good enough. Each person must decide. Verses 21–22 confirm the commitment to serve God on their own merits, by their own choice. That is what we all must do.

A Choice Must Be Made

A choice must be made in our lives to take God and His word seriously. Trying to avoid making a choice is a choice itself. If a person avoids the choice, they are saying, it is not important. The Bible is His word. In His word He commands us to read it.

> Of these things put them in remembrance, charging them before the Lord that they strive not about words to no profit, but to the subverting of the hearers. Study to shew thyself approved unto God, a workman that needeth not to be ashamed, rightly dividing the word of truth. But shun profane and vain babblings: for they will increase unto more ungodliness. (2 Timothy 2:14–16 KJV)

The Bible tells us here through Timothy that we need to be diligent. We must read and study His word so that we can learn the truth for ourselves. Learning the truth and studying the truth means that we do not have to defend ourselves and argue about individual petty things. Arguing about petty things is not good for those that do not know God well. This text says it will be ruin them. So many times, people who are young in Christ will be discouraged because of how other, older members act at church meetings or church conferences. Spiritual immaturity will lead to this strife.

The Bible Is the Best Guide for Our Lives

> But continue thou in the things which thou hast learned and hast been assured of, knowing of whom thou hast learned them; And that from a child thou hast known the holy scriptures, which are able to make thee wise unto salvation through faith which is in Christ Jesus. All scripture is given by inspiration of God, and is profitable for doctrine, for reproof, for correction, for instruction in righteousness: That the man of God may be perfect, thoroughly furnished unto all good works. (2 Timothy 3:14–17 KJV)

> Every word of God is pure: he is a shield unto them that put their trust in him. Add thou not unto his words, lest he reprove thee, and thou be found a liar. (Proverbs 30:5–6 KJV)

> Wherefore laying aside all malice, and all guile, and hypocrisies, and envies, and all evil speakings, As newborn babes, desire the sincere milk of the word, that ye may grow thereby: If so be ye have tasted that the Lord is gracious. (1 Peter 2:1–3 KJV)

Here we see that all scripture is good for us. We need it to grow. The Bible is from God Himself. We must trust that. Yes, there have been different writers, countries, cultures, and translations that have provided us with the Bibles we have today. However, if we believe in God, we must believe that the same God that spoke and created everything can assure that whatever is in our Bible today is just how He wished it to be from the beginning. It takes faith to believe that, and it takes faith to believe in God.

> But without faith it is impossible to please him: for he that cometh to God must believe that he is, and that he is a rewarder of them that diligently seek him. (Hebrews 11:6 KJV)

Faith is required to believe in God and His "Word." Believing that He truly is God means we must take into account the magnitude of how important the Bible is. It is worthy of our personal study. Diligent seeking is a requirement.

Necessities/Distractions/False Hurdles/Busyness

Our lives are full of things we do that some people have turned into seemingly life or death situations. How many people have to watch a soap opera, watch a certain television show, play certain video games, go to the movies, play a round of golf, work a crossword puzzle, or take a second job? The second job may be understandable if you need it to put food on the family table or to keep a roof over your head. Other than that, the list of things we like to do could go on and on and on. The entire list is fine if it does not become a false hurdle. These things occupy our time and make us feel as if no time is left in our day. How in the world can we squeeze in reading the Bible? The Bible must be a priority if we are going to have a relationship with God. A relationship is different than practicing a religion. We can go to a worship service once a week and get to "know about" God. However, to get to "know God," a person must spend more than once per week with Him. Any real relationship cannot flourish if you only spend time with the person two hours per week. Other things deemed to be important must be on the back burner relative to growing in grace with God.

> Come unto me, all ye that labour and are heavy laden, and I will give you rest. Take my yoke upon you, and learn of me; for I am meek and lowly in heart: and ye shall find rest unto your souls. For my yoke is easy, and my burden is light. (Matthew 11:28–30 KJV)

Learn, learn, learn, is what Jesus said. We are commanded to learn from God. How much would you study God's word to learn everything about Him, if you were promised one million dollars if you could pass a test on His word after studying the Bible? If the test was to be given in ninety days, how long would you spend studying each day? How many times would you try to review your notes? Well, there is something more valuable than one million dollars that you will get by studying the Bible. If you accept Him, you will receive eternal life.

> Being born again, not of corruptible seed, but of incorruptible, by the word of God, which liveth and abideth for ever. For all flesh is as grass, and all the glory of man as the flower of grass. The grass withereth, and the flower thereof falleth away: But the word of the Lord endureth for ever. And this is the word which by the gospel is preached unto you. (1 Peter 1:23–25 KJV)

The word of God has been delivered to our generation. It has endured. Everything else we know of will pass away over time. The tallest buildings will eventually decay like the relics in Egypt and Rome. However, the word of God will be with humanity as a beacon of light forever.

Therefore, Lord I repent for not caring enough to read the whole Bible for myself. I have not been reading it as I should. Lord, please forgive me, and help me to do better.

Chapter 3
I REPENT FOR BEING COVETOUS

The Tenth Commandment

Most people who are not Bible scholars probably cannot recite the Ten Commandments, which God Himself wrote on tablets of stone that He gave to Moses. Many people do, however, remember hearing thou shall not kill, thou shall not steal, and thou shall not commit adultery. Thou shall not covet is hardly on anyone's radar.

The Ten Commandments (Exodus 20):

- o No other gods before me.
- o Do not take the name of the Lord in vain.
- o Make no graven images.
- o Remember the Sabbath to keep it Holy.
- o Honor thy mother and father.
- o You shall not kill.
- o You shall not steal.
- o You shall not bear false witness (lie).
- o You shall not commit adultery.
- o You shall not covet.

How does covetousness wind up in the same list with lying, stealing, and murder? Humans have instituted laws that make it illegal for lying (perjury) stealing, and murder. There are people in prison today for lying, stealing, and murder. But no one is jailed for being covetous. Does God know something we do not know? Absolutely!

> For my thoughts are not your thoughts, neither are your ways my ways, saith the LORD. For as the heavens are higher than the earth, so are my ways higher than your ways, and my thoughts than your thoughts. For as the rain cometh down, and the snow from heaven, and returneth not thither, but watereth the earth, and maketh it bring forth and bud, that it may give seed to the sower, and bread to the eater: So shall my word be that goeth forth out of my mouth: it shall not return unto me void, but it shall accomplish that which I please, and it shall prosper in the thing whereto I sent it. (Isaiah 55:8–11 KJV)

God's ways and thoughts are so far above ours that we must consult His word to get some understanding about how covetousness made this list of sins. His word will not come back to Him void, so humankind should try to understand why it is important and stop overlooking it. How are we coveting? Why do we covet? How do we get in the habit of coveting? What harm does it do?

Compare and Contrast

In 1920, most Americans probably had a garden, one mule, one set of clothes for work, and perhaps one outfit for church on Sunday. Most things purchased were paid for using cash or perhaps a line of credit at the local country store. There was a garden in most back yards. A lot of people had small farms with a hog or two for killing, and maybe a cow for milking. Now, fast-forward to the next generation in 1960 when television commercials, radio commercials, and billboards became a larger part of our lives. The baby boom generation was just starting to generate a wave of movement, newness, and excitement. Like a surfer in the ocean, everyone wanted to catch the wave and have everything they saw. Gone were the days of sacrificing a long time for things and saving money in a cookie jar, when they could be bought using credit.

Many today have even taught their children that they deserve everything now. Elementary school children "have to have" cell phones now with monthly bills their parents sometimes struggle to pay for. There was a time when the first job was a newspaper route or at the local grocery store, and the income was saved for a first bicycle. Today teenagers feel they have the right to pout and show attitudes if they cannot get the desired kind of jeans or tennis shoes they desire. Of course, they must fit in with their peers, so nothing else will do. The lessons our grandmothers taught about saving for things we want and saving for a rainy day are gone.

It Matters to God; Everyone Is Guilty

> To whom shall I speak, and give warning, that they may hear? behold, their ear is uncircumcised, and they cannot hearken: behold, the word of the LORD is unto them a reproach; they have no delight in it. Therefore I am full of the fury of the LORD; I am weary with holding in: I will pour it out upon the children abroad, and upon the assembly of young men together: for even the husband with the wife shall be taken, the aged with him that is full of days. And their houses shall be turned unto others, with their fields and wives together: for I will stretch out my hand upon the inhabitants of the land, saith the LORD. For from the least of them even unto the greatest of them every one is given to covetousness; and from the prophet even unto the priest every one dealeth falsely. (Jeremiah 6:10–13 KJV)

This is a hard verse for us to read, but it does let us know that no one is exempt. Covetousness is a sin that we all must protect against. Unfortunately, in this text, it says that even clergy are guilty. That means we all must be cautious.

How Are We Coveting?

The word *covet* means to desire. However, all desire is not wrong. Every desire is not a sin. Desire for a pair of good shoes and coat to keep us warm and healthy in the winter is not wrong. Our desire for a meal is not a sin. Our desire for a safe boat to fish with if fishing is our profession is not a sin. Our desire to get decent clothes for our children is not wrong. Our desire for a home we can go to each night after working all day is not a sin. Jesus suggests to a large crowd that if one intends to build a tower, he would be wise to count the cost before the building begins (Luke 28–30). So, for most things a person must have a desire for something in order for it to come into existence. Gifts are fine to receive, but everything else must be worked for, saved for, planned for, and desired.

Jesus did not desire anything above and beyond His immediate necessities while He was here on earth. Think about it. We dress up, buy the biggest vehicle we can, and live in the largest house we can, and Jesus, the son of God, the Word with us, Emmanuel, the Prince of Peace, did not even have a place He called His personal home, while He was living here among us.

> And a certain scribe came, and said unto him, Master, I will follow thee whithersoever thou goest. And Jesus saith unto him, the foxes have holes, and the birds of the air have nests; but the Son of man hath not where to lay his head. (Matthew 8:19–20)

If Jesus was in the flesh with us today, we would expect anyone attracting the kinds of crowds He attracted to have a huge mansion. Jesus Christ is the humblest servant we know. He did not have anything to brag about except that He was sent by His Father. He did not ride into Jerusalem on a beautiful stallion. He rode in on a donkey. How many of our leaders take this humble approach? Jesus was demonstrating to us what is important. He did not covet anything the world had to offer.

Something else we must keep in mind is that "You shall not covet" is not only referring to items that can be purchased with money. Coveting is a sin in several venues.

You shall not covet your neighbor's house; you shall not covet your neighbor's wife, nor his male servant, nor his female servant, nor his ox, nor his donkey, nor anything that is your neighbor's. (Exodus 20:17 NKJV)

We covet when we desire another man's wife, his children, his business, his man cave, his facial hair, his personality, his charisma, or his life. We covet when we desire another woman's husband, her children, her business, her hair, her shape, her personality, her charisma, or her life.

Why Do We Covet?

The short answer is sin. The long answer requires a bit more soul searching or investigation. Why do you drive the vehicle you drive? Is it the most economical, roomy, or safe? Or is it the same kind of vehicle your neighbor has? Is it the one that has been advertised the most? Is your vehicle a status symbol? Do you yearn to drive a certain vehicle because the image will feed your pride and prestige? Will the public think you are a person with money and power if you live in a certain neighborhood? Why do you buy the clothes you choose to wear? Are they functional and the most comfortable? Or are they the name brand status symbol required to maintain an image? Why would one desire the husband of another woman? Are there no other men on earth that will suffice?

I want what somebody else has.

I want it because I really like what they have.	Jealousy
I want it because it makes me look good.	Pride
I want it just to keep them from having it.	Envy

35

I want it because I deserve it.	Entitlement
I want if because it really belongs to me.	Selfish

> What shall we say then? Is the law sin? God forbid. Nay, I had not known sin, but by the law: for I had not known lust, except the law had said, Thou shalt not covet. But sin, taking occasion by the commandment, wrought in me all manner of concupiscence. For without the law sin was dead. (Romans 7:7–8 KJV)

We buy needless stuff we don't need. We buy more expensive things than we need. We desire things that are not ours. The reason is personal, and it is sometimes born in sin.

The Effects

How does this innocent little sin affect our lives? After all, it is not murder. The Bible says that what we get paid for sin is death. Covetousness is a slow death. It steals time. We give away the most valuable (our time) for the most useless (things that will decay and be called old, out of date, and junk in the future). Time is the most valuable gift we have from God.

> Go to now, ye that say, Today or tomorrow we will go into such a city, and continue there a year, and buy and sell, and get gain: Whereas ye know not what shall be on the morrow. For what is your life? It is even a vapour, that appeareth for a little time, and then vanisheth away. For that ye ought to say, If the Lord will, we shall live, and do this, or that. But now ye rejoice in your boastings: all such rejoicing is evil. (James 4:13–16 KJV)

We ruin our credit so that we cannot afford to get the things we might really need like just a decent vehicle or an adequate house. Or because our credit is in such a shamble, we pay twice as much interest as we should have to. Some people are living paycheck to paycheck, paying bills on items to impress their neighbors and acquaintances. The rich get richer, and the poor get poorer because we are illiterate with our finances. We allow covetousness to control our lives. We got to have it, got to have it, got to have it!

We work two and three jobs to the detriment of our family life. We grow distant from our spouse and neglect our children coveting somebody else's wife. Would your own wife not be wonderful if you loved her like Christ loved the church? Children are affected by divorce because a woman covets another woman's husband. She claims it is love, but what about the love for her children that get damaged by the divorce? Covetousness is a horrible sin. It is an example of the iniquity God said would reach down to the third and fourth generation. That luxury automobile is not worth an intact family.

Young children learn from their parents and grow into teenagers willing to kill another teenager for a pair of tennis shoes or a nice jacket. The root of some bullying is because of covetousness. That is why wearing a uniform to school seems to alleviate the situation. Those children that can afford less do not get bullied as much.

Some people living in nice neighborhoods are still lying, scheming, and taking advantage of others, so they can make a fast buck and move into an even larger house or experience more extravagant vacations. Yes, even rich people covet other richer people. This is why so many professional athletes go broke shortly after their career ends. They make so much money relative to others in America, but they covet what others have so much that they still find a way to spend it all instead of setting themselves up for life.

Encouraging Ourselves to Be Covetous

How does it happen? We listen to one commercial and say, "I've got to have it." We talk to a friend with something new and say, "I've got to have it." We see a new car going down the road and say, "I've got to have it."

We listen to one smooth-talking salesman and say, "I've got to have it." We see one billboard and say, "I've got to have it." The culture in America encourages us to be covetous, but God warns us about letting this behavior become a part of our conduct.

> Let your conversation be without covetousness; and be content with such things as ye have: for he hath said, I will never leave thee, nor forsake thee. So that we may boldly say, The Lord is my helper, and I will not fear what man shall do unto me. (Hebrews 13:5–6 KJV)

Some Bible translations use the word *conversation*, instead of *conduct*, in this verse. It is not godly to even talk to each other about buying the flashiest car or the biggest house. Think of all the times when we pat each other on the back or praise someone for their "fine" car or their expensive bracelet. Sometimes, we act overjoyed almost to the point of worship over the new or expensive item. We talk about our friends and say, "Oh, they have a big house." When we use that in our conversation, our conduct or conversation is with covetousness. When we do, we are encouraging one another to focus on things that are not essential to life but that only feed our pride. God does not like pride (Proverbs 16:5).

Putting Money and Things We Covet into Perspective

> And one of the company said unto him, Master, speak to my brother, that he divide the inheritance with me. And he said unto him, Man, who made me a judge or a divider over you? And he said unto them, Take heed, and beware of covetousness: for a man's life consisteth not in the abundance of the things which he possesseth. And he spake a parable unto them, saying, The ground of a certain rich man brought forth plentifully: And he thought within himself, saying, What shall I do, because I have no room where to bestow my fruits? And he said, This will I do: I will pull down my barns, and build greater; and there will I bestow all my fruits and my goods. And I will say to my

soul, Soul, thou hast much goods laid up for many years; take thine ease, eat, drink, and be merry. But God said unto him, Thou fool, this night thy soul shall be required of thee: then whose shall those things be, which thou hast provided? (Luke 12:13–20 KJV)

Anytime people put their fleshly desires before the will of God, they are in error. Sin always has a harvest. When God instructed humanity not to covet in the Ten Commandments, He knew the pain, suffering, and death it would cause. All humankind should learn to be satisfied with the grace, mercy, and blessings God has afforded to come their way. Paul suggests in his letter to the Philippians that we have to learn to be full and hungry at the same time (Philippians 4:12). We must learn to have a desire for God and not a desire for things for ourselves.

Your neighbor has everything God has blessed your neighbor to have. Our mantra as Christians should be to rejoice when others rejoice. I should be happy, encouraged, and supportive that my neighbor has everything God has blessed him or her with. There is a fine line between desiring the things God desires for your life and desiring things that you want for your life because of your flesh, because someone else has it. God's Holy Spirit will guide you on what is appropriate. This great sin is a work in progress for all of us.

Therefore, Lord, I repent for being covetous. Lord, please forgive me, and help me to do better.

Chapter 4

I REPENT FOR NOT PRACTICING TRUE LOVE

I love my dog. I love my truck. I love my ring. I love him. I love her. I love chocolate and seeing the sun set over the ocean. I love a hot Midwestern steak. I love my children. I love country music, I love soul music, etcetera, etcetera, etcetera. Does the word *love* in these sentences portray the same meaning, feelings, and emotions? Or is this the same word implying different meaning, feelings, and emotions? What is love? How should we love? Love is important to us all. It should be demonstrated correctly.

We toss the word *love* around like pennies in a wishing well, or maybe not even that serious. Perhaps I should say we toss it around like the pennies I find on the ground from time to time. Someone has determined they are useless and threw them away. In other words, we say the words "I love you" like we appreciate the last raindrops that hit the ground two weeks ago. In some parts of the world, it rains a lot. If it rains a lot, individual raindrops will easily be taken for granted. We know it is important, but it is so easy to take the precipitation for granted when it is present. One individual raindrop means nothing. However, let it stop coming and suddenly we appreciate every wet forecast and every drop that hits the ground. Think of how different the precipitation is perceived and appreciated in an arid desert land. One drop of water means a lot there. That is what we have done by using the word *love* for everything. We use it so often that it has lost its impact. Therefore, blindsiding people into using the word, even in shallow circumstances.

Love Is Not What You Say; It Is What You Do

Saying "I love you" is important, but saying it and not showing it is like opening a Christmas present that turns out to be an empty box. How many pretty gift-wrapped boxes would you like to open like that in a row? There is a big red box. Surely that has a big stuffed animal or something. Nothing. There is a blue box. Maybe it has a nice warm blanket. Nothing. There is a small green box. It must have something expensive. Nothing. Each new box makes you think, "This is it; I'm finally getting to the real thing!" Only to find out that it is just another empty box. The word *love* is cast around so much that many have forgotten that simply saying the word is not what makes it important. Love is what you do.

If I say "I love you" but yet I curse at you, demean you, and physically abuse you, I absolutely do not love you. I am showing you how I really feel. I may be misguided or misdiagnosed, but for right now, I am demonstrating to you that I do not love you. A corporate chief executive officer (CEO) can say they love people and the community. However, if they knowingly allow their company to dump toxic chemicals into the local groundwater, then the CEO is demonstrating that they do not love the community nor the people. Drug dealers cannot claim that they love the people in their family and neighborhood if they are constantly selling substances that turn their neighbors into addicts, persons that sell women, and harlots. Turning a thirteen-year-old girl into a drug addict is not love. The young addicted girl will start selling her body to get drugs. This is abuse and greed. It is not love. The drug dealer is not innocent. A person cannot go to church service on Sunday, come out of the service, claim they are a Christian, and continue to verbally run down a less informed coworker. Remember, none of us were born perfect. All of us have had to grow in grace. The coworker needs compassion instead of contempt. Love means you will pray for your coworker. Love means you will encourage your coworker. Love means you will tell others to stop talking negatively about your coworker. Love means you will help that coworker to learn more about the love of God in you. Love means nothing unless the care, concern, and compassion for others is demonstrated by actions.

Love Is Not What You Get; It Is What You Give

America's pop culture has it all wrong. The songs on the radio say, "show me some love," "give me some love," or "don't hold back on your love." People have often told others, "If you love me, you will do this or do that." That is manipulation. True love is not what one gets; neither should it be graded by what is demanded. God has freely shown us love.

> And as Moses lifted up the serpent in the wilderness, even so must the Son of man be lifted up: That whosoever believeth in him should not perish, but have eternal life. For God so loved the world, that he gave his only begotten Son, that whosoever believeth in him should not perish, but have everlasting life. For God sent not his Son into the world to condemn the world; but that the world through him might be saved. (John 3:14–17 KJV)

The text here is clear that God has given us free will to accept a gift that He is offering for free. This is like a (free) Christmas present offered by a giver to an unknown receiver. All the receiver must do is accept the gift. It is unconditional. This is how God shows love. The New Covenant that has been established by the incarnation, birth, death, and resurrection of Jesus Christ is an unconditional gift from Almighty God. A person who loves someone else should be trying to find a way to give to that person. He or she should not be trying to find a way to get something from that person.

Love "Hard"

Love does not mean that you go along with everything someone does. Love does not mean you go along with everything someone says. God loved Jonah, but He arranged for him to be in the belly of a fish because he was hardheaded.

> So the shipmaster came to him, and said unto him, What meanest thou, O sleeper? arise, call upon thy God, if so be that God will think upon us, that we perish not. And they said every one to his fellow, Come, and let us cast lots, that we may know for whose cause this evil is upon us. So they cast lots, and the lot fell upon Jonah. Then said they unto him, Tell us, we pray thee, for whose cause this evil is upon us; What is thine occupation? and whence comest thou? what is thy country? and of what people art thou? And he said unto them, I am an Hebrew; and I fear the Lord, the God of heaven, which hath made the sea and the dry land. Then were the men exceedingly afraid, and said unto him. Why hast thou done this? For the men knew that he fled from the presence of the Lord, because he had told them. Then said they unto him, What shall we do unto thee, that the sea may be calm unto us? for the sea wrought, and was tempestuous. And he said unto them, Take me up, and cast me forth into the sea; so shall the sea be calm unto you: for I know that for my sake this great tempest is upon you. Nevertheless the men rowed hard to bring it to the land; but they could not: for the sea wrought, and was tempestuous against them. Wherefore they cried unto the Lord, and said, We beseech thee, O Lord, we beseech thee, let us not perish for this man's life, and lay not upon us innocent blood: for thou, O Lord, hast done as it pleased thee. So they took up Jonah, and cast him forth into the sea: and the sea ceased from her raging. Then the men feared the Lord exceedingly, and offered a sacrifice unto the Lord, and made vows. Now the Lord had prepared a great fish to swallow up Jonah. And Jonah was in the belly of the fish three days and three nights. (Jonah 1:6–17 KJV)

God loved Jonah. Jonah delivered a message that converted an entire nation for God. Despite that, God demonstrates to us that His will is not a suggestion. God lets us know in this text that getting along and being nice is not always the best way to show love. Some people call this "tough love." I call it loving, "Hard." Loving with all you have means you are doing whatever it takes to provide love to the recipient. Sometimes love does not look like chocolate, candy, and flowers. Sometimes love looks like refusing to let a teenager do something that will put him or her in harm's way. Sometimes love looks like refusing to enable an alcoholic spouse. They are enabled by buying their alcohol and lying to their boss, to cover up for their indiscretions. Love means I will not do it. Sometimes love looks like telling your aging parent that they cannot drive any more. Love looks like taking their keys so they will not hurt themselves and others. Love is not always easy. Love can be hard. Hard decisions must be made. Hard actions must be taken.

Love Is More Important

Love is more important than anything known to man. The love of one thing or another is the motivation for many things that have happened in the world. Sometimes the love is misguided, misused, or misdirected, but it is still the impetus for setting many things in motion.

> Though I speak with the tongues of men and of angels, and have not charity, I am become as sounding brass, or a tinkling cymbal. And though I have the gift of prophecy, and understand all mysteries, and all knowledge; and though I have all faith, so that I could remove mountains, and have not charity, I am nothing. And though I bestow all my goods to feed the poor, and though I give my body to be burned, and have not charity, it profiteth me nothing. (1 Corinthians 13:1–3 KJV)

This passage of scripture says anything we do without love is worthless. Good deeds done with the wrong motives are detrimental to all involved. The purpose for doing things without loving motives will be discovered and will lead to heartache and pain. The Bible is so important to us. It is the inspired word of God. The prophets in the Bible were all very important. Yet, Jesus said love was more important than all of them.

> Master, which is the great commandment in the law? Jesus said unto him, Thou shalt love the Lord thy God with all thy heart, and with all thy soul, and with all thy mind. This is the first and great commandment. And the second is like unto it, Thou shalt love thy neighbor as thyself. On these two commandments hang all the law and the prophets. (Matthew 22:36–40 KJV)

Every good thing that the laws taught us is secondary to loving God and loving your neighbor as yourself. Every prophet, his words, and his deeds are secondary to loving God and loving your neighbor as yourself. Everything is secondary to love.

Love Manifested in 1 Corinthians 13:4–8

The Bible says:

Verse 4: Love suffers long and is kind; love does not envy; love does not parade itself, is not puffed up; (NKJV). Are you patient with those you love? Then you love them. Are you kind to those you say you love? Then you love them. Do you talk with a soft, kind voice, or are you always talking mean to them? If you talk with a soft, kind voice, then you love them.

Are you happy when good things happen to those you love, or do you just want all the good things for yourself? If the first, then you love them. Do you ever stop bragging about yourself and acting like a big shot around those you are supposed to love? Then you love them.

Verse 5: Love does not behave rudely, does not seek its own, is not provoked, thinks no evil. (NKJV). Do you walk around acting rude just because you can? Do you act rude and claim it is just your personality? If you love somebody, you can't walk around acting like a rabid dog on attack mode all the time, forcing everybody around you to be afraid to say anything to you. Do you always have to have your way? If you love somebody, then you will be flexible and realize that you are not right all the time. Are you known as hotheaded? Do you live like you are waiting for something to tick you off every day? Then, you do not love the people around you. Are you always thinking of something evil to do? Do you constantly want to do something to cause others pain and aggravation? Then, you are not a loving person.

Verse 6: Love does not rejoice in iniquity but rejoices in the truth. (NKJV). In other words, if you love somebody, you can't be looking for opportunities to say, "*Gotcha!*" If you love someone, you are not happy to see that person caught up in sin. When you love someone, you want the person to do well. Looking for opportunities to point fingers is not love. Love means you tell people the truth because you know the truth sets them free from iniquity.

Verse 7: It bears all things, believes all things, hopes all things, endures all things. (NKJV). If we believe this verse, then many of the divorces that have occurred would never have happened. You should always maintain hope and be willing to endure whatever and however long it may take for somebody that you love to come around. Your loved ones may not be perfect, but neither are you. This "never give up" love is what God the Father demonstrated to the children of Israel though they turned their back on Him. They did not trust Him, time and time again (Exodus, Leviticus, Numbers, Deuteronomy). Hope is exemplified by one of the names for God: "Abba Father." A love like a child's love as they look up at their parents, knowing that everything is all right. Jesus endured for us on the cross. Suppose when the pain began to seem unbearable, He had said, "That's enough! I can't take it any longer! Call the angels! Get me off this cross!" No, He endured for us. That is love.

Verse 8 begins with: Love never fails. (NKJV). There is no such thing as temporary love. When you love somebody, the love never ends. Think about the parent of a child that commits a horrific crime. That parent may hate the crime and have much remorse, but they still love the child. That is the way all love should be.

Jesus's Summary

- Greater love has no man than this.

These things have I spoken unto you, that my joy might remain in you, and that your joy might be full. This is my commandment, that ye love one another, as I have loved you. Greater love hath no man than this, that a man lay down his life for his friends. Ye are my friends, if ye do whatsoever I command you. Henceforth I call you not servants; for the servant knoweth not what his lord doeth: but I have called you friends; for all things that I have heard of my Father I have made known unto you. (John 15:11–15 KJV)

- I am dying willingly.

Jesus answered, my kingdom is not of this world: if my kingdom were of this world, then would my servants fight, that I should not be delivered to the Jews: but now is my kingdom not from hence. Pilate therefore said unto him, Art thou a king then? Jesus answered, thou sayest that I am a king. To this end was I born, and for this cause came I into the world, that I should bear witness unto the truth. Every one that is of the truth heareth my voice. (John 18:36–37 KJV)

- He loves to the end.

Jesus, when he had cried again with a loud voice, yielded up the ghost. And, behold, the veil of the temple was rent in twain from the top to the bottom; and the earth did quake, and the rocks rent. (Matthew 27:50–51 KJV)

Therefore, we all need to use the word *love* with a little more respect. Love is not just a word. We can like many things. We can like the utility of many things. We can like how things perform, how they look, how they smell, how they taste, and how they feel. However, love should be reserved for God and other human beings. Jesus showed us what love is. He died for those He loves. I am not willing to die for my truck, or cheesecake, or a trip to Paris. I like the utility of my truck. I may like cheesecake. I may like and enjoy a trip to Paris. However, to say I love these things gives them too much power over my life and priorities.

Some say this is agape love. It is only the kind of love that God shows toward man. Well, as Christians, what are we supposed to be doing besides trying to be like Christ? If love means being willing to die for those you love, as Christ demonstrated, it should mean the same for us.

> If you dare use the word "love" in your vocabulary, then say what you mean and mean what you say.

Therefore, I repent for not practicing true love all the time, Lord. I have been using your word, "love," carelessly. Lord, please forgive me, and help me to do better.

Chapter 5
I REPENT FOR NOT WATCHING

When people watch a weather forecast calling for rain, they might grab an umbrella. When they watch a forecast calling for snow, they might traditionally go out and buy bread and milk. When a person watches the first fruit from their trees fall on the ground in the summer, they know it is time to harvest. When new parents watch their infant become a toddler, they know it is time to put safety locks on cabinets and a gate at the top of the stairway. Large manufacturing companies today practice Six Sigma as a way to maximize quality output. One of the main tenants of Six Sigma is to analyze (watch) the outcome as it is being produced. Many organizations today are using "evidence based practices" (EBP) to make recommendations for structuring future modes of operation. They are watching what the evidence tells them. Scientists use trial and error methodology to find solutions to some of the world's greatest problems. They watch what works, and then try something else. In other words, we purchase things, prepare things, develop things, do things, and change things based on what we watch and observe. How does watching apply to our Christian life? What should Christians be watching? What does Christian watching direct us to do?

Let It Be

Many people seem to live their lives as if they do not have a care in the world, and their life is just like a leaf blowing in the wind. They will go whichever way the wind blows. They seem to have no goals or direction. It is as if life is living them, instead of them living life. The repercussions of this lifestyle show up when a watchful eye could have alerted them to be aware of opportunities and catastrophes ahead. Not watching is like not caring. A Christian trying to live like Christ must care about things that might be on the horizon. A Christian must care about his or her own life and the life of others. Therefore, having their antenna up to learn, and to observe and see what is going on is a must. In fact, watching is what gives us the ability to practice the gift of discernment (1 Corinthians 12:10).

Christians Watching

Watching does not mean worry. God is taking care of everything. He blesses us. He provides for us. He protects us. He loves us. Watching is an awareness. Watching is being prepared. Watching is like going to school. There is always something to learn via observation. In the Christian life, watching is described and explained in several passages.

> Then shall the kingdom of heaven be likened unto ten virgins, which took their lamps, and went forth to meet the bridegroom. And five of them were wise, and five were foolish. They that were foolish took their lamps, and took no oil with them: But the wise took oil in their vessels with their lamps. While the bridegroom tarried, they all slumbered and slept. And at midnight there was a cry made, Behold, the bridegroom cometh; go ye out to meet him. Then all those virgins arose, and trimmed their lamps. And the foolish said unto the wise, Give us of your oil; for our lamps are gone out. But the wise answered, saying, Not so; lest there be not enough for us and you: but go ye rather to them that sell, and buy for yourselves. And while they went to buy, the bridegroom came; and they that were ready went in with him to the marriage: and the door was shut. Afterward came also the other virgins, saying, Lord, Lord, open to us. But he answered and said, Verily I say unto you, I know you not.

> Watch therefore, for ye know neither the day nor the hour wherein the Son of man cometh. (Matthew 25:1–13 KJV)

Two things must be noted about this text. First, how did the wise get their knowledge to be wise? Had they paid attention (watched) and seen a similar situation earlier? Second, verses 8–10 show the horrible panic and danger of not being watchful. Are we as Christians watching, waiting, preparing, and living as if we really believe God and His angels can count the hairs on our head and keep track of every word that comes out of our mouth? Are Christians today living as if Jesus is on His way back? Are we preparing for the wedding?

The Bible tells us to give honor to whom honor is due. Meaning, we should be watching other godly people to learn from them. Christians should imagine themselves in biblical stories so they can watch the actions of those that behave righteously and those that do not. How can we do what Jesus does if we do not watch what Jesus did in the scriptures?

Watching and living in expectation should make us wake up every day feeling that God is with us and something great is about to happen. Watching and living in expectation should give us immense joy. Watching and living in expectation should give us great peace and assurance that something wonderful may happen at any moment.

Watching for Information

> And there ran a man of Benjamin out of the army, and came to Shiloh the same day with his clothes rent, and with earth upon his head. And when he came, lo, Eli sat upon a seat by the wayside watching: for his heart trembled for the ark of God. And when the man came into the city, and told it, all the city cried out. (1Samuel 4:12–13 KJV)

In this text, Eli is waiting for news from the front lines of battle. He was concerned about the ark of God and his two sons. He was watching to get the news as soon as possible. Many people today shrink from watching the news, but it is reality. It can be a warning for what is coming. It is not something to worry about but something that God wants us to plan for. The people who lived during the time of Noah should have paid attention to the news about a huge boat being built. They should have reacted when all types of animals went into the ark, two by two. It was time to make a better and more realistic decision. God was making a move, and it was time to repent and get on board.

Watching for Protection

> He trusted in the LORD God of Israel; so that after him was none like him among all the kings of Judah, nor any that were before him. For he clave to the LORD, and departed not from following him, but kept his commandments, which the LORD commanded Moses. And the LORD was with him; and he prospered whithersoever he went forth: and he rebelled against the king of Assyria, and served him not. He smote the Philistines, even unto Gaza, and the borders thereof, from the tower of the watchmen to the fenced city. (2 Kings 18:5–8 KJV)

Hezekiah was one king of Israel that did not turn his back on God. This text demonstrates one of the reasons for his success. Verse 8 says that there must have been a watchtower or many watchtowers set up outside of the city to look for approaching enemies. Today we do not use watchtowers. However, it is feasible in our life to have many things designed to protect us from seen and unforeseen dangers. Security cameras are everywhere watching us. Things like auto, health, and life insurance serve as our watchtowers in case something happens. Savings and investment accounts serve as watchtowers to protect our financial stability.

Watching for Opportunity

> And it came to pass, when they were gone over, that Elijah said unto Elisha, Ask what I shall do for thee, before I be taken away from thee. And Elisha said, I pray thee, let a double portion of thy spirit be upon me. And he said, Thou hast asked a hard thing: nevertheless, if thou see me when I am taken from thee, it shall be so unto thee; but if not, it shall not be so. And it came to pass, as they still went on, and talked, that, behold, there appeared a chariot of fire, and horses of fire, and parted them both asunder; and Elijah went up by a whirlwind into heaven. And Elisha saw it, and he cried, My father, my father, the chariot of Israel, and the horsemen thereof. And he saw him no more: and he took hold of his own clothes, and rent them in two pieces. (2 Kings 2:9–12 KJV)

There is no better example of being blessed in all the Bible than this passage. Elisha is told all he must do to be blessed is watch Elijah. There are many people in this world today that have been blessed by watching what others do. Then, when the time comes, they are promoted. The shame comes when opportunity arrives, and a person has not been watching the mentor close enough to take over.

Watching to Be Aware of Your Enemies

> And David abode in the wilderness in strong holds, and remained in a mountain in the wilderness of Ziph. And Saul sought him every day, but God delivered him not into his hand. And David saw that Saul was come out to seek his life: and David was in the wilderness of Ziph in a wood. (1 Samuel 23:14–15 KJV)

David was anointed to replace Saul on the throne, but Saul was not willing to bow out peacefully. Saul tried to kill him many times. It is wise to be aware of where your enemies are so you will know how they may approach you.

Watching for Support and Encouragement

Any person with a child knows about this reason to watch. The self-esteem of a three-year-old goes over the top when Mom or Dad takes the time to listen to him or her recite a poem or perform a cartwheel in the middle of the living room floor. All of us, even adults, like to have someone in our corner for support.

> And he took with him Peter and the two sons of Zebedee, and began to be sorrowful and very heavy. Then saith he unto them, My soul is exceeding sorrowful, even unto death: tarry ye here, and watch with me. And he went a little farther, and fell on his face, and prayed, saying, O my Father, if it be possible, let this cup pass from me: nevertheless not as I will, but as thou wilt. And he cometh unto the disciples, and findeth them asleep, and saith unto Peter, What, could ye not watch with me one hour? Watch and pray, that ye enter not into temptation: the spirit indeed is willing, but the flesh is weak. (Matthew 26:37–41 KJV)

Here Jesus Christ, the Son of God, shows that even He could have used some support as His earthly body was preparing to go through merciless pain and suffering. Peter, James, and John were His closest allies, and He seemed to long for their support. Jesus also tells them to watch and pray because they would be weak. Watching is critical.

Watching for God's Return

God expects us to live always in expectation of His return. It says in the book of Revelation that He will return with the angels.

Let your loins be girded about, and your lights burning; And ye yourselves like unto men that wait for their lord, when he will return from the wedding; that when he cometh and knocketh, they may open unto him immediately. Blessed are those servants, whom the lord when he cometh shall find watching: verily I say unto you, that he shall gird himself, and make them to sit down to meat, and will come forth and serve them. And if he shall come in the second watch, or come in the third watch, and find them so, blessed are those servants. And this know, that if the goodman of the house had known what hour the thief would come, he would have watched, and not have suffered his house to be broken through. Be ye therefore ready also: for the Son of man cometh at an hour when ye think not. (Luke 12:35–40 KJV)

But and if that servant say in his heart, My lord delayeth his coming; and shall begin to beat the menservants and maidens, and to eat and drink, and to be drunken; The lord of that servant will come in a day when he looketh not for him, and at an hour when he is not aware, and will cut him in sunder, and will appoint him his portion with the unbelievers. (Luke 12:45–46 KJV)

Watch therefore: for ye know not what hour your Lord doth come. But know this, that if the goodman of the house had known in what watch the thief would come, he would have watched, and would not have suffered his house to be broken up. (Matthew 24:42–43 KJV)

And unto the angel of the church in Sardis write; These things saith he that hath the seven Spirits of God, and the seven stars; I know thy works, that thou hast a name that thou livest, and art dead. Be watchful, and strengthen the things which remain, that are ready to die: for I have not found thy works perfect before God. Remember therefore

> how thou hast received and heard, and hold fast, and repent. If therefore thou shalt not watch, I will come on thee as a thief, and thou shalt not know what hour I will come upon thee. (Revelation 3:1–3 KJV)

All these texts are talking about being ready for God's return. He uses an analogy that describes watching and being ready at all times because a person does not know when a thief is coming. The implication is that we should all be always watching. We should be mindful of our Christian character, attitude, actions, behavior, and demeanor at all times because God is paying attention.

> Behold, I come as a thief. Blessed is he that watcheth, and keepeth his garments, lest he walk naked, and they see his shame. And he gathered them together into a place called in the Hebrew tongue Armageddon. (Revelation 16:15–16 KJV)

We are blessed and given much for being the children of God. And unto whom much is given, there is much required. We should live in this world *watching*, with joy, peace, and great expectations.

Therefore, Lord, I repent for not watching and living in expectation. Lord, please forgive me, and help me to do better.

Chapter 6

I REPENT FOR SOMETIMES ACTING LIKE THERE ARE ALTERNATIVES TO GOD

When a person goes to the grocery store today, there are twenty types of bread to choose from. There are ten types of toothpaste. There are hundreds of types of floorings for a house. There are hundreds of types of house designs. There are thousands of makes and models of vehicles to choose from. There are many types of lipstick and hair styles. Society is used to having a choice. We are especially used to making our own decisions and choosing our own desires in America. Our destiny is in our own hands. Or is it? What about God? Do we have the option of choosing? Who cares? The Bible says that the God of Abraham, Isaac, and Jacob represents the Father. The Bible says Jesus Christ is the Son. The Bible says the Holy Spirit is with us as the Comforter, and He reveals all truth.

As the world sees it, there are choices for deity acknowledgment, worship, and reverence. This is obviously true because there are many different religions. Volumes have been written about many of them individually and in comparison. Choosing between these religions is beyond the scope of this book. For the purposes of this book as explained in the preface, this chapter assumes Christianity is the choice, not between religions but against everything else besides other religions. Therefore, this chapter is more a comparison of the devout Christian with nonbelievers and lukewarm Christians. In other words, there is the God of Abraham, Isaac, and Jacob, or there is nothing.

> I am the LORD, and there is none else, there is no God beside me: I girded thee, though thou hast not known me: That they may know from the rising of the sun, and from the west, that there is none beside me. I am the LORD, and there is none else. I form the light, and create darkness: I make peace, and create evil: I the LORD do all these things. (Isaiah 45:5–7 KJV)

The Godhead

The Godhead of Christianity is expressed as the Trinity. In the world there are many ways to experience water—rivers, saltwater oceans, streams, hot springs, fresh-water lakes, waterfalls, dew, fog, rain, and ponds. All these water forms can exist at the same time. This is also true of God. Each manifestation of God must be believed and received as words revealed by God.

> For there are three that bear record in heaven, the Father, the Word, and the Holy Ghost: and these three are one. And there are three that bear witness in earth, the Spirit, and the water, and the blood: and these three agree in one. (1 John 5:7–8 KJV)

> All the saints salute you. The grace of the Lord Jesus Christ, and the love of God, and the communion of the Holy Ghost, be with you all. Amen. (2 Corinthians 13:13–14 KJV)

To be a Christian means that you are a believer and follower of Jesus and His teachings. Jesus referred to and supported what was in the Old Testament. He stated that He did not come to destroy the law but to fulfill it. (Matthew 5:17). This links Jesus the Son to everything in the Old Testament. Jesus mentions scripture from the Old Testament many times in the gospels. Also, Jesus said that He was the only bridge for humanity to get to God the Father. He does not leave any alternatives or room for interpretation.

> Thomas saith unto him, Lord, we know not whither thou goest; and how can we know the way? Jesus saith unto him, I am the way, the truth, and the life: no man cometh unto the Father, but by me. If ye had known me, ye should have known my Father also: and from henceforth ye know him, and have seen him. Philip saith unto him, Lord, show us the Father, and it sufficeth us. Jesus saith unto him, Have I been so long time with you, and yet hast thou not known me, Philip? he that hath seen me hath seen the Father; and how sayest thou then, Show us the Father? Believest thou not that I am in the Father, and the Father in me? the words that I speak unto you I speak not of myself: but the Father that dwelleth in me, he doeth the works. Believe me that I am in the Father, and the Father in me: or else believe me for the very works' sake. (John 14:5–11 KJV)

Continuing in this same chapter, Jesus says that He will send us the Holy Spirit. We were not left orphans after He ascended. We have a Comforter. The Holy Spirit should not be ignored.

> And I will pray the Father, and he shall give you another Comforter, that he may abide with you for ever; Even the Spirit of truth; whom the world cannot receive, because it seeth him not, neither knoweth him: but ye know him; for he dwelleth with you, and shall be in you. I will not leave you comfortless: I will come to you. (John 14:16–18 KJV)

Many people try to say the Bible is confusing. These texts are not confusing. They are not vague. Therefore, there is no alternative to accepting the Trinity. Either it is all true, or it is all a lie.

Atheists and Agnostics

There are many things in this life that we attempt to put in God's place. The first thing is just busyness. "I have things to do and people to see," is a common quote. Our life is lived at a fast pace. humankind has always been trying to come up with things to occupy our minds. Atheists and agnostics let the physical and material things of this life occupy their entire being. There is no consideration for God.

Atheists and agnostics have a lot of faith. They believe that we who have body, soul, and spirit have arrived here at this place and at this time in the twenty-first century by pure accident or happenstance. That takes a lot of faith. One day we were not, and the next day we were, like *poff*! Like magic, we humans just appeared. That takes a lot of faith. Many that believe this way go about their lives ignoring their Creator.

> The fool hath said in his heart, There is no God. They are corrupt, they have done abominable works, there is none that doeth good. The LORD looked down from heaven upon the children of men, to see if there were any that did understand, and seek God. They are all gone aside, they are all together become filthy: there is none that doeth good, no, not one. (Psalm 14:1–3 KJV)

Also, some atheists and agnostics believe humans have arrived where we are today by evolution. Even Darwin didn't believe this. He said that if things were discovered to be more complicated than he was aware of in his day, then evolution would not be possible. Hence, the discovery of deoxyribonucleic acid, (DNA) in zygotes that give the code for our makeup is too complex to say it happened by accident. There is no alternative. There is a God. Atheists and agnostics are wayside seed. The word of the Lord may never even get a chance to take root in the ground of their mind.

> Hear ye therefore the parable of the sower. When any one heareth the word of the kingdom, and understandeth it not, then cometh the wicked one, and catcheth away that

which was sown in his heart. This is he which received seed by the way side. (Matthew 13:18–19 KJV)

Humanity is not on this earth by magic. Humanity may have evolved after our arrival, but humanity did not evolve from a pile of dirt by the ocean. Our DNA is too complex. The electrical impulse that makes our heart beat every day is a miracle every time it happens. Doctors do not know what switch drives it. What made the first heartbeat start beating? How did the chicken arrive first if there was no egg? How did the egg arrive first, if there was no chicken to lay it? Who created black holes in space? Where does the force of the gravitational pull come from? The answer to these and many other similar questions is that there is a God. There is no alternative to that belief. Every answer an atheist gives to questions about creation will always leave room for the next question: "And, where does that come from?"

Christian Substitutions

Before those people who claim to believe in God get too high and mighty, there is evidence that these same people also tend to ignore the Creator. Based on their fruit and their lifestyles, you would think they did not believe. That is why atheists and agnostics say Christians are hypocrites.

God has not called everyone to be a pastor, priest, elder, deacon, or bishop. So, it is wonderful and okay that we all have careers, visions, and goals that lead us into different walks of life. The issue comes when we live the life God has blessed us with and forget to include God in any of our recognitions, decision-making, planning, and time allowances.

> *Being blessed with a good job or career is a blessing from God. It is not an alternative to God.*

Each of the following categories are not necessarily bad or negative. They become problematic when they are taken out of context compared to God's way and desire for our lives. When our blessed life gets ahead of the God who does the blessing, then our priorities have become misaligned.

Money. The pursuit of money can be all-consuming. (See the chapter on worldliness.) It can take up all our time. If it becomes our goal in life, it will never be enough. Raising money can become a god to a person if they let it. When it is all said and done, after a lifetime of hoarding cash, a person will be left feeling empty, wanting more, and realizing there had to be more to life. Many wealthy people find themselves unhappy and looking for solace in a bottle of alcohol or pills.

Education. This author apologizes quickly for even putting education on this list. Knowledge is good. Knowledge is power. However, we do know that some people carry this to the extreme. Nothing is wrong with being an engineer, a doctor, a lawyer, a top-notch mechanic, or a top salesman. Every profession takes time out of our lives to study, practice, and enhance our skills. Especially if a person is going to be professional and successful in his or her endeavors. One should be mindful, however, as the days go by, whether the five master's degrees and two doctorates are really what God wants you to do in His kingdom. Do not neglect your family to go to every training to become a top-notch mechanic when this may be a time when your children need you at home. Sometimes it may be appropriate, and sometimes it may not be.

Laws and politicians. America is a wonderful country. We are fortunate now that the voices of everyone can be heard. However, being the fallible humans we are, sometimes humankind has been harmed by our own laws and politicians. Do not count on our laws and politicians to save your soul. You still need God for that. Ours laws and politicians are only as moral and godly as the men and women they represent. They cannot be a substitute for God.

Family pedigree. Suppose your family is the well-known rich family in the neighborhood. For three generations, your family has been the well-known aristocratic real or perceived community leader. Everyone in the community wants to know what your family thinks about an issue before they verbalize their own beliefs. Unfortunately, all that family pedigree cannot buy health, peace of mind, moral aptitude, or salvation. Sometimes, a scandal comes out about a family like that in the community, and everyone whispers about how they are so surprised about how it could happen in that family. The truth of the matter is that no one is exempt from sin and Satan. Family pedigree cannot replace a relationship with God.

Athleticism. A seventeen-year-old, 60 percent three-point basketball shooter should be able to count on his or her six-feet-seven frame to be a success. Especially if they have been playing AAU summer league ball and playing for their local school system since they were in the sixth grade. The future looks promising. It seems like graduation day will come, college will come, then a high payday will come, and life will be easy from then on. The reality is that one injury could sideline the dream. The injury could come in high school. It could come in college. It could come during the first year of their professional contract. When and if an injury occurs, it should not be a time to go off the deep end and go into a ten-year depression. Even though a person may be blessed with physical attributes and athleticism, it is best to take God along for the ride. If the young athlete is successful, great. He or she can give glory to God and bless His name. If the young athlete has an injury or gets sidelined for some other reason, great. It was still a good experience, and everything learned can be used to give glory to God.

Knowing the right people. An old saying is that "it's not what you know, but who you know." There is no question that knowing the right people and being in the right place at the right time can elevate a person. A person can have a highly successful life playing a sort of "follow the leader," when the leader is successful. However, the right person can also do something wrong and drag you down. Only people who are trying to be true Christians should be followed. The right people in the eye of the public does not mean they are trying to be righteous in the eyes of God.

Lottery, gambling, luck. Time and time again, we have heard this story. Someone wins the lottery or has a good hand on a Las Vegas blackjack table. A lot of money is won. Suddenly, it looks like the tables have turned. It looks like the family will be on easy street from now on. Statistics say that will not be the case. Many lottery winners live good for two to three years and wind up broke shortly thereafter. Gamblers may have a good hand or two, but then they hit a losing streak, and everything changes.

Hard work and a good career. Yes, hard work is required to be successful. As opposed to luck, hard work is the surest way to success. The only issue here is when the work becomes your life. Jobs and careers are different. Sometimes a person does have to work hard for a period or stay away from home for a time. Sacrifices often must be made to survive. That is understandable. The suggestion is to weigh your purpose in life with whatever your work is dictating to you at the moment. Has work taken over everything? How long will it last?

Illegal activities. You are not mistaken. This is a book designed for people who are at least leaning toward accepting Jesus Christ as their Lord and Savior to start a journey toward being like Christ and learning to love your neighbor as yourself. However, we all know that nobody arrives at being "super-Christian," immediately after their baptism. Becoming a Christian is a process. Therefore, since this chapter is about repenting for finding alternatives to God, perhaps someone reading this is currently doing something or considering doing something illegal to get ahead. This is not an alternative to God. Short-term gains will reap you a long-term harvest. God's word says, we reap what we sow. Do not let Satan tempt you. Resist him. Rebuke him. Tell him you serve a risen Savior that loves you. Seek help from other sources if necessary.

> Money, our pedigree, our stature, our looks, and what some may call luck or anything else mentioned here, (except illegal activities), could be a blessing from God. It is not meant to replace God.

As stated earlier, all these things are okay and not necessarily sinful. It may seem that I am taking the negative point of view in each of these cases. Some may say that the positive aspect of these scenarios could have occurred. That is absolutely true. Positive things could have occurred. However, like Jesus said, "They that are whole have no need of a physician" (Mark 2:17 KJV). If they do and all parties take God with them along life's journey, then life could be good and meaningful and blessed. The purpose of this chapter is to caution those that believe any of the items listed can give them solace in living a life without God. So many people who look successful have otherwise depressing or hard lives. Often, you might hear them say, "I felt like something was missing." Or "I have never been happy." There is no alternative to a life with God. Nothing can replace Him.

The Bible says:

1. Genesis 1:1 proposes that God made the earth from nothing. If He created everything you can stand on, everything you are surrounded by, everything you breath, and everything that you drink, doesn't it seem logical that we should worship Him and realize He is in full control.
2. Job 38–41 asks questions that point out the omnipotent power and design of God: God laid the axis and dimensions of the earth. Where were you when He did it? What is holding things together? Is any human intelligent enough to decide how many clouds should be in the sky at one time? Can anybody even fathom all the good things that come from water in the form of snow versus rain? For that matter, does hail provide something different and meaningful to our earth? Does anyone give each drop, flake, or ice pellet specific guidance about where to land? The Bible asks Job about the design of the wings of a peacock, the strong power of a horse, and decisions eagles make about their time to fly. The chapters ask if any human can reach all the places God can reach. They ask if any human can create anything close to a clap of thunder. No man or woman is even aware of all the parameters that are holding the universe together. Yet, these things cannot be ignored. There is no alternative to the awesome power of God; therefore, all we should do is respect it and humble ourselves before it.
3. The Bible also informs us in Hebrews 11:6 that understanding and believing anything about our creation and the universe we live in is impossible unless we have a measure of faith. The stretch between the awesome universe we are a part of and our limited

understanding is too wide. So, to all those that say Christianity does not make any sense and is too far-fetched to believe, you are exactly right. It takes faith. Since no one reading this book was alive over two thousand years ago, it takes faith to believe that a man named Jesus Christ lived and walked the earth. However, biblical and secular proof exists that He did. Our ability to understand and explain does not take away from the fact that something is real. For years humanity thought the earth was flat when it was the same earth we enjoy today, rotating around the sun.

If you are hoping to find a God to serve, consider God the Father of Abraham, Isaac, and Jacob, Jesus Christ, and the Holy Spirit. If you are hoping to find your ticket to make it through this life, consider the Trinity. Sometimes people are tempted to push God to the side and spend all the precious time in their lives doing other things. However, this will not bring us peace. There is no alternative.

Therefore, I repent for sometimes acting like there are other alternatives to God. Lord, please forgive me, and help me to do better.

Chapter 7

I REPENT FOR NOT ASKING

Being able to ask for something is a privilege. It means that you have someone to ask that you believe can provide something you need or desire to have more of. Whether real or perceived, there are some people living that believe they have no one to turn to. However, Christians have God to turn to for everything we desire that is within the will of God. We should not hesitate to ask God for our desires. We should ask respectfully and humbly.

What Should I Ask For?

> Verily, verily, I say unto you, He that believeth on me, the works that I do shall he do also; and greater works than these shall he do; because I go unto my Father. And whatsoever ye shall ask in my name, that will I do, that the Father may be glorified in the Son. If ye shall ask any thing in my name, I will do it. (John 14:12–14 KJV)

These verses are together in the Bible for a reason that is especially important when it comes to asking. Yes, verse 14 clearly states: ask and you shall receive. The Son of God has promised us that He will do it. Looking closely, though, we can see that the promise to receive is tied to: (1) belief in Jesus Christ and all that He stands for, and (2) the works that Jesus did that glorified God the Father. In other words, we cannot tie God to every whimsical idea that comes to mind that has nothing to do with glorifying

God and expect God to deliver just because we have asked. People asking God to bless them with their nightclub, brothel, or illegal drug ring are not going to receive any help from God. People acting like God is blessing them because they are getting away with embezzling money from the company they work for are very misinformed. People asking God for help with their finances, and then taking money off of a coworker's desk later that afternoon are not receiving an answer to prayer and a gift from God. That is stealing. Being determined to do something sinful may be allowed by God. Even though it is not His "perfect" will, it may be a part of His "permissive" will. Satan also wants to make things happen for you so that he can destroy you. Affirmative answers from God will be for things that will give glory to God. Some examples of biblical requests to God include:

Elisha asked for a double portion (2 Kings 2:9–11). In this text, Elisha is told by Elijah in verse 10 that he has asked for a hard thing. It is important for us to know that if what we ask for is within the will of God, then nothing is too hard for God. That is what God told Abraham about Sarah laughing. Even though she was beyond the age of childbearing, God promised them a child. (Genesis 18:13–14). If the God we believe in did anything, then that same God can do everything. Elisha's request was hard, but it was not too hard for God. God answered the request.

Hannah asked for a child (1Samuel 1:13–20). Hannah asked without her voice being heard. The Bible says she was praying in her heart. When it comes to asking God for something, He can read our hearts. This is awesome. When a person really starts to appreciate having a relationship with God, things will start to happen that the servant of God just thinks about without even voicing it out loud. Hence, your thoughts are important. God moves on the thoughts of your heart. Ask Him what you will.

Gideon asked for a sign from God twice (Judges 6:16–22 and Judges 6:36–40). While on a journey with God, there will always be new decisions to make as we grow in our trust. Remember how the first few plagues in Egypt made the Hebrews upset, and Moses had to keep returning to petition God about the situation. As we travel along this journey, take advantage of the access you have to God. Call on Him repeatedly.

Gideon asked the first time in verse 17 wanting assurance that he was God's person to fight the Midianites. He was unsure because he was not from a prominent family. Gideon asked the second time in verses 36 and 39 for assurance that he would get the victory. Both times God revealed an answer. God will sometimes just lead you to the next step without revealing the full picture.

Solomon asked for wisdom (1 Kings 3:5–14). Solomon was succeeding his father on the throne. His father David had been a highly successful warrior king. God asked Solomon in a dream what he wanted. Solomon could have asked for riches, a long life, or the defeat of his enemies. Instead, Solomon asked for an understanding heart to judge the people fairly. He was more concerned with his effect on others instead of selfishly being concerned with what was in it for him. God rewards us for caring about others. It gives glory to God. Solomon received the answer to his request and much more.

What We Should Not Ask For

> Then came to him the mother of Zebedee's children with her sons, worshipping him, and desiring a certain thing of him. And he said unto her, What wilt thou? She saith unto him, Grant that these my two sons may sit, the one on thy right hand, and the other on the left, in thy kingdom. But Jesus answered and said, Ye know not what ye ask. Are ye able to drink of the cup that I shall drink of, and to be baptized with the baptism that I am baptized with? They say unto him, We are able. And he saith unto them, Ye shall drink indeed of my cup, and be baptized with the baptism that I am baptized with: but to sit on my right hand, and on my left, is not mine to give, but it shall be given to them for whom it is prepared of my Father. And when the ten heard it, they were moved with indignation against the two brethren. But Jesus called them unto him, and said, Ye know that the princes of the

> Gentiles exercise dominion over them, and they that are great exercise authority upon them. But it shall not be so among you: but whosoever will be great among you, let him be your minister; And whosoever will be chief among you, let him be your servant: Even as the Son of man came not to be ministered unto, but to minister, and to give his life a ransom for many. (Matthew 20:20–28 KJV)

James and John's mother asked inappropriately. She asked for selfish reasons. An air of pride and self-righteousness led her to want her sons in a more prominent position than the other ten disciples. Asking God for selfish reasons is not going to work.

> From whence come wars and fightings among you? come they not hence, even of your lusts that war in your members? Ye lust, and have not: ye kill, and desire to have, and cannot obtain: ye fight and war, yet ye have not, because ye ask not. Ye ask, and receive not, because ye ask amiss, that ye may consume it upon your lusts. (James 4:1–3 KJV)

Asking God to bless you to open your nightclub may result in a resounding no from God. He will not bless your brothel, your strip club, or your drug business. Those that find themselves successful in these businesses may be getting help from the devil himself because he knows the outcome of these types of businesses. He knows the destruction and negative impact on lives that will occur.

Sometimes We May Not Know What to Ask For

> For we are saved by hope: but hope that is seen is not hope: for what a man seeth, why doth he yet hope for? But if we hope for that we see not, then do we with patience wait for it. Likewise the Spirit also helpeth our infirmities: for we know not what we should pray for as we ought: but

the Spirit itself maketh intercession for us with groanings which cannot be uttered. (Romans 8:24–26 KJV)

This is truly a blessing. Amid not being sure about what to do, God is still looking out for us. Verse 26 says that the Holy Spirit is blessing us. People who do not know what to ask and pray for can simply be still in the presence of God and be blessed.

The Hesitation to Ask

Too shy. Have you ever seen a small child when their parent is trying to teach them to ask for something they want? The child may shy away and hide behind the parent. Or the child may stand there and just not open their mouth. Perhaps the child will feel like they do not know how to ask correctly. Some children will finally say something but will mumble it as if it hurts them to ask. Meanwhile, a grandparent, aunt, uncle, friend, or neighbor is standing by just waiting to give the child what he or she wants. Even after doing this several times, some children still hesitate to ask. It is as if there is a magnet on the other end of their voice that is trying to keep them from getting the words out of their throat. Sometimes even adults seem to have the same magnet in their bodies. There is no reason to be shy before God. He knows you already. He created you.

Not taught. Have you ever considered why there is such hesitation for we as Christians to ask what we want from God? Truthfully, many people who have become Christians may not have had a good upbringing and were never taught the importance of asking with a please at the end of a request. Many people have never been taught and therefore do not understand the importance of approaching someone that has what we need and saying, "May I?" "Will you?" "Can I?" or "Can we?" Asking is important. Teach yourself to do it if you have not been taught. God instructs us and gives many examples to us about asking.

Too afraid. There also may be those that are afraid. They may be afraid that they are not worthy to ask. They may be afraid that their request will be refused. They may be afraid that they will make the potential giver angry just for asking. In this case, fear makes them hesitate. The person must be sensitive to why they are fearful. Past abuse or retribution for asking of any kind may warrant caution. Perhaps other issues need to be worked out prior to asking. On the other hand, one should not be afraid to ask because they feel unworthy or that they may receive a no answer. The crucial point is that the request must be asked to receive a yes, so ask. There is no reason to fear God.

Too proud. Lastly, there may be some who know that asking works, but they are so prideful that they refuse to humble themselves to receive something they may need. They may refuse to ask because they resent that someone else has something, and they have not figured out how to get it by themselves. Satan had a pride problem when it comes to God. Asking implies that the person asking is needy and Satan did not like that position. Humanity should realize that we are needy and therefore be willing to ask God.

Ask Respectfully and Humbly

God is our Creator. It is not meant for us to demand anything from Him. It is not appropriate for a child to demand what a parent should do or should not do. It is not appropriate for a child to demand what a parent should give or not give. It is the parent's responsibility to decide what is best for the child. Likewise, we must respect who God is.

> Woe unto him that striveth with his Maker! Let the potsherd strive with the potsherds of the earth. Shall the clay say to him that fashioneth it, What makest thou? or thy work, He hath no hands? Woe unto him that saith unto his father, What begettest thou? or to the woman, What hast thou brought forth? Thus saith the LORD, the Holy One of Israel, and his Maker, Ask me of things to come concerning my sons, and concerning the work of my hands command ye me. I have made the earth, and created man upon it: I, even my hands, have stretched out

the heavens, and all their host have I commanded. (Isaiah 45:9–12 KJV)

Jesus Himself demonstrated that He does not make demands of God the Father. In the Garden of Gethsemane, Jesus said He wanted God the Father's will to be done.

> And saith unto them, My soul is exceeding sorrowful unto death: tarry ye here, and watch. And he went forward a little, and fell on the ground, and prayed that, if it were possible, the hour might pass from him. And he said, Abba, Father, all things are possible unto thee; take away this cup from me: nevertheless not what I will, but what thou wilt. (Mark 14:34–36 KJV)

This is a perfect example. Jesus the son of God knew how to ask. He was very humble and willing to concede to whatever God the Father decided. We should do likewise.

Ask Believing

Sometimes things happen in a person's life that are simply by chance. Often Christians say there is no such thing as luck, but the Bible says differently.

> I returned, and saw under the sun, that the race is not to the swift, nor the battle to the strong, neither yet bread to the wise, nor yet riches to men of understanding, nor yet favour to men of skill; but time and chance happeneth to them all. For man also knoweth not his time: as the fishes that are taken in an evil net, and as the birds that are caught in the snare; so are the sons of men snared in an evil time, when it falleth suddenly upon them. This wisdom have I seen also under the sun, and it seemed great unto me. (Ecclesiastes 9:11–13 KJV)

Therefore, things can happen by pure chance. However, when a person asks for something, a decision has already been made to take the desired result out of the hands of chance. The reason for the request is to receive whatever is desired as an answer. A request is useless if one does not believe that whomever they are making the request to can deliver.

> If any of you lack wisdom, let him ask of God, that giveth to all men liberally, and upbraideth not; and it shall be given him. But let him ask in faith, nothing wavering. For he that wavereth is like a wave of the sea driven with the wind and tossed. For let not that man think that he shall receive any thing of the Lord. (James 1:5–7 KJV)

> And Jesus answering saith unto them, Have faith in God. For verily I say unto you, That whosoever shall say unto this mountain, Be thou removed, and be thou cast into the sea; and shall not doubt in his heart, but shall believe that those things which he saith shall come to pass; he shall have whatsoever he saith. Therefore I say unto you, What things soever ye desire, when ye pray, believe that ye receive them, and ye shall have them. (Mark 11: 22–24 KJV)

It is almost as if asking is like a person looking for a job. Going to the interview with slumped shoulders and a "Whoa is me" demeanor will not land a person the position when he or she is competing with others that have a good, positive, can-do attitude. Asking from God is much more serious, but believing that it is possible to receive the answer is a prerequisite.

Keep on Asking

Shy children were mentioned earlier in this chapter. On the other hand, some children are not afraid to ask for anything they want. In fact, children that are not afraid or shy are usually the most persistent about their desires. Many will ask something four or five times to get an answer. "Where are we going?" Are we there yet?" "May I have it?" "Well, may I have it if …?" "May I go with my friend?" "Why not?" "All my other friends are going." There is something to be said for persistence when it comes to asking.

> Then He spoke a parable to them, that men always ought to pray and not lose heart, saying: "There was in a certain city a judge who did not fear God nor regard man. Now there was a widow in that city; and she came to him, saying; "Get justice for me from my adversary." And he would not for a while; but afterward he said within himself, "Though I do not fear God nor regard man, yet because this widow troubles me I will avenge her, lest by her continual coming she weary me." Then the Lord said, "Hear what the unjust judge said. And shall God not avenge His own elect who cry out day and night to Him, though He bears long with them? I tell you that He will avenge them speedily. Nevertheless, when the Son of Man comes, will He really find faith on the earth?" (Luke 18:1–8)

Jesus told this parable, which suggests that we keep asking. Some people say that asking again is not trusting. The Bible does not suggest that. Sometimes it took many years before God responded to some prayer request. In fact, earlier in the Gospel of Luke, in chapter 11, there are many verses dedicated to the positive results from continuing to ask. The first thirteen verses are all about asking. The chapter starts off with the model prayer wherein Jesus suggests that we ask for what we need for the day. The prayer also asks to be forgiven, to be able to avoid temptation, and to be delivered from evil. These are specific things every Christian should ask for, every day. Then, Jesus explains a specific parable about asking. The friend of someone comes asking for bread at midnight. The analogy teaches that the friend eventually gets what he wants, not because it makes sense, but because of the persistence and late-night hour of the request. It turns out that the friendship itself is not enough. Perhaps, we should all petition God after midnight. Perhaps we should all keep on knocking. Finally, these verses end with a lesson on the omniscience of God. He knows what we need, and He will give us what is best for us. So, keep on asking.

The Response

> Ask, and it shall be given you; seek, and ye shall find; knock, and it shall be opened unto you: For every one that asketh receiveth; and he that seeketh findeth; and to him that knocketh it shall be opened. Or what man is there of you, whom if his son ask bread, will he give him a stone? Or if he ask a fish, will he give him a serpent? If ye then, being evil, know how to give good gifts unto your children, how much more shall your Father which is in heaven give good things to them that ask him? (Matthew 7:7–11)

God is waiting to bless us. He is waiting to answer our godly request. There is only one way to guarantee you will "not" receive anything unless it is left up to pure chance; and that is *by not asking*.

Therefore, I repent for not asking. I ask for your wisdom. I ask for a righteous world, nation, city, and home. I ask that our nation will repent, like Nineveh, with sackcloth and ashes. Lord, please forgive me, and help me to do better with my asking.

Chapter 8

I REPENT FOR NOT ACKNOWLEDGING THE FRUITS OF THE SPIRIT WITHIN ME

The God that Christians serve is a triune God as mentioned in other chapters. Jehovah God is the Father. Jesus Christ is the Son. The Holy Spirit is the third part of the Trinity. The Holy Spirit is inside of us when we accept Jesus Christ as our Savior. Galatians 5 tells us what the fruits of the Holy Spirit are. It tells us what should be showing up in our lives because of the indwelling. For our Christian fruit to show up, we must turn our past loose and stop ignoring the God that is now in us.

It Is in Us

Planting an apple tree or a peach tree will not render you a good harvest of walnuts. Likewise, you can love cucumbers all you want. You can dream about cucumbers. You can go the grocery store and buy them and put them all over your house. However, if you want to grow some cucumbers you will never be able to get them from a tomato plant. Apple trees yield apples. Peach trees yield peaches. Tomato plants yield tomatoes.

> Know ye not that ye are the temple of God, and that the Spirit of God dwelleth in you? If any man defiles the temple of God, him shall God destroy; for the temple of

God is holy, which temple ye are. (1 Corinthians 3:16–17 KJV)

Same branch with different fruit. This should not be. A watermelon, banana, and apple cannot grow together. How can you be a Christian with strange fruit? Pride, arrogance, hatred, malice, witchcraft, and idolatry do not belong on the branch of a Christian. What fruit on your branch needs to be removed?

The fruits of the Spirit are diverse, but they are the same. They all show love and reverence to God and love for fellow human beings. Some of the fruit may not be as developed as others, but the Holy Spirit in us is working on that. All the fruit has the same purpose.

If the truth be known, we should be producing the fruit of the new Spirit that is dwelling in us once we accept Jesus Christ. New fruit that we need to acknowledge twenty-four hours a day, seven days a week, for 365 days a year. This new fruit is powerful.

> Because the carnal mind is enmity against God: for it is not subject to the law of God, neither indeed can be. So then they that are in the flesh cannot please God. But ye are not in the flesh, but in the Spirit, if so be that the Spirit of God dwell in you. Now if any man have not the Spirit of Christ, he is none of his. And if Christ be in you, the body is dead because of sin; but the Spirit is life because of righteousness. But if the Spirit of him that raised up Jesus from the dead dwell in you, he that raised up Christ from the dead shall also quicken your mortal bodies by his Spirit that dwelleth in you. (Romans 8:7–11 KJV)

The Holy Spirit indwells believers. Verse 11 clearly states that the same power that raised Jesus from the dead can also control our bodies.

The Fruits

People should be able to look at our lives and see that we are striving to be more like Christ. No one can claim to have arrived at being a perfect Christian, but that is the goal. In the meantime, as a person that loves the Lord is growing in grace, there should be more Christian fruit showing up today than there was ten years ago.

> Ye have heard that it hath been said, Thou shalt love thy neighbour, and hate thine enemy. But I say unto you, Love your enemies, bless them that curse you, do good to them that hate you, and pray for them which despitefully use you, and persecute you; That ye may be the children of your Father which is in heaven: for he maketh his sun to rise on the evil and on the good, and sendeth rain on the just and on the unjust. For if ye love them which love

> you, what reward have ye? do not even the publicans the same? And if ye salute your brethren only, what do ye more than others? do not even the publicans so? Be ye therefore perfect, even as your Father which is in heaven is perfect. (Matthew 5:43–48 KJV)

God calls all of us to strive for perfection. In the Greek translation, *perfection* means maturity. We should have more Christian fruit today than we had five years ago. We should be approaching maturity like an exponential line approaching infinity. Every day there should be less sinful behavior and a little more spiritual fruit resonating from our being.

> Now the works of the flesh are evident, which are: adultery, fornication, uncleanness, lewdness, idolatry, sorcery, hatred, contentions, jealousies, outbursts of wrath, selfish ambitions, dissensions, heresies, envy, murders, drunkenness, revelries, and the like; of which I tell you beforehand, just as I also told you in time past, that those who practice such things will not inherit the kingdom of God. But the fruit of the Spirit is love, joy peace, longsuffering, kindness, goodness, faithfulness, gentleness, self-control. Against such there is no law. (Galatians 5:19–23 NKJV)

Love. People should be able to see, feel, and hear genuine love coming from anyone claiming to be a Christian. All things that are done should reflect the love described in 1 Corinthians 13:4–8. True love is never focused on self. That is selfishness and vanity.

Joy. The joy of God is manifested on the inside of a person and is then revealed on the outside of a person. This joy cannot be removed by happenings that occur around or outside of a person.

Peace. According to Matthew 5:9, peacemakers are due a special blessing from God. They will be especially designated as children of God. Christians should always be the type of person seeking peace.

Long-suffering. Christians cannot always be impatient. Sometimes things may have to be resolved in a hurry for various reasons. However, most of the time a Christian should be willing to take all the time necessary to bring someone else along. Remember how long-suffering God the Father was with the Israelites of the Old Testament. Repeatedly, they turned their backs on Him, but He kept on being patient and making a way for them. Remember how patient God was with you, to get you where you are today.

Kindness. Not enough can be said about this important word. How many marriages could be saved by having a kind attitude and response to a spouse's question. Instead of barking like a mad dog and biting someone's head off each time you speak, a kind word is much better.

Goodness. What does it mean to be good? In Matthew 19:17, Jesus once said, "Why do you call Me good? No one is good but One, that is God. But if you want to enter into life, keep the commandments." Jesus the Son of God says here that no one earns the right to call themselves good. You can call yourself a good person or say you have done good deeds, but it will not earn you a place in the kingdom. Even though this is true, the Spirit in us should make us long to do things that are good for God and for humanity.

Faithfulness. The Holy Spirit inside of you will constantly teach you the ways and will of God. People then have the opportunity to show themselves faithful to God as they mature as Christians. Hebrews 5:12–14 talks about young Christians needing milk like a baby, implying they are not ready for solid food. The text says, "Solid food belongs to those who are of full age." That means those that are spiritually mature. In other words, you must believe in faith and have proven yourself faithful.

Gentleness. Remember when you or someone in your family brought home a newborn baby. It is impossible to believe how small they can be unless you have held one. Even big nine- or ten-pound babies remind us of how delicate we are when we arrive. People are so careful when handling the newborn. The baby is laid down gently and picked up gently. The bed is made to be soft. The covers are soft. Everything around the baby is arranged or designed to make any contact with the infant to be as soft as possible. Can you imagine how gently the mother of Moses laid her infant son in the small basket she made to put him in the Nile? (Exodus 2:1–8). As Christians, we should all be that sensitive with one another. People have feelings, issues, and concerns. People should be treated gently because you never know what they may have been through on any given day.

Self-control. The Bible has a lot of drama, but Jesus in the face of Pilate had to be an awesome scene. Pilate did not realize that he was in the presence of someone with more power than him.

> Then saith Pilate unto him, Speakest thou not unto me? knowest thou not that I have power to crucify thee, and have power to release thee? Jesus answered, Thou couldest have no power at all against me, except it were given thee from above: therefore he that delivered me unto thee hath the greater sin. (John 19:10–11 KJV)

This is one of the most dramatic, intense moments in the Bible. Jesus and Pilate are face-to-face. Pilate is the supreme ruler of the land, and he represents the strongest country in the world at the time—Rome. And yet, here is this Jew (a second-class citizen compared to Roman citizens), staring him down. This slave that was betrayed by his own people has the nerve to question Pilate's power. Jesus Christ, the Son of God who could call down legions of angels, shows the ultimate example of self-control. All Christians that want to be like Christ are given a perfect example of controlling your mouth and your actions no matter what.

Walk in It

All these fruits of the Spirit are important. In other words, these are the apples that should be growing from every Christian's apple tree. We are Christians. And our fruit should be love, joy, peace, long-suffering, kindness, gentleness, goodness, faithfulness, and self-control. Anything else that shows up in our character is the wrong fruit coming from the wrong tree. We should not be proud and boastful when we see the wrong fruit. We should be working and longing to produce the right fruit.

And they that are Christ's have crucified the flesh with the affections and lusts. If we live in the Spirit, let us also walk in the Spirit. Let us not be desirous of vain glory, provoking one another, envying one another. (Galatians 5:24–26 KJV)

Shaking the Past

The Holy Spirit is a gift from God. People should be proud of it instead of how we acted in the past. Most children would be more anxious to play with their latest toy that they just asked for, as opposed to the one they received three years ago. It may really be time to give up the old toy because the child has outgrown it.

> Therefore if any man be in Christ, he is a new creature: old things are passed away; behold, all things are become new. And all things are of God, who hath reconciled us to himself by Jesus Christ, and hath given to us the ministry of reconciliation; To wit, that God was in Christ, reconciling the world unto himself, not imputing their trespasses unto them; and hath committed unto us the word of reconciliation. (2 Corinthians 5:17–19 KJV)

We are not our past selves. We are not the same person that we were before we accepted Christ. We are no longer isolated from God. We have been reconciled to Him in the resurrection of Jesus Christ.

> Ye shall know them by their fruits. Do men gather grapes of thorns, or figs of thistles? Even so every good tree bringeth forth good fruit; but a corrupt tree bringeth forth evil fruit. A good tree cannot bring forth evil fruit, neither can a corrupt tree bring forth good fruit. Every tree that bringeth not forth good fruit is hewn down, and cast into the fire. Wherefore by their fruits ye shall know them. (Matthew 7:16–20 KJV)

Ignoring the Fruits of the Spirit

So, why do we as Christians seem to revel in our bad attitudes as if we are proud of them? Some even say, "I almost lost my religion." Or "They better be glad I'm saved." It's like we are bragging about the bad dog that is still buried deep within us. Then we threaten to bring it out as if that is our major and most important weapon to defend ourselves with. We act like the Holy Spirit in us has no power at all. We ignore the Holy Spirit that has been given to us.

Someone has a successful business. It is not failing, but neither is it excelling. It is just surviving from month to month. Then, one day, the owner comes up with an exciting new idea. A trip is made to the bank, and a loan is approved to start production of the new idea. The owner now has more than enough financing to launch and advertise the new invention. However, weeks, months, and even years go by, and the new loan line of credit is never tapped. The new idea is still on a piece of paper stashed with other papers in the owner's desk. An opportunity has been wasted. Every month the bank sends a statement showing we have access to the extended line of credit, but it is ignored.

A person buys some exercise equipment: a treadmill, a stationary bike, and some weights. The goal is to improve his or her stamina, agility, and overall health. The equipment will help the person walk with more assurance and self-esteem. However, this equipment has been in the basement for two years. It has never been used. The price tag is still hanging on the handlebars of the exercise bike. On top of that, there is no real intention of using the equipment anytime soon. The person laughs and tells jokes about the unused equipment and would rather talk seriously about the entire cake he or she ate in one sitting last week. The exercise equipment is getting ignored and dusty.

The Holy Spirit may be set aside and ignored, but it is not weak. Christians must make a choice daily to be like Christ or not.

> Ye are of God, little children, and have overcome them: because greater is he that is in you, than he that is in the world. They are of the world: therefore speak they of the world, and the world heareth them. (1 John 4:4–5 KJV)

He is inside of us when we are baptized. We just need to acknowledge that He is in there and honor His presence. We often talk about God the Father and Jesus the Son. It seems people try to ignore the Holy Spirit.

Therefore, I repent for not acknowledging the fruits of the Spirit within me. Lord, please forgive me, and help me to do better.

Chapter 9

I REPENT FOR BEING SO SELFISH THAT I FORGET THE PLIGHT OF THE POOR

It is easy to forget the plight of the poor because we do not often run in the same circles. I am not homeless, so I have a bed to sleep in tonight. My cabinets and refrigerator are not empty, so I have food to eat today. How is it that we can be so preoccupied that we do not realize someone is about to be homeless? How is it that we can be so preoccupied that we do not realize someone does not have food in their cabinets or refrigerator? How is it that we can be so preoccupied that we do not pay attention to children wearing the same smelly, raggedy clothes day after day? Have we become accustomed to ignoring it? Do we attempt to forget it? There are a few issues when it comes to helping the poor. Some say it is their own fault that they are poor. Helping the poor is inconvenient and time consuming. However, helping the poor shows our true love for humanity.

Ignoring Their Plight

Many television commercials, especially on Christian stations, portray disadvantaged children in Africa, India, or South America. The children are portrayed hungry, malnourished, and living in poor conditions. Some of the commercials say menial amounts of money will feed a child for a month. All these dire situations are real. No doubt, there are many disadvantaged children in many foreign lands.

Likewise, we see the same type of commercials for mistreated dogs. Many dogs have been abandoned. Many dogs have been malnourished. There is no doubt that there are mistreated animals all over the world.

However, when have you seen a commercial about hungry, malnourished, and poor children on "A" Avenue, "B" Street, or "C" Boulevard that live just one or two blocks from where you live. Somehow, it's easier to turn the channel when the problem is "over there." Somehow the problem is easier to ignore when it is in a foreign country. Somehow it is easier to go to our nice, well-decorated worship buildings on Sunday morning than to go into the subsidized housing or the projects in your city on Saturday night to address the physical needs that people have right down the street from us. It is easier to zone the city so that subsidized housing and projects are on the other side of town, and we do not even have to look at them. Some laws and ordinances seem to be passed to keep people away—out of sight and out of mind. It is easier for people to detach from poor human beings when the problem is somewhere else (foreign) or not us (dogs).

> Hearken, my beloved brethren, Hath not God chosen the poor of this world rich in faith, and heirs of the kingdom which he hath promised to them that love him? But ye have despised the poor. Do not rich men oppress you, and draw you before the judgment seats? (James 2:5–6 KJV)

God deeply cares about poor people all over the world. That includes those that live right next door to us. God knows when the poor are taken advantage of. The poor are not ignored by God.

> If a brother or sister be naked, and destitute of daily food, And one of you say unto them, Depart in peace, be ye warmed and filled; notwithstanding ye give them not those things which are needful to the body; what doth it profit? Even so faith, if it hath not works, is dead, being alone. (James 2:15–17 KJV)

It is not enough just to realize the poor are there. They should not be ignored. Christians are called to do something about it. Our society says get more, take more, and go more, when some among us are just trying to find some food to eat tonight. Our quest for the nicer car, the best-groomed poodle, the most prestigious vacation, the nicest restaurant has made us turn a blind eye to the poorest among us.

Forgetting Their Plight

Except for sporting events or concerts, classes in America do not often mix. People tend to hang out with people of the same class. Wealthy people send their children to elite private schools and colleges. The rich invite other rich people to their weddings. Middle-class and poor people also attend family and friend gatherings with people in their socioeconomic genre. Of course, these are general statements. Lines do cross periodically. Not every rich person goes to a private school. However, it is so easy to be living a life that allows you to get comfortable and think everybody is living your type of life situation. That is a myth. Each class will have different setbacks, concerns, and goals in life. Consider these scenarios.

Scenario 1—rich. Last night the men at the Green Club voted to include me in the organization. It is going to be fun from now on. That means my wife will be included with their wives when they go shopping in exclusive shopping malls all over the world. My wife will now wear the finest clothes. As for me, I have a teatime with the guys this afternoon. A game of golf can take all day. Three to four hours on the front nine and then, four hours on the back nine with lunch in between. Life is busy. Especially, since I work ten- to twelve-hour days, six days a week. Now maybe, since I received this promotion, we can move to a nicer neighborhood. I hope we can find a nanny.

Scenario 2—middle class. During football season, I do not have any time for myself. My oldest daughter is in the band now, at Alamance High. My son is a senior football player. My youngest daughter is taking gymnastics. On top of all that, Lois, my next-door neighbor, wants me to go with her to the flea market every Saturday this summer to help her sell some of her deco mesh reefs. That is not going to bother me because there should be enough room on the display table for me to show off my handmade aprons. A lot of people at the church really seem to like them. I hope my husband can get the car fixed for me to do some of the driving with Lois, since I will be selling some items also.

Scenario 3—poor. Today is the last time I must go to this boring finance class. They want to tell you what to do like they know everything. Anyhow, that is the only way I qualified for the $300 stipend they were giving away. I need to be at home to see if that apartment maintenance man is coming today. He has been lying to me about fixing that refrigerator for six weeks. With my food stamps, we may make it until the twentieth before we run out of food this month. I am glad my sixteen-year-old son is close enough to school to walk to football practice. And I wish my daughter would stop acting like she has an attitude because I cannot afford her school pictures. She should know we do not have it like that.

These scenarios are vastly different. Neither necessarily frames the people as bad or good, but they are different. The point is that each scenario demonstrates how anyone can get so caught up in the details of their day that they must plan to and purposefully think about how others are living.

Affluent people may worry about where to get the Rolls Royce, Lincoln, Mercedes, Lamborghini, or Cadillac washed and detailed. One of the top concerns for affluent people may be where to leave the poodle while we fly to Paris for the weekend. Middle-class people may be concerned with taking the car to their local mechanic so all the kids can get to their soccer game. Middle-class people may splurge on a night out and go to a fancy bistro restaurant once a quarter or twice a year.

However, a poor person may not get to decide on a luxury to choose from. There is no Paris vacation and no poodle. Poodles cost too much to get groomed. Not to mention vet charges. There may not even be a family sedan to take to a mechanic. The car better be something I can fix in the back yard. The soccer game better be within walking distance, or the bus will have to pick me up. A poor person may never have been to a bistro restaurant.

So, what is the difference between an affluent person, a middle-class person, and a poor person? The poor person may not get to eat tonight. The poor person may not have heat in the winter or air conditioning in the summer. The poor person may have the water turned off by the city for failure to pay the water bill. The poor person may be homeless.

Some Say Poor People Are Lazy, So It Is Their Own Fault

What does it take to be poor? In the age of the recent pandemic, this question has been answered loudly. Prior to this pandemic, many said poor decisions and laziness were the cause for poverty. It was said that people just like welfare and living for handouts. Well, now the pandemic God allowed has answered this question with a response that many seem to have forgotten. Sometimes bad things do happen to good people. If a bad thing can happen to the entire world at one time, it can certainly happen on a micro scale in one state, in one town, in one industry, or on one job. Many people have had bad things happen to them. Some people have had many bad things happen to them. Perhaps we did not know about it because it was not as newsworthy as the recent pandemic.

It is sad when a higher-class person in society assumes that all poor people, or those of a lower class, decide to be poor and that they are less than them because of their poverty.

> And being in Bethany in the house of Simon the leper, as he sat at meat, there came a woman having an alabaster box of ointment of spikenard very precious; and she brake the box, and poured it on his head. And there were some that had indignation within themselves, and said, Why was this waste of the ointment made? For it might have been sold for more than three hundred pence, and have been given to the poor. And they murmured against her. And Jesus said, Let her alone; why trouble ye her? she hath

> wrought a good work on me. For ye have the poor with you always, and whensoever ye will ye may do them good: but me ye have not always. (Mark 14:3–7 KJV)

Many young people are growing up in poverty today. These young people are learning, making decisions, eating, and sleeping in everyday poverty. To blame a child for making bad decisions when he or she is going to bed hungry is like blaming a rape victim for being raped. Many seniors today live in poverty. According to a recent survey, prior to the COVID pandemic that swept the world, "A staggering 1 in 6 Americans said that they could not afford 'food' at times within the past year."[9] Some have tried to say that others buy what they want to when they want to. That implies everybody has a choice about everything that can be purchased. That is not the case. Some people are in situations wherein they absolutely cannot afford some things right now, and their humanity should be considered.

Another important point out of this text is that since the poor are with us all the time, Band-Aids do not work. Giving someone a gift at Christmastime may be nice, and it may make us feel good, but it does not solve the problem when a child is sitting at home two days after Christmas with nothing to eat. Giving children a backpack is not a permanent fix either. When people are poor and have lost hope, they may need help on many levels. It is not an easy fix.

Helping the Poor Is Inconvenient and Costly

Old preachers years ago used to say, "In order to be a shepherd, you have to be willing to smell like sheep." The poor are a "needy" bunch. They need food, clothing, and a ride to somewhere. They may need something for their children or a down payment for something or for somebody to get them to their appointment on time. How ashamed and embarrassed do they need to be before we are willing to help? Do people honestly believe that someone less fortunate than them is worthy? Christians should be willing to do all they can for the poor to set them free from their situation.

> And if thy brother be waxen poor, and fallen in decay with thee; then thou shalt relieve him: yea, though he be a stranger, or a sojourner; that he may live with thee. Take thou no usury of him, or increase: but fear thy God; that thy brother may live with thee. Thou shalt not give him thy money upon usury, nor lend him thy victuals for increase. I am the LORD your God, which brought you forth out of the land of Egypt, to give you the land of Canaan, and to be your God. And if thy brother that dwelleth by thee be waxen poor, and be sold unto thee; thou shalt not compel him to serve as a bondservant: But as an hired servant, and as a sojourner, he shall be with thee, and shall serve thee unto the year of jubilee. And then shall he depart from thee, both he and his children with him, and shall return unto his own family, and unto the possession of his fathers shall he return. For they are my servants, which I brought forth out of the land of Egypt: they shall not be sold as bondmen. Thou shalt not rule over him with rigor; but shalt fear thy God. (Leviticus 25:35–43 KJV)

So much is said in this Old Testament text. People are not supposed to take advantage of others due to their financial situation. People should not use other people for a profit if they have fallen into poverty. People and their families were never meant to be long-term slaves for a profit. God reminds us that He is the one that saves us. He is the one that should be in charge of other people.

Helping the Poor Is Love

"God is love" (1 John 4:8 KJV). This is a recurring theme in the Bible and throughout this book. Jesus suggested that being fake when it comes to poverty and people in need is not going to fool Him when it comes to how we handle the poor. When discussing dividing the true sheep of God from the goats that don't really care, Jesus explained it this way.

When the Son of man shall come in his glory, and all the holy angels with him, then shall he sit upon the throne of his glory:

And before him shall be gathered all nations: and he shall separate them one from another, as a shepherd divides his sheep from the goats:

And he shall set the sheep on his right hand, but the goats on the left.

Then shall the King say unto them on his right hand, Come, ye blessed of my Father, inherit the kingdom prepared for you from the foundation of the world:

For I was an hungred, and ye gave me meat: I was thirsty, and ye gave me drink: I was a stranger, and ye took me in:

Naked, and ye clothed me: I was sick, and ye visited me: I was in prison, and ye came unto me.

Then shall the righteous answer him, saying, Lord, when saw we thee an hungred, and fed thee? or thirsty, and gave thee drink?

When saw we thee a stranger, and took thee in? or naked, and clothed thee?

Or when saw we thee sick, or in prison, and came unto thee?

And the King shall answer and say unto them, Verily I say unto you, inasmuch as ye have done it unto one of the least of these my brethren, ye have done it unto me.

> Then shall he say also unto them on the left hand, depart from me, ye cursed, into everlasting fire, prepared for the devil and his angels:
>
> For I was an hungred, and ye gave me no meat: I was thirsty, and ye gave me no drink:
>
> I was a stranger, and ye took me not in: naked, and ye clothed me not: sick, and in prison, and ye visited me not.
>
> Then shall they also answer him, saying, Lord, when saw we thee an hungred, or athirst, or a stranger, or naked, or sick, or in prison, and did not minister unto thee?
>
> Then shall he answer them, saying, Verily I say unto you, inasmuch as ye did it not to one of the least of these, ye did it not to me.
>
> And these shall go away into everlasting punishment: but the righteous into life eternal. (Matthew 25:31–46 KJV)

Someone that is hungry, thirsty, without clothes and without a place to stay sounds like a poor person to me. Jesus is clear on how we should treat them and the repercussions if we do not. He makes it clear that being self-righteous and going to a church building on Sunday does not matter. For Christians, helping the poor is more important than the poodle, fancy restaurant, luxury vehicle, and expensive vacation. People matter more.

> Let brotherly love continue. Be not forgetful to entertain strangers: for thereby some have entertained angels unawares. Remember them that are in bonds, as bound with them; and them which suffer adversity, as being yourselves also in the body. (Hebrews 13:1–3 KJV)

Treat every poor person as if they are going to win a multimillion-dollar lottery tomorrow. It would be very nice for that lottery winner to know that you helped them in their time of need. In God's eyes that person has already won the lottery. In God's eyes that person is already valuable and loved. Your reward for helping them will come from God.

> Hereby perceive we the love of God, because he laid down his life for us: and we ought to lay down our lives for the brethren. But whoso hath this world's good, and seeth his brother have need, and shutteth up his bowels of compassion from him, how dwelleth the love of God in him? My little children, let us not love in word, neither in tongue; but in deed and in truth. (1 John 3:16–18 KJV)

Poor people are right next door. They live in the next house or two blocks away. Some cannot afford food. Some cannot afford decent clothes. They may even try to not let people know they are hurting. Our own selfishness is the only thing that would keep us from seeing it.

Therefore, Lord, I repent for being so selfish that sometimes I forget the plight of the poor. Lord, please forgive me, and help me to do better. Help me to remember that people right down the street may be hungry.

Chapter 10

I REPENT FOR USING GOD LIKE A VENDING MACHINE

A vending machine really means nothing to me. I do not care if it is dented, red, blue or black. I don't care if it is a machine sitting inside a store or outside in the cold or heat. I really do not care if it has rust on the outside. Yes, it probably will attract me to it if it looks nice and pretty. The only thing I really care about is if I will get exactly what I want out of it at the precise time I want it. If the vending machine is designed to keep things cold, then I want them cold or else I will complain. If it is made to serve hot food or beverage items, then I want them hot. If it is a snack machine, then I just want the items to fall out when they are supposed to. That is how some people treat God. They act like they do not have to get along with God to receive the blessings of God. They act like they do not need to have a relationship with God to receive His benefits.

Time for a Snack

When it comes to catastrophic events or emergency situations, many people whom you would never hear say anything about God will call His name. During a catastrophic event, people who never say anything about God will say, "We need your prayers." Or they will say, "Please pray for us." Fires in the West, tornados in the Midwest, hurricanes coming up the

East Coast, planes hitting the World Trade Center, and a global pandemic all make the world stop and say, "Lord have mercy."

On a microscale, when sickness or death comes to a particular family, they may suddenly acquire more religious habits, gatherings, or group prayers. The circumstance is pressing the family to behave differently for a time. When the circumstance is removed, the behavior goes back to normal. A visit is made to the vending machine (God), to fill a void for a time.

> And it came to pass, that, as they went in the way, a certain man said unto him, Lord, I will follow thee whithersoever thou goes. And Jesus said unto him, Foxes have holes, and birds of the air have nests; but the Son of man hath not where to lay his head. And he said unto another, Follow me. But he said, Lord, suffer me first to go and bury my father. Jesus said unto him, Let the dead bury their dead: but go thou and preach the kingdom of God. And another also said, Lord, I will follow thee; but let me first go bid them farewell, which are at home at my house. And Jesus said unto him, no man, having put his hand to the plough, and looking back, is fit for the kingdom of God. (Luke 9:57–62 KJV)

Jesus informs us in this text that part-time, temporary, religious, even supposedly "good" activity is not sufficient to please God. Being a follower of Jesus should be considered a full-time, all-consuming occupation. It should not be something that a person or group picks up just because of a crisis. It should not be something that is done sporadically, periodically, or when a person can fit it in.

The Irony

Asking for prayers without a relationship with God is like me asking a rich man to pay my bills this month. Sure, he has the ability. He has the ability many times over. He could pay my current bills for the rest of my life, plus give me anything else I wanted financially. However, I have no relationship with him. So why should this rich person give me the time of day? On the other hand, this rich person's son or daughter will have access to all his riches because of their relationship.

Asking for prayers without a relationship with God is like a sporting team asking for the championship trophy when they have never bothered to learn the rules of the game. They do not practice. They do not wear the proper gear. The coaches are laughable. In fact, suppose the team is barely even organized. A group of people just get together on the day before the championship awards ceremony and walk up to the podium and demand the trophy. This scene would be hilarious. The team would not know the announcer, the other athletes that had demonstrated prowess and dedication to the game, or most of the fan base. That is roughly what some people do to God when they pray to Him and expect Him to cater to their needs when they have made no effort to be involved with Him in the past.

They Missed It

The Israelites that were slaves in Egypt missed the opportunity to have a trusting relationship with God in the promised land. They had prayed for a deliverer to lead them out of slavery. At one point they believed God had provided the answer to their prayer.

> And the LORD said to Aaron, Go into the wilderness to meet Moses. And he went, and met him in the mount of God, and kissed him. And Moses told Aaron all the words of the LORD who had sent him, and all the signs which he had commanded him. And Moses and Aaron went and gathered together all the elders of the children of Israel: And Aaron spoke all the words which the LORD had spoken unto Moses, and did the signs in the sight of the people. And the people believed: and when they heard that the LORD had visited the children of Israel, and that he had looked upon their affliction, then they bowed their heads and worshipped. (Exodus 4:27–31 KJV)

Verse 31 here says that the Israelite leaders believed. When God is accepted into our life, a journey begins. They saw the signs God had shared with Moses. When God reveals Himself to a person, He should be trusted from then on. However, the Israelites chose to treat God like a vending machine.

This chart shows how the Israelites complained and doubted God from the time God shared with them that He was going to get them out of the bondage of Egypt until they were about to enter the promised land of Canaan.

Rebellion	God's Response
1. Exodus 5:15–21. Israelites question Moses, Aaron, and God because they are told to make bricks without straw.	Exodus 6:1–9. God repeats the promises He made to Abraham, Isaac, and Jacob. God says, I am the Lord.
2. Exodus 14:10–12. After God performs ten miraculous plagues in Egypt, the Israelites rebel and question God at the banks of the Red Sea.	Exodus 14:13–31. God opens the Red Sea so that the children of Israel can pass on dry land.
3. Exodus 15:23–24. The water at Marah is bitter. The Israelites complained against Moses.	Exodus 15:25. A tree is cast into the water, and it made the water sweet.
4. Exodus 16:2–3 The Israelites complained against Moses and Aaron. They bragged about how good they ate in Egypt.	Exodus 16:8–18. God blessed the people of Israel with manna in the morning and quail in the evening.
5. Exodus 17:1–3. The Israelites had no water in Rephidim. They complained to Moses and said he brought them out of Egypt to die of thirst.	Exodus 17:5–6. Moses smites the rock at Horeb and water comes out of the rock.

6. Exodus 32. The very Israelites God had rescued from Egypt got impatient with Moses and God and built a golden calf to worship. Moses was away on the mountain talking to God.	Exodus 32. Moses intercedes against the wrath of God. The two tablets of the Ten Commandments are broken. Many die when Moses asks, "Who is on the Lord's side?"
7. Numbers 11:1–3. The people of Israel were generally complaining, and the Lord heard it and was angry.	Numbers 11:1–3. Fire from the Lord consumed those on the outer edges of the camp.
8. Numbers 11:4–35. The people of Israel complained saying they had fish, cucumbers, melons, leeks, onions, and garlic to eat in Egypt. They complained about the manna from God.	Numbers 11:31–34. God sent an overabundance of quail and a plague.
9. Numbers 12:1–3. Miriam and Aaron question God's leadership decision.	Numbers 12:4–15. Miriam becomes leprous, and the cloud that guided them during the day left the tabernacle.
10. Numbers 13–14. After the reports of twelve spies are delivered to the Israelites in Numbers 13, they began to cry and complain to Moses and Aaron. They start talking about returning to Egypt.	Numbers 14:22–45. God is provoked, and Moses intercedes on their behalf. God says that they will not be allowed into the promised land. Some test God and are killed.

Ten times the people of Israel doubted and complained about God after they were so happy that they were about to be delivered. God was so patient with His chosen people. They complained and complained. He gave them whatever they were crying for at the time. Their tears and complaints were the coins for the vending machine. Once they received whatever they cried about, there appears to be no new trust in their relationship with God because they continued to doubt Him. They missed their opportunity to get to the Promised Land. The text below mentions these ten times and how God rebuked the people.

> Because all these men who have seen My glory and the signs which I did in Egypt and in the wilderness, and have put Me to the test now *these ten times*, and have not heeded My voice, they certainly shall not see the land of which I swore to their fathers, nor shall any of those who rejected Me see it. But My servant Caleb, because he has a different spirit in him and has followed Me fully, I will bring in the land where he went, and his descendants shall inherit it. Now the Amalekites and the Canaanites dwell in the valley; tomorrow turn and move out into the wilderness by the Way of the Red Sea. (Numbers 14:22–25 NKJV)

Some Characteristics Are Similar

- **A vending machine is stationary, convenient, and available.**

Just like a vending machine, a person can count on God being there whenever He is needed. God is always there. He can be summoned if a car accident occurs. People assume that they do know where God can be located. They just do not need Him to be on their mind all the time. However, God is omnipresent. Unlike a vending machine, some people mistakenly believe that God is only at a church building, or only in the mind of the clergy. Unlike a vending machine, a person cannot leave God in another room.

> Whither shall I go from thy spirit? or whither shall I flee from thy presence? If I ascend up into heaven, thou art there: if I make my bed in hell, behold, thou art there. If I take the wings of the morning, and dwell in the uttermost parts of the sea; Even there shall thy hand lead me, and thy right hand shall hold me. If I say, Surely the darkness shall cover me; even the night shall be light about me. Yea, the darkness hides not from thee; but the night shineth as

the day: the darkness and the light are both alike to thee.
(Psalm 139:7–12 KJV)

- **Selection**

Any good vending machine will have a selection to choose from. Some seem to act like God should be on standby with financial blessings, a good spouse, successful children, and good health. When something goes wrong, they expect God to bless them with protection and healing. They also expect God to fight their battles when necessary.

> Then Moses said to God, "Indeed, when I come to the children of Israel and say to them, 'The God of your fathers has sent me to you,' and they say to me, 'What is His name?' What shall I tell them?" And God said to Moses, "I AM WHO I AM." And He said, "Thus you shall say to the children of Israel, 'I AM' has sent me to you.'" (Exodus 3:13–14 NKJV)

For those who have a relationship with God, the selection is infinite. God said to the Israelites, "I AM everything you need. Whatever your needs are, I am all of it." This is not true for those that do not believe. Jesus says in Matthew 21:22 that a person must pray believing to receive.

- **The payment**

Those that treat God like a vending machine will serve God the way they want to. They will go to the weekly service if they choose to. They will give in the offering if they decide to. They will participate on committees and organizations if there is something in it for them. They have no compelling desire to do what they do because of a relationship with God. Anything done to support ministry is mostly fitting in with a herd mentality. Things done for God or for the ministry are looked at as a favor to God or the ministry. This is not satisfactory to God.

> And Samuel said, When thou wast little in thine own sight, wast thou not made the head of the tribes of Israel,

> and the LORD anointed thee king over Israel? And the LORD sent thee on a journey, and said, Go and utterly destroy the sinners the Amalekites, and fight against them until they be consumed. Wherefore then didst thou not obey the voice of the LORD, but didst fly upon the spoil, and didst evil in the sight of the LORD? And Saul said unto Samuel, Yea, I have obeyed the voice of the LORD, and have gone the way which the LORD sent me, and have brought Agag the king of Amalek, and have utterly destroyed the Amalekites. But the people took of the spoil, sheep and oxen, the chief of the things which should have been utterly destroyed, to sacrifice unto the LORD thy God in Gilgal. And Samuel said, Hath the LORD as great delight in burnt offerings and sacrifices, as in obeying the voice of the LORD? Behold, to obey is better than sacrifice, and to hearken than the fat of rams. For rebellion is as the sin of witchcraft, and stubbornness is as iniquity and idolatry. Because thou hast rejected the word of the LORD, he hath also rejected thee from being king. (1 Samuel 15:17–23 KJV)

This text makes it clear that God is not interested in anything done for His church as a mandate. God is not interested in things done for ritualistic or "herd mentality" reasons. The law said sacrifice lambs and oxen, but the purpose was to remind humanity to get their relationship right with God. The purpose was not to make sure the right number of lambs and oxen were killed each year. When people have a relationship with God, they understand that God loves us and that He wants us to obey Him because it is best for us, not Him.

> The sacrifice of the wicked is an abomination to the LORD: but the prayer of the upright is his delight. The way of the wicked is an abomination unto the LORD: but he loveth him that followeth after righteousness. (Proverbs 15:8–9 KJV)

The vending machine model was never God's design. God's design is for us to constantly draw closer to Him and have a relationship with Him. In the Old Testament God says, "And ye shall be my people, and I shall be your God" (Jeremiah 30:22 KJV). In the New Testament God says, "And I, if I be lifted up from the earth, will draw all men unto me" (John 12:32 KJV). This is talking about a close relationship.

Therefore, I repent for treating You like a vending machine. Lord, please forgive me, and help me to do better.

Chapter 11

I Repent for Misusing and Abusing My Fellow Man and Fellow Woman

Even people who do not claim to be Christians have heard of the Golden Rule: "Do unto others as you would have them do unto you." That quote comes from the Bible.

> If ye then, being evil, know how to give good gifts unto your children, how much more shall your Father which is in heaven give good things to them that ask him? Therefore all things whatsoever ye would that men should do to you, do ye even so to them: for this is the law and the prophets. (Matthew 7:11–12 KJV)

Treating people the way you want to be treated seems like it would almost be a natural thing to do. It seems like it would be an easy road map concerning how one would handle business and daily transactions. Yet the world is full of people inappropriately using people. It is full of people taking advantage of other people. There are various reasons this occurs, and the repercussions can stretch through generations.

Examples of misuse and abuse and their "generic" potential cause:

- ✓ Price gouging—money
- ✓ Older adults using children to sell drugs—money
- ✓ Children's credit to buy things because your own credit is bad—money
- ✓ Love lies for sex—sex
- ✓ Ponzi schemes—money
- ✓ Child porn—sexual deviant, money
- ✓ Sex trafficking—money
- ✓ Gold diggers, purposely relating with someone for financial gain—money
- ✓ Borrowing with no intention of paying money back—money
- ✓ Getting somebody else to do your work—lazy
- ✓ Murder for insurance—money
- ✓ Rape—sex, power, anger
- ✓ Get somebody to repeatedly run your errands—manipulation, money
- ✓ Constantly borrowing instead of buying your own—money, manipulation
- ✓ Never reciprocating when others continue to show you favors—conniving
- ✓ Child labor—money
- ✓ Internet scams—money
- ✓ Murder for hire—money, revenge, other
- ✓ Falsely advertised products for sale—money
- ✓ Overzealous salesman that prey on the elderly and uniformed—money
- ✓ Nonfiduciary unscrupulous salesman—money

Prominent Reasons for Abuse and Misuse

Selfishness—the most ubiquitous reason. Humanity seems to have a great disassociation between self and everybody else. Oftentimes this is evident when we observe bystanders picking sides in a fight. When a family member has a disagreement with somebody, most people line up with their family member before they even get all the details of the situation. The other nonfamily member is wrong until proven right. This is a part of our tendency to see others as the unfamiliar suspect, thus making it easier for our feelings to become detached from that person.

When the contact is personal, most people come to the situation with a "what's in it for me" (WIIFM) attitude. Many people do not approach others with an open mind to consider the other person's perspective and plight. The Bible, on the other hand, states that we should not only see other people as our equals but see them as better than ourselves.

> Therefore if there is any consolation in Christ, if any comfort of love, if any fellowship of the Spirit, if any affection and mercy, fulfill my joy by being like-minded, having the same love, being of one accord, of one mind. Let nothing be done through selfish ambition or conceit, but in lowliness of mind let each esteem others better than himself. Let each of you look out not only for his own interest, but also for the interests of others. (Philippians 2:1–4 NKJV)

When we fail to do this and detach our feelings from the plight of others, then it becomes easier to have a "just so I get mine" attitude. It becomes easier to see other people as objects for your personal gain versus fellow human beings deserving equal treatment. God continued to remind the Israelites to remember where they came from, so they would not look down on others less fortunate. The Bible suggests that instead of taking advantage of others, Christians should be trying to actively find a way to provide for those that are less fortunate.

> Thou shalt not pervert the judgment of the stranger, nor of the fatherless; nor take a widow's raiment to pledge: But thou shalt remember that thou wast a bondman in Egypt, and the LORD thy God redeemed thee thence: therefore I command thee to do this thing. When thou cuttest down

> thine harvest in thy field, and hast forgot a sheaf in the field, thou shalt not go again to fetch it: it shall be for the stranger, for the fatherless, and for the widow: that the LORD thy God may bless thee in all the work of thine hands. When thou beatest thine olive tree, thou shalt not go over the boughs again: it shall be for the stranger, for the fatherless, and for the widow. When thou gatherest the grapes of thy vineyard, thou shalt not glean it afterward: it shall be for the stranger, for the fatherless, and for the widow. And thou shalt remember that thou wast a bondman in the land of Egypt: therefore, I command thee to do this thing. (Deuteronomy 24:17–22 KJV)

Self-effacing reflection was God's way of reminding the chosen Israelites to not look down on others. He tells them not only to care for others but to care for their belongings.

> Thou shalt not see thy brother's ox or his sheep go astray, and hide thyself from them: thou shalt in any case bring them again unto thy brother. And if thy brother be not nigh unto thee, or if thou know him not, then thou shalt bring it unto thine own house, and it shall be with thee until thy brother seek after it, and thou shalt restore it to him again. In like manner shalt thou do with his ass; and so shalt thou do with his raiment; and with all lost thing of thy brother's, which he hath lost, and thou hast found, shalt thou do likewise: thou mayest not hide thyself. Thou shalt not see thy brother's ass or his ox fall down by the way, and hide thyself from them: thou shalt surely help him to lift them up again. (Deuteronomy 22:1–4 KJV)

This level of care and reflection demonstrates what the New Testament calls love. "Love is kind." "Love does not seek its own." That is what it takes to pick up someone's belongings and rightly take care of them and return them.

Money— the most common reason. The list of examples of misuse and abuse shown previously certainly makes us understand what the Bible says in 1 Timothy about money. Money seems to be the largest reason people are misused and abused. The sum of money does not seem to make a difference. People are misused and abused for small and large sums of money.

> But they that will be rich fall into temptation and a snare, and into many foolish and hurtful lusts, which drown men in destruction and perdition. For the love of money is the root of all evil: which while some coveted after, they have erred from the faith, and pierced themselves through with many sorrows. (1 Timothy 6:9–10 KJV)

Yes, unfortunately, money makes many people do many things that are deceitful against others. In the days when scales and weights were used more often to determine what was being purchased and how much was owed, the Bible instructed the Israelites to treat each other fairly.

> Thou shalt not have in thy bag divers weights, a great and a small. Thou shalt not have in thine house divers measures, a great and a small. But thou shalt have a perfect and just weight, a perfect and just measure shalt thou have: that thy days may be lengthened in the land which the LORD thy God giveth thee. For all that do such things, and all that do unrighteously, are an abomination unto the LORD thy God. (Deuteronomy 25:13–16 KJV)

During the "Year of Jubilee," when all debts were to be canceled and everything was to be returned to the original owner, the Bible mentions selling items at a reasonable price. God is implying that there is a "best" way to treat each other financially. Perhaps if we did things God's way, we would not have so many homeless people all over the country now.

> And if thou sell ought unto thy neighbor, or buyest ought of thy neighbor's hand, ye shall not oppress one another: According to the number of years after the jubilee thou

> shalt buy of thy neighbor, and according unto the number of years of the fruits he shall sell unto thee: According to the multitude of years thou shalt increase the price thereof, and according to the fewness of years thou shalt diminish the price of it: for according to the number of the years of the fruits doth he sell unto thee. Ye shall not therefore oppress one another; but thou shalt fear thy God: for I am the Lord your God. (Leviticus 25:14–17 KJV)

The Bible even suggests that some family members should not be charged interest if they need a loan. All this is designed to keep us from taking advantage of others in need.

> Thou shalt not lend upon usury to thy brother; usury of money, usury of victuals, usury of anything that is lent upon usury: Unto a stranger thou mayest lend upon usury; but unto thy brother thou shalt not lend upon usury: that the Lord thy God may bless thee in all that thou settest thine hand to in the land whither thou goest to possess it. (Deuteronomy 23:19–20 KJV)

In addition to that, instead of browbeating people that are poor and taking advantage of them, the Bible also suggests a lot of leniencies to those that cannot pay due to hard times.

> When thou dost lend thy brother anything, thou shalt not go into his house to fetch his pledge. Thou shalt stand abroad, and the man to whom thou dost lend shall bring out the pledge abroad unto thee. And if the man be poor, thou shalt not sleep with his pledge: In any case thou shalt deliver him the pledge again when the sun goeth down, that he may sleep in his own raiment, and bless thee: and it shall be righteousness unto thee before the Lord thy God. Thou shalt not oppress an hired servant that is poor and needy, whether he be of thy brethren, or of thy strangers that are in thy land within thy gates: At his day

> thou shalt give him his hire, neither shall the sun go down upon it; for he is poor, and setteth his heart upon it: lest he cry against thee unto the LORD, and it be sin unto thee. (Deuteronomy 24:10–15 KJV)

Here again the Bible is consistent in recommending no misuse or abuse should be doled out to people when hard times are present. They should not be chased to their home for payment, and their last bit of goods should not be taken from them. Finally, this text says, it is a sin to anyone that misuses and abuses people in this way.

Sex—the most personal reason. Children and adults, males and females, are misused and abused for sex. The sexual misuse and abuse may be the result of a combination of misguided motivations, including anger, revenge, money, power, or just the physical pleasure of the sex act. In many cases, the victim feels used, unappreciated, and maybe even depressed. God created everything involved in our sexual nature. He is not surprised at any aspect of it. He did, however, create parameters.

> If a man find a damsel that is a virgin, which is not betrothed, and lay hold on her, and lie with her, and they be found; Then the man that lay with her shall give unto the damsel's father fifty shekels of silver, and she shall be his wife; because he hath humbled her, he may not put her away all his days. (Deuteronomy 22:28–29 KJV)

This text simply demonstrates that God designed sex to be more than physical in our lives. God designed it to have boundaries and stipulations. The sex act ties in with our soul and spirit. Therefore, sexual abuse of any kind is not a way to demonstrate God's love. See the chapters on promiscuity and adultery for more on this matter.

Power—the most ruthless reason. Some people misuse and abuse others just because they can. They see it as a way to demonstrate their power. However, power over others was never meant to misuse or abuse them.

> There is no man that hath power over the spirit to retain the spirit; neither hath he power in the day of death: and there is no discharge in that war; neither shall wickedness deliver those that are given to it. All this have I seen, and applied my heart unto every work that is done under the sun: there is a time wherein one man ruleth over another to his own hurt. And so I saw the wicked buried, who had come and gone from the place of the holy, and they were forgotten in the city where they had so done: this is also vanity. Because sentence against an evil work is not executed speedily, therefore the heart of the sons of men is fully set in them to do evil. Though a sinner do evil an hundred times, and his days be prolonged, yet surely I know that it shall be well with them that fear God, which fear before him: But it shall not be well with the wicked, neither shall he prolong his days, which are as a shadow; because he feareth not before God. (Ecclesiastes 8:8–13 KJV)

In this text, the writer states that wickedness persists but having that power can be to the detriment of the person with the power. This is true when the power is used to take advantage of persons that are weaker. Often, justice seems like it will not come because it may not be immediate, but it will come.

Accountability

> For yet a little while, and the wicked shall not be: yea, thou shalt diligently consider his place, and it shall not be. But the meek shall inherit the earth; and shall delight themselves in the abundance of peace. The wicked plotteth against the just, and gnasheth upon him with his teeth. The Lord shall laugh at him: for he seeth that his day is coming. The wicked have drawn out the sword, and have bent their bow, to cast down the poor and needy, and to slay

such as be of upright conversation. Their sword shall enter into their own heart, and their bows shall be broken. A little that a righteous man hath is better than the riches of many wicked. For the arms of the wicked shall be broken: but the LORD upholdeth the righteous. (Psalm 37:10–17 KJV)

Those that choose to misuse and abuse others will have to pay for their deeds. God will bless those that are on His side, and He will punish those that choose to oppress His children.

> An Ammonite or Moabite shall not enter into the congregation of the LORD; even to their tenth generation shall they not enter into the congregation of the LORD forever: Because they met you not with bread and with water in the way, when ye came forth out of Egypt; and because they hired against thee Balaam the son of Beor of Pethor of Mesopotamia, to curse thee. Nevertheless the LORD thy God would not hearken unto Balaam; but the LORD thy God turned the curse into a blessing unto thee, because the LORD thy God loved thee. Thou shalt not seek their peace nor their prosperity all thy days for ever. (Deuteronomy 23:3–6 KJV)

God holds those that do not help and those that wish bad on His people accountable. The Ammonites and Moabites were descendants of Lot. That means they were relatives of Abraham. However, this text demonstrates that God did not like how they behaved when the Israelites came out of Egypt.

Repercussions

Class, society, and generational poverty. The rich get richer, and the poor get poorer. This is like going on a trip and taking a wrong turn. The longer a person keeps driving in the wrong direction, it usually means that they are getting further and further away from their destination. When we do not treat each other fairly, we exacerbate an environment of have and have-nots. Often the effects of misuse and abuse are not a straight line. They are usually cumulative and/or show up exponentially. In the book *Bridges Out Of Poverty*[10], the author discusses rules used by people in poverty, versus people in middle class, versus people in wealth. People form habits that influence their short-term and long-term decisions and actions. Therefore, it is almost as if spending time in one of the classes almost becomes a self-perpetuating invitation for the next generation to experience the same thing. That implies that misusing or abusing one person could have effects on their future and their children's future. Over time that would cause greater income disparities and lead to more people subject to misuse and abuse. It would lead to more people being psychologically scarred. It would lead to more dissension between the classes.

God remembers the abusers. The Bible says vengeance belongs to God. He remembers those that choose to take advantage of and abuse others. He will repay.

> Remember what Amalek did unto thee by the way, when ye were come forth out of Egypt; How he met thee by the way, and smote the hindmost of thee, even all that were feeble behind thee, when thou wast faint and weary; and he feared not God. Therefore it shall be, when the LORD thy God hath given thee rest from all thine enemies round about, in the land which the LORD thy God giveth thee for an inheritance to possess it, that thou shalt blot out the remembrance of Amalek from under heaven; thou shalt not forget it. (Deuteronomy 25:17–19 KJV)

God holds us accountable when we misuse and abuse others. It does not go unnoticed. There are repercussions that effect our entire society. It can cause a lot of heartache and turmoil among diverse groups of people. There is not an easy solution to what the Bible suggests to us in this chapter. It is something that will have to be thought out, prayed about, and worked on. Being fair to everyone is a burden on the wealthy, powerful, and strong.

Therefore, Dear God, I repent for misusing and abusing my fellow man or fellow woman. Lord, please forgive me, and help me to do better.

Chapter 12

I REPENT FOR ALLOWING RACISM TO CONTINUE IN MY PRESENCE

I wish I could just weep enough for everyone involved to make this issue go away. One of the most polarizing issues in America today is still racism. When it comes to race, some people must think God made a mistake with His creation. Maybe God wasn't clever enough to create only one race of people. He created many species of flowers, trees, antelopes, cats, dogs, and even fish. There are even different types of rocks and even different types of dirt, but when it comes to humanity, do we really believe God made a mistake? Why would God make one generic man when He put so much variety into the rest of His creation? The book of Genesis says that at the end of every day of creation that God looked back on his day of creation and said it was good. Christians need to share that notion. God is intentional. He knows that He created different races in His image.

This chapter, in this book, is not long enough, nor is it intended to thoroughly cover all the details about racism in America. This chapter, like all the others, assumes the reader is a Christian trying to do better and live according to God's word and God's will.

Race issues in America are tied to the Middle Passage, slavery, the Civil War, white supremacy, the Native American "Trail of Tears," the Chinese

Exclusion Act[11], Reconstruction, Jim Crow laws, separate but equal, the Japanese American internment after the bombing of Pearl Harbor, the civil rights movement, white flight, white backlash, redlining, Black Panthers, the war on drugs, mass incarceration, Charlottesville's Unite the Right Rally, and gentrification. Other evils could be added to this list. Each issue is identified by one thing—the skin color or body features of a race of people created by God.

So, how can we still be talking about racism? Particularly, how can we still be talking about racism, over 160 years after the bloodiest war America has ever fought to protect slavery? The Civil War caused the death of over six hundred thousand American people in four years. Compare that to other wars America has fought. Did we not learn anything from all that bloodshed? Unfortunately, lives are still being lost today. Unfortunately, negative laws, policies, and systems are still being put in place today because of race.

The Civil War was not the only time people in America have been killed because of race. Additionally, the bloodshed has not been confined to just one race. Native Americans, Blacks, Whites, Asians, Latin Americans, and Middle Easterners have been bloodied in this country because of race. Further, all kinds of horrid atrocities have been carried out in America because of racial differences: lynchings, shootings, burnings, property destruction, property confiscation, unequal incarceration, forced internment, forced migration, housing discrimination, education discrimination, and financial discrimination. Racism has been a part of America since the country's inception and continues today.

A lot of ill will has taken place due to race. However, *racism is still just a sin*. It is no more detrimental or outlandish than any other sin. It is a sin whose wages are death, just like every other sin. It is a sin that can kill quickly like a car accident. It is also a sin that can kill quietly and slowly like high blood pressure. A racist wants us to think racism is "my heritage" or "my right to free speech." Satan wants us to think it is more than just a sin. Racists have even used God as a supporter of their sin. As usual, Satan has used deception to prolong direct confrontation with who God is. The Bible says, "God is love" (1 John 4:8 KJV). That means that anyone who does not love their fellow man, does not love God. Racism is a sin that reveals how hypocritical many people are that proclaim to be Bible-believing .

Sin, Without a Doubt

Scripture proof 1. Racism is a sin. Hatred is an "over the top" version of dislike. Hatred is dislike on steroids. Hatred implies a tendency to be aggressive and violent. Extreme prejudice is hatred. Now, consider where hatred is in the Bible.

> Now the works of the flesh are evident, which are: adultery, fornication, uncleanness, lewdness, idolatry, sorcery, hatred, contentions, jealousies, outbursts, of wrath, selfish ambitions, dissensions, heresies, envy, murders, drunkenness, revelries, and the like; of which I tell you beforehand, just as I also told you in time past, that those who practice such things will not inherit the kingdom of God. (Galatians 5:19–21 NKJV)

There it is. Hatred is right in there with idolatry and murder. However, it is not the only sin in this biblical list that can be identified with racism. Contentions, jealousies, outbursts of wrath, selfish ambitions, dissensions, envy, and murders can all be associated with racism. How can anyone who claims to believe in the love of Jesus Christ justify being a racist when so many aspects of racism are listed as sins?

Scripture proof 2. We all know that the Holy Spirit in us will affect how a mature Christian treats people. A true Christian standing before God on judgment day will not be able to convince God that any part of treating a person like a slave or with a racist attitude is Christian.

> And Jesus answering said, A certain man went down from Jerusalem to Jericho, and fell among thieves, which stripped him of his raiment, and wounded him, and departed, leaving him half dead. And by chance there

> came down a certain priest that way: and when he saw him, he passed by on the other side. And likewise a Levite, when he was at the place, came and looked on him, and passed by on the other side. But a certain Samaritan, as he journeyed, came where he was: and when he saw him, he had compassion on him, And went to him, and bound up his wounds, pouring in oil and wine, and set him on his own beast, and brought him to an inn, and took care of him.
>
> And on the morrow when he departed, he took out two pence, and gave them to the host, and said unto him, Take care of him; and whatsoever thou spendest more, when I come again, I will repay thee. Which now of these three, thinkest thou, was neighbour unto him that fell among the thieves? And he said, He that shewed mercy on him. Then said Jesus unto him, Go, and do thou likewise. (Luke 10:30–37 KJV)

Will the racist try to convince God that he or she is justified in not doing what could be done to help the less fortunate? The Samaritan in this text helped someone that he normally would not deal with. The Samaritan was considered another race because of ancestry.

Scripture proof 3.

> A new commandment I give unto you, That ye love one another; as I have loved you, that ye also love one another. By this shall all men know that ye are my disciples, if ye have love one to another. (John 13:34–35 KJV)

Once we learn who our neighbor is, we are accountable. We are told to love one another. Will the racist then try to convince God that the different skin tone, or hair, or eye configuration made the person unworthy of love?

Scripture proof 4. Unfortunately, God has been used throughout history to support racism. God has been accused of supporting one race over another. This is not true. God chose the Israelites to demonstrate what it means to love someone, despite how the recipient of the love behaves. He demonstrated His love by supporting and providing for them regardless of their behavior. That was only for our example (1 Corinthians 10:1–11). Now that we know what love is, we are commanded to love our brother.

> If a man say, I love God, and hateth his brother, he is a liar: for he that loveth not his brother whom he hath seen, how can he love God whom he hath not seen? And this commandment have we from him, That he who loveth God love his brother also. (1 John 4:20–21 KJV)

Scripture proof 5.

> Let nothing be done through strife or vainglory; but in lowliness of mind let each esteem other better than themselves. Look not every man on his own things, but every man also on the things of others. Let this mind be in you, which was also in Christ Jesus: Who, being in the form of God, thought it not robbery to be equal with God: But made himself of no reputation, and took upon him the form of a servant, and was made in the likeness of men: And being found in fashion as a man, he humbled himself, and became obedient unto death, even the death of the cross. (Philippians 2:3–8 KJV)

Are we allowed to think God was only referring to those of our own race in this text? Jesus Christ Himself demonstrates humility for the sake of others. No matter who it is, this scripture says we should love them and treat them like they are royalty, more important than we are ourselves.

Scripture proof 6. In Acts 10:10, Peter fell into a trance. He received a vision that he was not sure what the meaning was, but as events unfolded in later verses, it became very clear.

> Then called he them in, and lodged them. And on the morrow Peter went away with them, and certain brethren

> from Joppa accompanied him. And the morrow after they entered into Caesarea. And Cornelius waited for them, and he had called together his kinsmen and near friends. And as Peter was coming in, Cornelius met him, and fell down at his feet, and worshipped him. But Peter took him up, saying, Stand up; I myself also am a man. And as he talked with him, he went in, and found many that were come together. And he said unto them, Ye know how that it is an unlawful thing for a man that is a Jew to keep company, or come unto one of another nation; but God hath shewed me that I should not call any man common or unclean. Therefore came I unto you without gainsaying, as soon as I was sent for: I ask therefore for what intent ye have sent for me? (Acts 10:23–29 KJV)

Later, Peter continues.

> Then Peter opened his mouth, and said, Of a truth I perceive that God is no respecter of persons: But in every nation he that feareth him, and worketh righteousness, is accepted with him. (Acts 10:34–35 KJV)

This chapter should have been the end of all racism for all time. God invited the Gentiles to receive His Holy Spirit just like the Jews. The Bible demonstrates here that God does not see a separation because of race.

These six texts prove that a person cannot be a racist and a Christian at the same time. Actually, the converse is true. If a person is a racist, he or she is not practicing Christianity. If a person is a racist, he or she is not following Jesus Christ but is worshipping some other god. The Bible is full of texts that point to God loving all people. Racism is simply a sin and should be seen as such.

God the Father, Jesus the Son, and the Holy Spirit

Looking at the landscape of the entire Bible, you can see the love of God for His creation. It is ironic that even though God has allowed humankind to kill, murder, and maim each other, He still loves us. Man has been murdering other men since Cain killed Abel. Murdering, slandering and being mean to each other is just a symptom. The cause of the symptom is sin. When we plant enough sin, the harvest we will reap is everything evil one can imagine that humanity will commit against humanity. God, on the other hand, is all about love. "God is love" (1 John 4:8 KJV).

> Beloved, let us love one another: for love is of God; and every one that loveth is born of God, and knoweth God. He that loveth not knoweth not God; for God is love. In this was manifested the love of God toward us, because that God sent his only begotten Son into the world, that we might live through him. Herein is love, not that we loved God, but that he loved us, and sent his Son to be the propitiation for our sins. Beloved, if God so loved us, we ought also to love one another. No man hath seen God at any time. If we love one another, God dwelleth in us, and his love is perfected in us. Hereby know we that we dwell in him, and he in us, because he hath given us of his Spirit. And we have seen and do testify that the Father sent the Son to be the Savior of the world. Whosoever shall confess that Jesus is the Son of God, God dwelleth in him, and he in God. And we have known and believed the love that God hath to us. God is love; and he that dwelleth in love dwelleth in God, and God in him. (1 John 4:7–16 KJV)

This text explains to us the nature of God and His love. Verse 8 specifies that if we do not love one another, we do not know God. Verse 11 says that we owe it to God to love one another because He has loved us. These verses are inclusive. They do not suggest that our love should extend only to a race of people who look like us.

Jesus Christ Himself points out that love for our fellow man is supremely important. In fact, it is second only to loving God the Father.

> Then one of them, which was a lawyer, asked him a question, tempting him, and saying, Master, which is the great commandment in the law? Jesus said unto him, Thou shalt love the Lord thy God with all thy heart, and with all thy soul, and with all thy mind. This is the first and great commandment. And the second is like unto it, Thou shalt love thy neighbor as thyself. On these two commandments hang all the law and the prophets. (Matthew 22:35–40 KJV)

The second most important verse in all the Bible is to love my fellow man. It does not say love only the fellow man of your own race. How can people be racists and say they believe in the Bible?

Racism and Slavery

In America, race was used to identify slaves. Slaves mentioned in the Bible were not identified by race. Slaves were identified by which country conquered another. Citizens of the losing country became slaves to the victors. Using race as an identifier has caused immense bloodshed, anguish, and turmoil in America. It is a trick of Satan to divide humanity that was never meant to be. Jesus did not "fix" the slavery issue while He was here but, neither did He fix sexism, wars, and all illness. What He did do was give us a formula and a solution for our maladies. Concerning race, He taught us what a neighbor was, regardless of race (see Scripture Proof 2).

In the book of Philemon, Onesimus is a runaway slave who has accepted Christ. Paul asks Philemon to accept Onesimus back as a Christian brother and not as a slave. In the Old Testament, slaves were not even to be returned to their masters if they ran away.

> Thou shalt not deliver unto his master the servant which is escaped from his master unto thee: He shall dwell with

thee, even among you, in that place which he shall choose in one of thy gates, where it liketh him best: thou shalt not oppress him. (Deuteronomy 23:15–16 KJV)

In this text it is plain to see that even slaves were supposed to be treated humanely in the Old Testament. By the time America and other countries allowed race and mistreatment to become a standard operation in the slave trade, Satan had taken the country on a terrible and abusive tangent. Nevertheless, slavery and the memories from those horrible times are still just sins that can be replaced by love like all other sins.

Hard to Finish

Emotions seem to run high on the topic of racism. People who hate one race or another seem to be totally intolerant. There is no middle ground. There is no, "live and let live." Therefore, it is hard to reason with the hater. Even in this difficult-to-have conversation, God suggests we talk.

> Wash you, make you clean; put away the evil of your doings from before mine eyes; cease to do evil; Learn to do well; seek judgment, relieve the oppressed, judge the fatherless, plead for the widow. Come now, and let us reason together, saith the Lord: though your sins be as scarlet, they shall be as white as snow; though they be red like crimson, they shall be as wool. (Isaiah 1:16–18 KJV)

Here, God is talking to the Israelites through His prophet Isaiah, seemingly asking for a "cease-fire," among warring parties. It would be wonderful if humanity would stop all the evilness for a moment and have a conversation. We all need to reason together about what is right and what is wrong. The oppressed are here in this same text with an offer of forgiveness for the evil perpetrators.

One of the main problems with the racial issue is that it is a sin that has never been confronted as a sin. Therefore, it has gone on for hundreds of years in America. It is a sin that has festered, almost as if it is something other than just a sin.

People who claim to know the God of Abraham, Isaac, and Jacob should be able to talk about racism thoroughly. Too many suns have gone down on this sin without seeing that it as an issue that is more about God instead of skin color.

> Wherefore putting away lying, speak every man truth with his neighbor: for we are members one of another. Be ye angry, and sin not: let not the sun go down upon your wrath. (Ephesians 4:25–26 KJV)

It has been hard to finish the race conversation, but it must be done. If we are Christian and we love all humanity like God has commanded us to do, then this sin of racism must be talked about for what it is. It is a direct contradiction to being a Christian.

This Has Never Officially Happened

Executive Order 9066 was passed based on fear and racism. Shortly after the bombing of Pearl Harbor, President Roosevelt signed the order in February 1942[12]. Approximately 120,000 Asian Americans were interned in camps. Many were second and third generation Americans. The country saw fit to acknowledge this wrong in 1988 when then President Ronald Reagan signed the Civil Liberties Act. Interned Asian Americans and their heirs were paid for the wrong that had been done to them by the government.

> Ye have heard that it was said of them of old time, Thou shalt not kill; and whosoever shall kill shall be in danger of the judgment: But I say unto you, That whosoever is angry with his brother without a cause shall be in danger of the judgment: and whosoever shall say to his brother, Raca, shall be in danger of the council: but whosoever shall say, Thou fool, shall be in danger of hell fire. Therefore if

thou bring thy gift to the altar, and there remember that thy brother hath ought against thee; Leave there thy gift before the altar, and go thy way; first be reconciled to thy brother, and then come and offer thy gift. (Matthew 5:21–24 KJV)

If America and its race relations were a marriage, and they could go to a marriage counselor, the first thing the counselor would likely tell them is to sit down and apologize for the wrong that has been done. In the case of Asian Americans, this has been done. We are not discussing politics in this book, but it has not been done on behalf of the several other races mentioned earlier that have been wronged in this country. The only reason it is being mentioned here is to point out that it does make it difficult to move forward. Even though racism still exists, many of the worst atrocities were committed by people who have been deceased for a long time. Christians in America should pray about this issue. The Bible says reconciliation should take place even before offering further gifts to God. Taking $10,000 to church will not be a remedy for the person wronged, nor will it please Almighty God.

No one race has a 100 percent guilt or 100 percent innocence when it comes to race relations. So, if a person has a brother that commits a crime, should that person feel guilty and apologize for what the brother did? Look in the mirror on this one. How many times have we as Christians made sure we apologized to everyone that might have been hurt by our children, siblings, other relatives, and friends? Are people wearing guilt, even if they are not guilty?

On the other hand, forgiveness is a requirement for Christians. This is not easy.

> Then came Peter to him, and said, Lord, how oft shall my brother sin against me, and I forgive him? till seven times? Jesus saith unto him, I say not unto thee, Until seven times: but, Until seventy times seven. (Matthew 18:21–22 KJV)

Since Christians should not judge, any apology given should be forgiven and accepted. It is a step forward for America. Individually and/or collectively, Christians should demonstrate how to make this happen.

Relics

Mount Rushmore on stolen Native land	No Mount Rushmore on stolen Native land
Sports Mascots	No Sports Mascots
Statues	No Statues
Monuments	No Monuments
Confederate Flags	No Confederate Flags

Memories that remind are endearing to some and repulsive to others. Is it heritage or hate? What would Jesus do? Where do we go from here? The scenarios below are for conversation.

Scenario 1. My father was a child molester. Strong evidence proves that he molested three neighborhood children continuously over a nine-year period. He was caught after murdering the parents of one of the children. He is currently serving a total of eighty-seven years for the crimes. He has eighty-three more years to go. My father was able to molest the children because he had started a highly successful kids camp in the community. The camp was well known and had won many accolades from community leaders for the work they were doing. The camp is still open. I am now running it. I am twenty-four years old now, and I am guessing that I will never see my father outside of prison anymore for the rest of my life. That is my heritage in this town. I have not done anything wrong, but I feel the eyes of people on me whenever I leave home around here. I have framed relics and plaques in my den of my father with the kids from the camp, (including a beautiful eleven-by-seventeen framed plaque and picture with one of the kids that was molested.) What should I do with these relics? It is a part of my heritage. How would the family of that child feel if they ever happened to come to my house and wind up in the den?

Scenario 2. A husband and wife argue about whether he put a red T-shirt in the washing machine with white clothes. Bleach was used, and the red shirt ruined all the white clothes. They all came out pink. At first the husband could not remember doing it, but later he relented. He did remember he had grabbed the bleach before grabbing the liquid detergent, and he must have thrown the red T-shirt in by accident because he remembers being hot.

The couple have been married nine years and heretofore have been fairly happy. Then imagine after the disagreement that the wife insisted upon tacking a pink T-shirt over his mirror in the bathroom as a memento to remind her of her superior memory and debate skills. What needs to happen for this couple to stay happily married for at least another nine years?

> Owe no man anything, but to love one another: for he that loveth another hath fulfilled the law. For this, Thou shalt not commit adultery, Thou shalt not kill, Thou shalt not steal, Thou shalt not bear false witness, Thou shalt not covet; and if there be any other commandment, it is briefly comprehended in this saying, namely, Thou shalt love thy neighbor as thyself. Love worketh no ill to his neighbor: therefore love is the fulfilling of the law. (Romans 13:8–10 KJV)

Verse 10 here is super powerful and is one of the most important verses in all the Bible. If Christian love is in the heart of a person, then everything they do should be sifted through the eyes of what is good for that person. This verse should take away all thoughts or attempts at selfishness. A Christian cannot do anything that is harmful, in any way, to another person for selfish reasons.

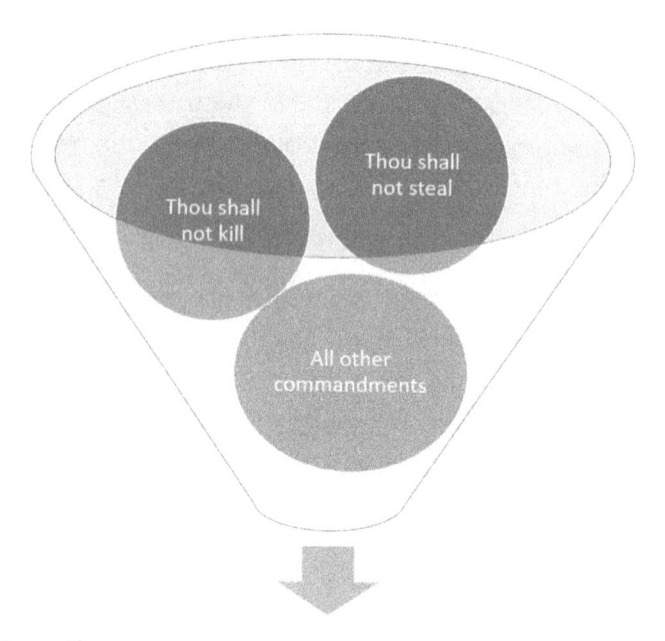

LOVE YOUR NEIGHBOR AS YOURSELF
Love does no harm to a neighbor

This diagram demonstrates a combination of everything God says about love. Matthew 22:37–39 says that love is the most important thing in the Bible—love for God and love for your fellow humans. This verse in Romans points out exactly what loving one's neighbor means. You cannot love and hate at the same time. A person cannot be a Christian and hate another human being regardless of race.

Speaking Up

Racism has manifested itself in many ways for all to see. Some may ask, why me? Why do I have to be the one to speak up? Somebody else will handle it. It is not my job. I do not like tension. I would rather just leave it alone. I do not like to argue. Sometimes these statements may be valid. There certainly is a time to speak up and a time to be quiet. (See chapter 17: "I Repent for Not Speaking up about Sin and Evil.")

However, racism is like many other sins; the seeds of it are often sown in secret. Sin is often done in the dark, in the back room. Where were the Christians when the decision was made to kill Native Americans during battle after battle after battle? Did anyone stand up to say, "These are children of God?" When the decision was made to send all Asian Americans to internment camps, where was the voice to say, "This is racist"? Where was the voice to put an end to the thought before the first American citizens were gathered? Was there not one person that loved God enough to absolutely protest and fight while a slave was being hoisted on a tree? I wonder if either of the other policemen standing around George Floyd's murder ever went to church on Sunday, or any other day for that matter.

People become accomplices when they let racism exist in their presence. By not speaking up and standing up, there is no resistance to Satan at the exact time when his lies begin to spread in private conversations or meetings.

To all the Christians out there reading or listening to this, I must first say that God always has, and still does, call for His followers to be different from the rest of the world. We are called to be the light and the lamp. We must stand up for what is right, regardless of the circumstances. Racism would die a slow death if zealous Christians would resist, rebuke, and cast Satan behind them, each time it is mentioned by their own friends and family members.

> I beseech you therefore, brethren, by the mercies of God, that ye present your bodies a living sacrifice, holy, acceptable unto God, which is your reasonable service. And be not conformed to this world: but be ye transformed by the renewing of your mind, that ye may prove what is that good, and acceptable, and perfect, will of God. (Romans 12:1–2 KJV)

We cannot conform to the world of our friends, our neighbors, or even our families. We are Christian. Our bodies should be a living testimony and sacrifice for God Almighty. The time to stop a fire is when it is small. It can be contained when it is small. Oftentimes when racist comments, jokes, and acts are done among family or close friends, the fire is still small. Perhaps an opportunity to share the gospel should be taken. It is much easier to do it then, as opposed to waiting until hateful mobs are gathered on the streets. The pastor cannot be there to tell the perpetrator of a racist joke that it is not funny, but many times, people who profess to be Christians are there.

The truth is that racism can never be fixed unless people speak up in private situations. Many of the atrocities that have been done to others throughout history are the result of schemes and decisions. The true repercussions may not be revealed until years later. Covert laws, policies, and procedures discussed privately on the golf course, at a family gathering, or in a private office can always be developed to work on Satan's behalf. You may be the only one present to rebuke Satan in his tracks. The Bible describes this action.

> Put on the whole armour of God, that ye may be able to stand against the wiles of the devil. For we wrestle not against flesh and blood, but against principalities, against powers, against the rulers of the darkness of this world, against spiritual wickedness in high places. (Ephesians 6:11–12 KJV)

Satan is fighting spiritual warfare. He never fights fair. He always starts his fire with just a little flame. Because he knows how uncontrollable it will be when it grows.

Racism Summary

It saddens me so much to imagine that America can become like the ongoing battles we see in the Middle East wherein hatred and skirmishes just seem to keep passing from one generation to the next. If we teach hatred, then hatred will most certainly wind up killing our children and grandchildren as they continue to take advantage of and brutalize each other. Biblical prophets, civil rights leaders, and others can only speak to the people concerning what needs to be done in their era to earn a few basic equal rights in that specific era. However, changing the hearts of humanity can last forever. Proper behavior and restraint have always been needed to love people for who they are. It is still needed today, and that will only come with a true Christian heart. People are still working for civil rights today, but it will only be short-lived if a heart change does not go along with the policy and law changes.

If the truth be known, we Christians hold the only long-term answer to the racial dilemma in America. Obviously, laws and legislation help. However, they can never solve the problem if it is not solved in the hearts of people. Being able to live in a certain neighborhood does not help if neighbors continue to hate and disdain your existence. Eventually, the situation will boil over. Legislation that allowed children to go to any school was a great step forward. However, without changing the hearts of people, new schools will be opened (a lot of private schools in the '60s and '70s), and new stipulations and new rules and regulations will be put in place that are still aimed at keeping learning children apart. People will move out of town into the suburbs just to stay segregated. Changing hearts is the one and only solution to racism.

Therefore, I repent for allowing racism to continue in my presence. I need to do everything I can to rebuke this sin. When I have the opportunity, I should speak up. Lord, please forgive me, and help me to do better.

Chapter 13

I REPENT FOR ACCEPTING PROMISCUITY AND ADULTERY IN OUR SOCIETY

The Bible is clear about our omnipotent, omniscient, omnipresent God being holy and righteous. Everything He created is good. Everything He has done for us is because of His love for us. He did not create us to be puppets but has given us free will to choose to believe in Him and serve Him. Just as a child adores and serves loving parents because of all they have done for him or her, so should Christians have a desire to say Abba Father to God, expressing a deep love for God. With this love in place, God uses His Word to speak to us about His purity and our sinfulness, His righteousness and our filthy rags, His Spirit and our flesh. Also, even though the Bible refers to women as virgins, harlots, and prostitutes, the sexual sins of our culture are equally carried out by men as well. Men and women both have flesh and must deal with their own fleshly lust. Women are supposed to be chaste virgins, while men get to go out and "sow their wild oats." Satan has lied to us. If the Bible commands that women should not be harlots and adulterers, then that pretty much limits men to their own spouses. God uses marriage and the sexual relationship between a man and woman to explain His relationship to humanity and the church. We will survey the Bible and some of these texts. Sexual sins are nothing new to humanity.

God Is Married to Us

> Do not fear, for you will not be ashamed; neither be disgraced, for you will not be put to shame; for you will forget the shame of your youth, and will not remember the reproach of your widowhood anymore. For your Maker is your husband; the Lord of hosts is His name; and your Redeemer is the Holy One of Israel; He is called the God of the whole earth. (Isaiah 54:4–5 NKJV)

The statement in verse 5 is very clear. Our relationship to God is a marriage. Many theologians divide the interpretation of the entire book of the Song of Solomon into two categories. One is an actual physical and sexual relationship between Solomon and his wife, (early in his reign before lust enticed him to gather seven hundred wives and three hundred concubines), and the other is an expression of God's love for Israel and/or the church. The Song of Solomon champions sex as something between a married man and woman. Almost the entire chapter of Ezekiel 16 is about the marriage relationship between God and Israel. Some other texts that refer to our relationship with God and the church being similar to a marriage include Hosea 2:16–23, Ephesians 5:15–32, and Revelation 22:13–17. This is not a complete list of all such verses.

> Only acknowledge thine iniquity, that thou hast transgressed against the Lord thy God, and hast scattered thy ways to the strangers under every green tree, and ye have not obeyed my voice, saith the Lord. Turn, O backsliding children, saith the Lord; for I am married unto you: and I will take you one of a city, and two of a family, and I will bring you to Zion. (Jeremiah 3:13–14 KJV)

Once again, God uses the analogy of a married relationship with His chosen people, thus, pointing out the importance of the integrity of this relationship without promiscuity, adultery, and harlotry. In verse 13, we hear God pleading with an unfaithful wife who has "scattered her charms" to others.

Survey

When preparing a sermon, before one gets to the contextual analysis and the detailed analysis of the scripture, a good preacher will take a survey of the entire Bible, testament, and book that the text is coming from. To be interpreted correctly everything must be considered and be in agreement. Sometimes this takes a lot of study, prayer, and understanding to make sure the message is accurate. One way of conducting this survey is to consider repetitive phrases and words. For instance, considering our topic, many associated words are used several times throughout the Bible. The words in the table below deal with the topic in this chapter.[13]

Adulterer	3
Adulterers	9
Adulteress	5
Adulteresses	3
Adulteries	5
Adulterous	4
Adultery	40
Fornication	36
Fornications	3
Fornicator	3
Fornicators	5
Harlot	56
Harlot's	4
Harlotry	50
Harlotries	4
Harlots	9
Infidelity	1
Immorality	2
Played the harlot	16
Prostitute	4
Sexually immoral	2
Virgin	33

Virginity	9
Virgin's	1
Virgins	22
Total	**329**

Do we really think God made some mistake by using these words? Did God use a bad analogy to make the points He was trying to make in His word? When God talks about a chaste virgin without spot or wrinkle and compares it to the church He is coming back for, is that something we can just ignore because this is the twenty-first century? Where is the outrage? Words with sexual connotations are used 329 times in the Bible relating to the behavior of humanity. It cannot be a mistake that our sexual behavior has a message we need to adhere to. These words span from Genesis to Revelation, from the Old Testament to the New Testament, for those that are unmarried and those that are married. In other words, our sexual lives matter to God. Our sexual lives are in the Bible as a sign from God that how we behave is important.

How Did America Get Here?

Nothing new. The Bible says there is nothing new under the sun (Ecclesiastes 1:9). Sexual sins, promiscuity, and adultery have been with us throughout humanity's history. Like all sin, if humans are present, sin is present also. Prostitution is considered the oldest profession. Adultery is one of the Ten Commandments just like murder and stealing, but when is the last time you saw somebody get prosecuted or go to prison for adultery? Sexual sins are like many moral sins that cannot be appropriately addressed by human laws. However, God will hold us accountable.

> Know ye not that the unrighteous shall not inherit the kingdom of God? Be not deceived: neither fornicators, nor idolaters, nor adulterers, nor effeminate, nor abusers of themselves with mankind, Nor thieves, nor covetous, nor drunkards, nor revilers, nor extortioners, shall inherit the kingdom of God. (1 Corinthians 6:9–10 KJV)

Gradually. The current debauchery in our culture today did not happen in one generation. It happened over time. Now, everybody wants to be sexy. Looking elegant, nice, and respectful is not enough. Every movie producer wants to push the envelope just a little further now that our eyes have been opened (thanks to Eve, the invention of film and movies). Now, we have developed an appetite for things of the flesh. The Bible says sin is passed down from one generation to the next. The problem with that is that each new generation starts off with a lowered threshold for what is sinful and what is not. Consider these changes that have occurred since the beginning of the twentieth century:

- ✓ Women wearing pants as a mainstay, (hot pants, leggings, yoga)
- ✓ Hemlines get shorter, necklines get lower
- ✓ Nickelodeons and movie theaters become common
- ✓ The fashion industry learns to advertise
- ✓ Invention of birth control pills
- ✓ Television becomes commonplace
- ✓ Television channels allow more selections
- ✓ Some television commercials become more risqué
- ✓ Daytime soap operas normalize adultery and fornication
- ✓ Playboy and Hustler magazine
- ✓ Romance novels
- ✓ R-rated, X-rated movies, XXX-rated movies, no rating movies
- ✓ Sixties sexual revolution
- ✓ Half-dressed cheerleaders
- ✓ Many of our own broken families became examples for our children
- ✓ Pornography in our hands (cell phones and computers)
- ✓ Sports figures performing in outfits that are more risqué than a prostitute in a red-light district
- ✓ Internet arrives

All the industries that came of age in the twentieth century were visualized, organized, and run by men for most of the century, so that means in many cases (not all), their lust for seeing flesh helped drive our society to the next level of decadence.

Today's worldly influences. Today we gossip and smirk about things that people were ashamed of in the past. We read about couples breaking up and remarrying in the tabloids. Hollywood movies, television shows, soap operas, and celebrity lifestyles all add credence to and sometimes glamorize promiscuity and adultery. Now a person can even access pornography in the palm of their hands on a cell phone. We are living in the twenty-first century, and our culture in America today has become its own biggest perpetrator of sexual immorality. Sex trafficking is known to reach the highest levels of our society. Today, even church attendees are taking God's word for granted so much that we are saying it's just life. No, it is not just life. The wages of sin are still death in the Bible. It is not life. It is death. Some pastors have dared to divorce their wives, marry someone else in the same congregation, and keep on pastoring. My Christian friends, God is still the same God—yesterday, today, and tomorrow. Previously, sexual sins were always looked at as the "seedy" stuff that occurs on the other side of the tracks. A few generations ago, girls were sent out of town to live with another relative if they got pregnant out of wedlock. There was a certain stigma and shame about letting the community know about the pregnancy. Today it seems to be accepted as ordinary. Now we no longer introduce someone as my husband or my wife. Now, we say, "my baby's daddy," or "my baby's momma." People comment today: "Teenagers will do what teenagers will do." "People in their twenties and thirties will shack up." "It is okay for anybody of any age to hook up." The internet and the ability to google anything has given children access to pornography. Movie stars and porn stars kiss, fondle, and have sex with each other on screen, and our culture supports it by the tickets we purchase or the views we give it on social media. Risqué pictures on social media sites are commonplace. A person following Christ cannot justify supporting this. After listing several sins, Paul writes:

> Who knowing the judgment of God, that they which commit such things are worthy of death, not only do the same, but have pleasure in them that do them. Therefore thou art inexcusable, O man, whosoever thou art that judgest: for wherein thou judgest another, thou condemnest thyself; for thou that judgest doest the

> same things. But we are sure that the judgment of God is according to truth against them which commit such things. And thinkest thou this, O man, that judgest them which do such things, and doest the same, that thou shalt escape the judgment of God? Or despisest thou the riches of his goodness and forbearance and longsuffering; not knowing that the goodness of God leadeth thee to repentance? (Romans 1:32 through Romans 2:1–4 KJV)

Verse 32 points out that as Christians we should not be financially supporting industries that promote sinful behavior. Christians should not be finding pleasure in the sinful things being done. Verse 3 reminds us that we will be held accountable. Yet, it appears, based on the behavior of some people, that they have swallowed the whole bait on this sex trap from Satan, as they say in fishing terminology, "hook, line, and sinker." Promiscuity among teens and hooking up and shacking up among adults seems to be expected, ordinary, and nothing to get all shook up about in our culture today. Sexual sins may be the most pervasive, silently accepted sin that Satan has fooled us into accepting. Even though this may be the case, that does not mean that we should not resist.

The Bible Speaks

- **Old Testament**

  > You shall not make any cuttings in your flesh for the dead, nor tattoo any marks on you: I am the Lord. Do not prostitute your daughter, to cause her to be a harlot, lest the land fall into harlotry, and the land become full of wickedness. (Leviticus 19:28–29 NKJV)

Some people say that some things in the Bible are vague and not clear. This verse, however, is clear and direct and even has a warning that we are witnessing in our culture today. Our land has turned into one that is full of harlotry and wickedness. As an example, what do we do in our society? During ring dance and prom season, we dress our sixteen-, seventeen-, and eighteen-year-old daughters up in scant, revealing clothes and send them out to dances with painted faces to listen to loud, provocative music and then act surprised when they say they are pregnant a few weeks later. Shame on us. Some may call them "coming of age" parties or a "rite of passage." However, in terms of the sin being promoted, it could more accurately be deemed a "gotcha" party.

> There shall be no ritual harlot of the daughters of Israel, or a perverted one of the sons of Israel. You shall not bring the wages of a harlot or the price of a dog to the house of the Lord your God for any vowed offering, for both of these are an abomination to the Lord your God. (Deuteronomy 23:17–18 NKJV)

God is so disgusted with sexual promiscuity that He says He does not want the money from their sinful profession. This is like man's laws against laundering dirty money that comes from drug dealing or embezzlement. Using the dirty money implies you are complicit with whatever efforts were used to raise it. God cannot be bought.

> To keep thee from the evil woman, from the flattery of the tongue of a strange woman. Lust not after her beauty in thine heart; neither let her take thee with her eyelids. For by means of a whorish woman a man is brought to a piece of bread: and the adulteress will hunt for the precious life. Can a man take fire in his bosom, and his clothes not be burned? Can one go upon hot coals, and his feet not be burned? So he that goeth in to his neighbor's wife; whosoever toucheth her shall not be innocent. Men do not despise a thief, if he steals to satisfy his soul when he is hungry; But if he be found, he shall restore sevenfold; he shall give all the substance of his house. But whoso committeth adultery with a woman lacketh understanding: he that doeth it destroyeth his own soul. A wound and dishonor shall he get; and his reproach shall not be wiped away. For jealousy is the rage of a man:

> therefore, he will not spare in the day of vengeance. He will not regard any ransom; neither will he rest content, though thou givest many gifts. (Proverbs 6:24–35 KJV)

Prior to this text, verse 20 instructs a son to listen to his parents and bind these instructions in his heart. This is serious instruction. We should heed the warning today. Falling for the harlot who gives herself to all men is a trap. The same is true for a woman that falls for a man that gives himself to all women. It is a trap. Also, this verse explains why adultery has so many people in the grave. The jealous rage resulting from a love triangle cannot be easily put out.

- **New Testament**

> Ye have heard that it was said by them of old time, Thou shalt not commit adultery: But I say unto you, That whosoever looketh on a woman to lust after her hath committed adultery with her already in his heart. (Matthew 5:27–28 KJV)

Jesus sets the record straight. This is the same look of lust that David had that led to his adultery with Bathsheba (2 Samuel 11:1–4). Consider all the things in our American culture that are specifically designed to encourage lust. How many industries in America would have to change the way they operate? Christian men and women should be mindful of what they are doing and saying to encourage lust in others because if lust starts with a look, there will eventually be a harvest.

> It hath been said, Whosoever shall put away his wife, let him give her a writing of divorcement: But I say unto you, That whosoever shall put away his wife, saving for the cause of fornication, causeth her to commit adultery: and whosoever shall marry her that is divorced committeth adultery. (Matthew 5:31–32 KJV)

Just think how many marriages would get back together if somebody else wasn't waiting right around the corner to go to bed with the estranged wife or husband. The sex drive God created may encourage many marriages to reconcile if our culture did not make it so acceptable to divorce and move on to the next one. This is a moral issue and most likely cannot be easily enforced by legislation.

> All things are lawful unto me, but all things are not expedient: all things are lawful for me, but I will not be brought under the power of any. Meats for the belly, and the belly for meats: but God shall destroy both it and them. Now the body is not for fornication, but for the Lord; and the Lord for the body. And God hath both raised up the Lord, and will also raise up us by his own power. Know ye not that your bodies are the members of Christ? shall I then take the members of Christ, and make them the members of an harlot? God forbid. What? know ye not that he which is joined to an harlot is one body? for two, saith he, shall be one flesh. But he that is joined unto the Lord is one spirit. (1 Corinthians 6:12–17 KJV)

This text makes it clear that God is in us when we are baptized in Christ. It then compares the absurdity of taking the same body and using it as a man with an unworthy harlot. The inference being that the two should not mix. Clearly being with a harlot is not presented as a good thing. Verse 13 plainly states that our temple and sexual immorality should not exist in the same body.

> Flee fornication. Every sin that a man doeth is without the body; but he that committeth fornication sinneth against his own body. What? know ye not that your body is the temple of the Holy Ghost which is in you, which ye have of God, and ye are not your own? For ye are bought with a price: therefore glorify God in your body, and in your spirit, which are God's. (1 Corinthians 6:18–20 KJV)

Continuing with Paul's letter to the church at Corinth, it becomes clear once again that immoral acts such as promiscuity and adultery should not be carried out in the same body that has become the temple of God. Jesus redeemed our flesh from the devil when He "bought" it on the cross. Jesus paid for us to be free from the things Satan wants us to do.

Other Considerations

God and order. Paul addressed speaking in tongues to the Corinthians and he said, "Let all things be done decently and in order" (1 Corinthians 14:40 KJV). Even though the subject was different, it still points out God's desire for order. This is also evident in how God told Moses to design the tabernacle.

> And the Lord spake unto Moses, saying, On the first day of the first month shalt thou set up the tabernacle of the tent of the congregation. And thou shalt put therein the ark of the testimony, and cover the ark with the vail. And thou shalt bring in the table, and set in order the things that are to be set in order upon it; and thou shalt bring in the candlestick, and light the lamps thereof. And thou shalt set the altar of gold for the incense before the ark of the testimony, and put the hanging of the door to the tabernacle. And thou shalt set the altar of the burnt offering before the door of the tabernacle of the tent of the congregation. (Exodus 40:1–6 KJV)

Look at all this detail about how things should be done. The text goes on to talk about the laver, water to be put in it, the court, the screen at the court gate, and anointing oil among other things. God likes order and detail. It is easy to surmise that He prefers the same for our lives.

God's Way, Ordered Side	Corruption Way
Baby born totally helpless to two married, loving parents, and both are there and dedicated to help. **The parents were virgins when they got married.**	Baby born totally helpless out of wedlock (promiscuity) or divorce (Jesus said only for adultery), so baby is reared by one parent. In some cases, due to multiple sex partners, mother may not know who the father is. Throughout life, past sexual partners may intervene, interrupt, or cause many arguments.
Child grows to adulthood being reared, encouraged, and chastised by two loving parents.	Child grows to adulthood maybe seeing both parents or maybe not. Weekend visits are in place or maybe not. Custody battles may occur inside or outside of a courtroom. Grandparents may have to step in and help rear the children. Subsequent lack of attention and all the socioeconomic things that go along with single parenting may apply. Guilt feelings by one or both parents may prevent fervent discipline of the child. If one parent has another significant other, then step parent issues may apply.
Child is now adult.	Child is now an adult that may have some trauma or psychological scars, feeling firsthand in their heart that single parenting is normal.

Consider all the extra things that must be dealt with on the right side of this chart. The Bible says, "For he who sows to his flesh will of the flesh reap corruption" (Galatians 6:8). What you see on the right side is the unnecessary corruption that may result due to the sexual sins of promiscuity and adultery. Of course, this chart is not absolute. Yes, everything does not have to turn out perfect on the left side and everything does not have to turn out negative on the right side; however, in general, statistically, the odds improve greatly by doing things God's way—decently and in order.

Gravity. (Like apostle Paul once said, this section is the author's opinion only). Gravity is a proven scientific fact even though we cannot see it. We know it exists because we see the results of it. How do we know what God has put between the sexual connection of a man and a woman when it says in the Bible that "the two shall become one?" When two virgins meet, get married, and have intercourse for the first time, does God do something special to cement that bond? Otherwise, why do intimate sexual partners matter anymore than the thousands of people a person shakes hands with. Why do we feel something special about the intimacy of sexual intercourse? With the absence of that special bond, the complete opposite of everything taught in this chapter so far would be constant orgy possibilities with everyone you meet, at any time, with no feelings, attitudes, or repercussions—just like a handshake. That also would nullify what will be discussed in the next section. I believe God does have something special that happens during sexual intercourse that we cannot see. Perhaps, like other sins, we can grieve the Holy Spirit and seer our conscience so that we cannot tell if this special gift God puts in place is there anymore, but that does not mean it was not present to begin with.

Used car parts—The disassociated and detached body parts. The secular world views sex as something "nasty" and vulgar instead of the personal, private, loving connection God has intended it to be. Our culture has deemed our sexual organs to be mere replacement parts from an auto parts store. Sex driven only by fleshly lust can settle for a used auto part from any store available (orgies, one-night stands, hookups, etc.). We use the parts and totally ignore that God's creation is body, soul, and spirit. Having "just" sex means we are using only the physical body. What happens to the soul of the person? What happens to the spirit within the person? Our culture would have us think that the soul and spirit of a person do not matter.

This body, soul, and spirit realization is why the "Me Too" movement is so important to many people who were used like spare parts when they were underage. Their message is so powerful because the trauma they experienced has touched their soul. None of these victims would be speaking up if their soul had not been impacted. Now, years later, the perpetrators must face the truth that the bodies they were misusing had a soul and spirit attached that should not have been disregarded. This is another way that it becomes evident that something else takes place during the sex act. No child suffers trauma from shaking hands with someone when they were six, eight or twelve years old. However, the intimacy of the sex act touches the soul and spirit of the individual. Even promiscuous adults find themselves longing for more, and emotionally attached when their coconspirator proves to be just in it for the lust of the flesh. When one person finds out that the use of their body is interchangeable, not meant to be long term and easily replaceable, it often results in many tears, emotional depression, suicidal tendencies, and perhaps even murder-suicides.

I have already made a mistake; it is too late. This is one of the biggest lies and misconceptions that get people into trouble. Using this as a reason for promiscuity is like having a bowl or pot of hot soup that you are transporting from the stove to the table and after slightly tripping and spilling a drop or two one decides to say, oh well, and just pours the rest of it on the floor. Past mistakes do not warrant giving in to this sin. Every time a wrong seed of iniquity is planted, there will be harvest. God's grace should not be taken for granted. The adulteress woman accused before Jesus was taught this lesson. He told her to go and sin no more.

> When Jesus had lifted up himself, and saw none but the woman, he said unto her, Woman, where are those thine accusers? hath no man condemned thee? She said, No man, Lord. And Jesus said unto her, Neither do I condemn thee: go, and sin no more. (John 8:10–11)

The word *mistake* should be used cautiously once a person knows what God says about this subject. The sex act is no longer a mistake. The sex is something done on purpose unless rape is involved. The mistake would be a mistake in judgment concerning the repercussions from God. The mistake is disrespecting God or perhaps your parents (in the case of a teenager), when they have told you not to have premarital sex.

Everybody is doing it. You obviously need a new set of friends and acquaintances if you believe this. Look around your school or workplace. The person that may be trying to live a godly life in regard to this sin of promiscuity and adultery will not be the "life of the party" type of person. They may seem somewhat subdued, but later on in life, that subdued, humble person could wind up much more successful than others because they avoided lifelong mistakes, trauma, and sleepless nights. Every married person does not believe they have to have an affair for affirmation in our American culture. Some couples have been married for many years without either party committing adultery. Satan wants people to believe everybody is doing it, but that is a lie.

The Aftermath

What is our acceptance of these sexual sins doing to our society? In addition to the preceding table showing corruption, there are many repercussions. All sins lead to death, but promiscuity and adultery allow Satan to disrupt God's biblical design for a family unit, in a special way. Children are often affected. Many children have in the past and are still today growing up without one of their biological parents in their home because of sexual sins. The foundation that surrounds the child is different from the way God designed it. Not to mention all the in-law and extended family drama that come with not doing things God's way. This is not just everyday drama but lifelong drama at all family events like graduations, weddings, and funerals. This is a sin that Satan allows to keep on paying.

Sexual sins have ruined the reputation of many powerful men and women. Ungodly men and women have supported, encouraged, and profited from sexual sins. Sex trafficking and pornography have grown because of humanity's fleshly appetite for behavior outside of the will of God. Many people are in graves today because of love triangles. Many abortions would not even be necessary if our culture did not embrace promiscuity like it does.

Psychologically and mentally, people will be impacted by their decision to be promiscuous. A precedent is set. Imagine that you are a person that really likes chocolate ice cream. It has been your favorite since you were five. Now, at age twenty-two, the doctor tells you that the chocolate is bad for you. You can still have ice cream but just not chocolate. Now when you eat any kind of ice cream, it makes you think about the chocolate. In the spiritual realm, your memory and soul will have to deal with the memories of premarital promiscuity. Your spouse can never be chocolate ice cream for you. Now, you are left longing for something you cannot and should not want any longer. Does having already tasted it make it harder to resist now?

Summary

Sex is a gift from God. He created it just like He created everything else. "Every good gift and every perfect gift is from above and comes down from the Father of lights, with whom there is no variation or shadow of turning" (James 1:17 NKJV). Like all gifts, they are wonderful when used correctly. A river in its banks brings wonderment and life to everything it touches. However, when the same river gets out of its banks, it will soon become destructive. A river out of its banks can destroy things and get things out of position. When a river gets out of its banks, a lot of mud will have to be removed, and if it enters your house, some furniture may have to be thrown away, and sheetrock and carpet may have to be ripped up and thrown out. God's design for sex works the same way. Inside a committed marriage like God's marriage to His people, it is a wonderful thing. Outside of the bounds of a married relationship it will have repercussions that someone will reap—you, your spouse, or your children.

Thou shall not commit adultery is the seventh of the Ten Commandments. Our American culture has allowed it to become a temporary contract that can be swept under the rug. In the Levitical laws, early in God's revelation about who He is and who we are to Him, guilty parties may have been put to death. Jesus came and told us about grace, love, and forgiveness, but could it be that God the Father wanted us to know how serious this matter is in the Old Testament. Contemplate what would be different in our culture if premarital sex and adultery were thought to be as serious as a sudden twenty-thousand-foot drop in an airplane flying over the ocean? Would some marriages (kids and families) get back together if absolutely no one would marry a divorced person? Has our culture made it too easy to get out of marriage? One thing we know for sure is that God cares.

Therefore, I repent for accepting promiscuity and adultery in our society. Help me to be firm in my beliefs about this issue Father. Lord, please forgive me, and help me to do better.

Chapter 14

I Repent for Failing to Call Sin, Sin

On the surface, it seems that we would always point out something that is morally wrong and hazardous to our health. However, that is not the case. It is interesting that we do not when many Christians go to some organized religious service on a regular basis. People grow up listening to their religious leader tell them right from wrong. People grow up listening to their teacher tell them right from wrong. People grow up listening to their parents and grandparents tell them right from wrong. Yet, people still do wrong. How could this be? Then, on top of that, how can those that have learned better stand by and not point out when sin is occurring and calling it the devasting event, thought, or practice that it is? Christians should be compelled to call sin, sin. Christians must call sin out for us all to be healed. Our American culture makes this difficult, but it must be done.

Why We Do Not Call It Out

We did it too. Considering the years of our brief existence in this life, most grade-school children do not get in serious moral trouble. The bulk of what most of us would call real serious trouble does not start until the teenage years. Those are the years when young people have gained enough mobility and autonomy to begin to test what they have heard and what they have decided to abide by. All adults have lived through this period of youthful exuberance when life seems like it will go on forever. Everyone is telling these young people that they are the future, and they know that they are the "up-and-comers." All adults that are honest will agree that they not only lived through those youthful years, but we also did some of the same things we wish our children and grandchildren would not do. That is part of the problem. Christians mature spiritually over time. One does not become an instant mature Christian when exiting the baptismal pool. It is a process. So now, our sinful flesh reminds us and encourages us to look back. The devil uses our memory to remember only fond memories of our sinful past. He does not remind us of the devastation, depression, and reason why we grew away from the past situation.

> Do not say, "Why were the former days better than these?" For you do not inquire wisely concerning this. (Ecclesiastes 7:10 NKJV)

The truth is that many of us must admit that we are still battling the seeds of the demon that were sown in our youth, which became habits way too quickly. That makes it hard to tell someone else not to do something when we know in our spirit that we could easily still be in the world doing the same thing. Every Christian should know for sure that there is no turning back.

> For if after they have escaped the pollutions of the world through the knowledge of the Lord and Savior Jesus Christ, they are again entangled therein, and overcome, the latter end is worse with them than the beginning. For it had been better for them not to have known the way of righteousness, than, after they have known it, to turn from the holy commandment delivered unto them. But it is happened unto them according to the true proverb, The dog is turned to his own vomit again; and the sow that was washed to her wallowing in the mire. (2 Peter 2:20–22 KJV)

Therefore, it is so important to walk humbly as a Christian. That way, when people say, "I want to be like you," you can respond by saying, "There is only one man that is worthy of trying to mimic, and they nailed him to a cross." That will let people know up front that you are not perfect either. Let people know that you have made mistakes also. That gives you room to still try to help someone else.

> And the prayer of faith shall save the sick, and the Lord shall raise him up; and if he have committed sins, they shall be forgiven him. Confess your faults one to another, and pray one for another, that ye may be healed. The effectual fervent prayer of a righteous man availeth much. (James 5:15–16 KJV)

Easier not to speak up. With no resistance, water will always flow downhill. The force of gravity makes it go in one direction. Now if a pump is applied, which is an alternate force, or the water is heated, the water will have a force of its own. Humanity's relationship with sin mimics the attributes of water. When Christians are silent or trying to be politically correct with our worldly culture, we are taking the easy route. We are flowing with the outside forces of sin and Satan and letting them dictate our life and environment. We are complicit with the devil and his workings.

Do not want to have arguments, hurt feelings, or lose friends. Some people have an amiable personality and do not like conflict. For those people, hurting someone's feelings creates conflict that will lead to an unwanted argument. Someone that grew up as a single child may not be used to the same amount of conflict and noise as a child that grew up in a family with five siblings. Some may fear abandonment or isolation. Some people may feel like they will not be listened to anyway, because of self-esteem issues. So, this type of person may do as one of my old deacons used to say, "Go along to get along." Sadly, this person may behave like an abused spouse when it comes to standing up for themselves and getting out of a bad situation.

Sin sometimes seems so pervasive that there is no way that it can be defeated and pushed back. However, all Christians must realize that all sin left unchecked will grow and spread even further. Jesus said, "I did not come to bring peace, but a sword" (Matthew 10:34). We must learn to find our strength and speak up. All Christians should grow to understand their spiritual gift and use it to stand for righteousness.

Blind and ignorant to repercussions. When a three-year-old walks into a swimming pool or into a busy street, that does not mean the three-year-old would not be an intelligent adult someday. It simply means that at that age they do not understand the danger. They do not understand the serious repercussions that could result from such actions. In some impoverished countries where children might not have the opportunity to go to school and learn about gravity, it does not mean that the force of gravity does not still apply. The same is true for any sinful activity, practice, or behavior that is allowed to go unchecked.

A teenager experimenting with their first drink cannot imagine that twenty years later they will become the alcoholic on the street that they sneer at today. That is because they do not know that the first drink will lead to the second, which leads to more, which leads to alcohol being a gateway to experiment with marijuana, which leads to experimentation with narcotics, which leads to theft, which leads to prison time, which leads to broken relationships and loss of employment, which leads to being the alcoholic on the street. Satan will kill you fast, or he will kill you in slow motion. He does not care. He will often seduce you with something that seems nonconsequential and irrelevant because we have no idea how bad things can get when we do not follow God.

> Now the serpent was more subtle than any beast of the field which the Lord God had made. And he said unto the woman, Yea, hath God said, Ye shall not eat of every tree of the garden? And the woman said unto the serpent, We may eat of the fruit of the trees of the garden: But of the fruit of the tree which is in the midst of the garden, God hath said, Ye shall not eat of it, neither shall ye touch

it, lest ye die. And the serpent said unto the woman, Ye shall not surely die: For God doth know that in the day ye eat thereof, then your eyes shall be opened, and ye shall be as gods, knowing good and evil. And when the woman saw that the tree was good for food, and that it was pleasant to the eyes, and a tree to be desired to make one wise, she took of the fruit thereof, and did eat, and gave also unto her husband with her; and he did eat. (Genesis 3:1–6 KJV)

What if Eve and Adam could have looked through history and seen the repercussions of this one time that they chose not to obey God? Oftentimes we cannot see the wrecked cars, addictions, hangovers, unwanted pregnancies, sexually transmitted diseases, immediate death, prison time, crying children, arguments, loss of income, or broken marriages until the harvest from the sin is ripe. Therefore, the Bible tells us to study. We as Christians need discernment. We must pray, fast, and study God's word so we can recognize and point out sin when we see it. Being blind and ignorant causes seen and unseen dangers.

Still Guilty

The truth is that if we Christians are not part of the solution to all the secular, irreverent behavior going on in society today, then our complicity does not mean we are innocent. The prophets of God pleaded and pleaded with the nations of Israel and Judah, but the people would not listen. What if there had been even more people speaking up like Jeremiah, Isaiah, Ezekiel, and Daniel. What if there was a mass of people working together today to promote Christianity? So, our sitting at home Monday through Saturday allows the devil to have free reign.

Our hands are not clean. We can wash them all we want by going to a church service on Sunday morning. However, we are still guilty if we do not play our part in calling out sin. Pilate tried to wash his hands before the people to say, "I am not guilty," but he still played a role in the crucifixion. It was not just Aaron that messed up. It was the entire nation out there singing and dancing naked in front of the calf. Why didn't somebody speak up?

Why We Should Call Sin, Sin

If God has blessed us with discernment to see sin, it becomes our task as a Christian to call it out because the spiritual discernment of others may not be where ours is. "Therefore, to him that knoweth to do good, and doeth it not, to him it is sin" (James 4:17 KJV). Also, if we love our fellow man and woman, we must call sin, sin to protect them. We who are Christian realize that "the wages of sin is death" (Romans 6:23 KJV).

> And we have known and believed the love that God has
> for us. God is love, and he who abides in love abides in

> God, and God in him. Love has been perfected among us in this: that we may have boldness in the day of judgment; because as He is, so are we in this world. There is no fear in love; but perfect love casts out fear, because fear involves torment. But he who fears has not been made perfect in love. (1 John 4:16–18 NKJV)

We are told in verse 18 that love should make us bold. Love for our fellow human beings should be so engrained in us that we are willing to call sin, sin.

Why We Must Call Sin, Sin

> Ye are the salt of the earth: but if the salt have lost his savour, wherewith shall it be salted? it is thenceforth good for nothing, but to be cast out, and to be trodden under foot of men. Ye are the light of the world. A city that is set on an hill cannot be hid. (Matthew 5:13–14 KJV)

In other words, if we are Christians, we are called to speak up and be seen by the world. In fact, this text points out that speaking truth is exactly what we are here for.

> No man can serve two masters: for either he will hate the one, and love the other; or else he will hold to the one, and despise the other. Ye cannot serve God and mammon. Therefore I say unto you, Take no thought for your life, what ye shall eat, or what ye shall drink; nor yet for your body, what ye shall put on. Is not the life more than meat, and the body than raiment? (Matthew 6:24–25 KJV)

A person can go to church every Sunday all their life and still miss heaven. Being a Christian by definition means we have made, and are still required to make, the choice every day to speak boldly and represent God's word.

> For what shall it profit a man, if he shall gain the whole world, and lose his own soul? Or what shall a man give in exchange for his soul? Whosoever therefore shall be ashamed of me and of my words in this adulterous and sinful generation; of him also shall the Son of man be ashamed, when he cometh in the glory of his Father with the holy angels. (Mark 8:36–38 KJV)

Now is not the time to be bashful and ashamed. Now is the time to speak up and let everyone know that the Bible calls that a sin.

The Culture Trap

As a married man, if I say, "She's sexy," when talking about another woman other than my wife; what am I really saying? The definition of the word *sexy* basically describes a kind of attractiveness that has something to do with a desire for sex. It means looking appealing for sexual reasons. Yet, this phrase is used daily by married and unmarried men and women. If I say, "I'm only human," what am I really saying? Does a person being human, "flesh," give them an excuse to do whatever they feel like doing? If I concede to some act or behavior and say, "That's life," what am I really saying? What I am really saying is that we have to accept it because we can't stop it or change it. If I say what the movie *Love Story* said years ago, which is, "Love means never having to say you are sorry," I am really suggesting that I am never wrong. All these statements should be rebuked. All these statements represent erroneous quotes and philosophies used daily.

Many statements, actions, and behaviors like these have become a part of our culture. Our songs, friends, TV shows, movies, and social media can very easily have us start to repeat things without contemplating what we are really saying. Many people wind up laughing, quoting, or mimicking cultural nuances before they are screened by their spiritual discernment. Sometimes we allow Satan to put words in our mouths, and we can very easily find ourselves repeating them without thinking. What we hear and what we quote is vital to our well-being. The Bible says every word that comes out of our mouth will someday be judged. I cannot assume the language of the popular culture and let words and actions become a part of my behavior when they are against God's word. It is our job as Christians to call sin, sin and point it out to the world.

> Ye adulterers and adulteresses, know ye not that the friendship of the world is enmity with God? whosoever therefore will be a friend of the world is the enemy of God. Do ye think that the scripture saith in vain, The spirit that dwelleth in us lusteth to envy? But he giveth more grace. Wherefore he saith, God resisteth the proud, but giveth grace unto the humble. Submit yourselves therefore to God. Resist the devil, and he will flee from you. Draw nigh to God, and he will draw nigh to you. Cleanse your hands, ye sinners; and purify your hearts, ye double minded. Be afflicted, and mourn, and weep: let your laughter be turned to mourning, and your joy to heaviness. Humble yourselves in the sight of the Lord, and he shall lift you up. (James 4:4–10 KJV)

God's words here are harsh and direct. We cannot be "buddy-buddy," with the world. Christians are to resist the draw of the devil. We must cleanse our hearts and stop laughing at things that are not funny. Sometimes, it may be sin, and we need to be the person(s) to point it out and call it what it is.

Therefore, my Father, I repent for failing to call sin, sin. It must be called out for what it is. Lord, please forgive me, and help me to do better.

Chapter 15

I Repent for Lying

Lying may be one of the coldest, most egregious, devious, demonic, and harmful sins of all. That is because lying is a sin that can lay in wait for somebody for one week or one month or ten years. The innocent can be affected and not even know that a trap has been set. Lying is a sin we sometimes overlook as if it is more palatable than murder or robbery. On the surface, lying seems sort of mundane and somewhat innocent. After all, nobody goes to jail for any long sentences just for lying. What difference does it make? What harm does it really do? We will take a closer look at this God-hated sin.

2 for 2 for 2

Lying is what I call a "2 for 2 for 2" sin. That means that lying always affects at least two parties; it usually assures the creation of two issues instead of one, and it is mentioned in the Bible as two of the seven things God hates.

- **Two parties**

Unless you are lying to yourself, which is a possibility, but that would belong under another subject, lying will always affect at least two parties. The person or group telling the lie and the person or group being lied to. Detrimental effects occur to both.

First, the person lying is emboldened with pride and stress at the same time. This is because a lie is like a pot of water sitting on a hot stove. It can sit there one day or one week, but it will always have the potential of getting hot and boiling over. Therefore, the liar always must be mindful of the condition of the pot. At any moment the lie could be revealed. Satan will never let the person forget that he or she harboring a lie. It will be like a ransom note for Satan to badger the liar. That may lead someone to become a perpetual liar and lead to other sins.

Second, the person or group being lied to will first of all probably get their feelings hurt. Not only do they have to deal with whatever was lied about but they also must deal with not being able to trust someone they believed and had confidence in. The repercussions of the lie itself could be anywhere from minor to drastic.

- **Two issues**

This is what is so sad about lies. People often forget that the lie itself is a second sin. I am sure you have heard the saying, "two wrongs don't make a right." A lie is a second wrong that can never make a right. As a child, at least a time or two I remember my parents telling me that if I did something wrong it was best to tell the truth about it. If I chose to lie about it, then I was going to get a spanking. When a person steals something from a store but then is standing at the door the next morning in remorse to return it, then a second sin has been averted. If a child accidently breaks a vase, (one that is not too expensive), and quickly admits it when the parent gets home then only one mistake has occurred. If the child lies about it for two weeks until his or her mother pieces together enough in-house detective work to figure out what happened, then the anger and punishment will be the result of the broken vase and the lie. Even in our courtrooms today, a defendant will normally get more leniency by showing remorse and admitting to the criminal behavior instead of lying and claiming innocence if the person in fact is guilty. That is because lying is an additional wrongdoing on top of the original crime.

- **Two of seven**

    > These six things doth the LORD hate: yea, seven are an abomination unto him: A proud look, a lying tongue, and hands that shed innocent blood, An heart that deviseth wicked imaginations, feet that be swift in running to mischief, A false witness that speaketh lies, and he that soweth discord among brethren. (Proverbs 6:16–19 KJV)

Notice verse 17 (a lying tongue), and verse 19 (a false witness who speaks lies). According to these verses, God calls lying an abomination. Lying is not something we should take lightly. It is huge, and the implications should not be underestimated.

Scenarios

The eighteen-year-old college freshman. A young, female, college freshman named Alice Beris was new to the campus of Example University. Her father and mother had never gone to college. Scholarships seemed to be harder to find back then. Alice grew up on her parents' dairy farm, and she was ecstatic to be out of that environment. Now, the straight A student was looking forward to her degree and a life away from the farm. One day in the library, she met an upperclassman named David Lawson. He was a fraternity man, two years ahead of Alice. They soon began to enjoy each other's company and started dating. Even though both grew up going to church, it was not long before things became intimate.

The seemingly happy couple were doing fine until one day they were studying together in the basement of the fraternity house. Alice noticed that an old chalkboard was hidden behind a shoddy makeshift covering. Alice was close to it, so she pulled it open before David could stop her. The bulletin board revealed a "Knock-Knock" challenge with frat brothers' names beside girls' names and dates. Alice was devastated because she recognized the date on the board as the first time that she and David had been intimate. After studying that night, Alice was planning to tell David what she had just confirmed. She was six weeks pregnant, already legally too late to get an abortion, even if she wanted one, in her state.

The two buddies. Two friends in their thirties have been really close since high school. They grew up on the same block and had once played ball together on a state championship football team. Nate was a starter on that team, but Jamal was what is known as a benchwarmer. That never did seem to matter to them after all these years. Nate would visit Jamal, and Jamal would visit Nate even though they were two states away from each other now. Two or three times a year, both of them always seemed to find a reason to get together. Nate had moved to Columbus, Ohio, while Jamal was still residing in their hometown of St Louis, Missouri. Although miles apart now, the only real difference between the two men was that Nate now had a new wife and an eight-month-old son.

One day the two friends were talking in more detail about starting the furniture moving business they had toyed with many times over the years. Both men had jobs but neither seemed to be satisfied with them enough to consider them as their lifetime careers. Jamal was a diesel mechanic and could very easily do all the work required on the trucks for their new business. Nate could take care of getting customers and the paperwork for the business. Sure enough, they both commit this time. Four months down the road, Nate has left his job and moved his young family back to St. Louis. Nine months down the road, Nate has used the money from his 401K to put a down payment on two trucks, get them painted, rent a small office space, and buy a computer and a few other office supplies. For some reason, Jamal never leaves his current job, and he never comes over to the new office. He seems to like to talk about their friendship, but without explanation, three years down the road he has never helped with the struggling furniture moving company.

Scenario results. Did David tell Alice a lie? What impact will it have on her life? Did Jamal tell Nate a lie? What impact will it have on his life? Could David in scenario one and Jamal in scenario two rightly explain away their behavior. Lies can take many forms and can impact many lives. Lies have put some people in a position from which they can never recover for the rest of their lives. It is like putting a ball and chain on someone's ankle and saying, "Here, this belongs to you." Lies are not without consequence. God will repay those that do others wrong.

Some examples of lying opportunities:

- ✓ signing up for things on credit, when we know we will not be able to pay for them
- ✓ embezzling funds over a period of time
- ✓ to a spouse about an adulterous relationship
- ✓ to a spouse about money spent, outside of discussed budget
- ✓ taxes
- ✓ political lies and half-truths to get elected
- ✓ breaking a promise or breaking a vow
- ✓ professing love
- ✓ unscrupulous businesses
- ✓ products for sale
- ✓ nonfiduciary investment brokers
- ✓ charities for outreach that are scams
- ✓ in a courtroom under oath
- ✓ to protect someone

Examples of Lies in the Bible	
Type or Justification for Lie	**Person(s) that Committed the Lie**
Omission	Genesis 20. Abraham about Sarah being his sister.
Commission	Act 5:1–11. (Especially verse 4) Ananias and Sapphira lie to Peter and to God.
Manipulation	2 Samuel 11. David acting like he was a friend to Uriah; when he was trying to kill him.

Peer pressure	1 Kings 18:20–40. All the fake prophets that were trying to burn an offering before Elijah.
Postpone or put off consequences	Judges 16. Samson keeps lying to his nemesis Delilah.
Gain advantage	Genesis 27:1–29. Jacob and his mother for Esau's blessing.
Avoid harm or punishment	John 18:13–27. Peter said, "I do not know him."
Protect someone	Joshua 2, James 2:25. Rahab lies to protect the spies of Israel.

Our Bible is so thorough that nothing is sugarcoated. We do not just get the bright side of the story. We get lies and other bad occurrences. The entire Bible is good for our edification. We should all learn from these biblical lies. All had consequences.

A Little White Lie

What if it is just a "little white lie"? What does that even mean in our society? Sometimes people will suggest that little white lies are those little harmless lies people say that do not hurt anyone. They are perceived as okay just to get away with something small, perhaps. Consider the following text.

> Like a madman who throws firebrands, arrows and death,
> is the man who deceives his neighbor, and says, "I was just joking!" (Proverbs 26:18–19 NKJV)

This text is very clear about how God feels about any type of lie. Think about this in terms of how Satan likes to deceive us. He did not present himself in the Garden of Eden and announce to Eve that he was the enemy of God who had been thrown out of heaven. He isolated Eve, started a conversation, and toyed with her passions to be wise. Herein lies the danger of playing with Satan when God gives an absolute. We are not allowed to rewrite God's word and say, "It's okay to lie in certain circumstances."

Consider Santa Claus, the Tooth Fairy, Halloween goblins and the Boogey Man. Why has our culture made up these lies? What is the real purpose? Do we really have to lie to our kids to make them behave for one day—Christmas Eve? Tradition says children are told they will not receive gifts the next morning if they do not behave. What are we teaching? Why? What are we enforcing? Why? It would work just as well to tell them that we are practicing our Christianity, and we give gifts at Christmastime to commemorate the wise men that brought gifts to Jesus. Otherwise, when the child goes to bed on Christmas Day, he or she has learned two things: (1) how to play with their favorite toy, and (2) it is okay to tell a lie. Children are watching and learning all the time. It is not fair to train children that lying is okay and then spank them three weeks later because they eat a forbidden cookie out of the cookie jar and proceed to say they did not do it. That is hypocrisy.

Reaping the Harvest

For the liar, there will be guilt, shame, stress, and loss of respect. A liar will teach others not to trust him or her and shatter the person's reputation as people begin to realize they are being lied to. Eventually, a liar will be abandoned. How many friendships and relationships that were otherwise fruitful in life were ended because of a lie?

As pointed out in the scenarios earlier, the person or persons lied to will reap an unknown harvest. It could be minor, or it could be severe. It could be tomorrow, or it could be the rest of their life. Lying is a horrendous sin, and anyone that makes it a habit is working with the devil himself. Jesus spoke about lies in the book of John.

> Why do ye not understand my speech? even because ye cannot hear my word. Ye are of your father the devil, and the lusts of your father ye will do. He was a murderer from the beginning, and abode not in the truth, because there is no truth in him. When he speaketh a lie, he speaketh of his own: for he is a liar, and the father of it. And because I tell you the truth, ye believe me not. (John 8:43–45 KJV)

The devil wants to ruin people's lives now and for eternity. The father of lies has tried to make people think that lying is not as bad as murder and some other sins, when in fact the Bible says lying will keep a person out of heaven.

> He who overcomes shall inherit all things, and I will be his God and he shall be My son. But the cowardly, unbelieving, abominable, murderers, sexually immoral, sorcerers, idolaters, and all liars shall have their part in the lake which burns with fire and brimstone, which is the second death. (Revelation 21:7–8 NKJV)

This text once again points out how serious lying is to God. While humanity may have degrees of what is a good sin and what is a bad sin, the Bible has liars and murderers in the same sentence. Lying should be resisted on all levels. It is a horrible sin.

Battling the Demons

> Wherefore take unto you the whole armor of God, that ye may be able to withstand in the evil day, and having done all, to stand. Stand therefore, having your loins girt about with truth, and having on the breastplate of righteousness. (Ephesians 6:13–14 KJV)

Any lie to another human being is a lie to Almighty God. God is the one that commands us not to bear false witness. However, God gives us a way to defeat the devil. He tells us to put on His whole armor, which starts with truth.

Therefore, Lord, we repent for lying. It hurts everybody. Lord, please forgive us, and help us to do better.

Chapter 16

I REPENT FOR ACCEPTING THE LGBTQ LIFESTYLE AS A GOD-APPROVED WAY OF LIFE

In this twenty-first century culture we are living in, the first question about this issue may be, why point out this particular sin? First, this book is about repentance. There are forty chapters herein about different atrocities we are committing before God. So, this sin is one of many. It is a sexual sin, (see chapter on promiscuity and adultery). Lesbian, gay, bisexual, transvestite, queer, (LGBTQ) is in the same category, biblically. However, our twenty-first century culture today is saying just accept it. If not, you must be a hater. There is a difference between God's moral law and man's legal rights. Does love give us any answers about this?

Just Accept It

In that regard, it seems that LGBTQ is the only particular sin in our society today that is being pushed into our American culture in such a way that everyone is being forced as a Christian to either accept it and throw their Bible away, or hold on to their religion and their Bible and be ostracized. Nobody is requiring people to accept a murderer and let him or her murder whenever that person feels compelled because of being born a murderer. Nobody is requiring people to accept a thief and let him or her steal because of being born a thief. Even adultery, as pervasive as it is, most still agree that it is not right and sinful. However, society is being asked to accept homosexuality being taught in our schools as an acceptable way of life. It is being forced on society if we choose to watch television and some Hollywood producer chooses to put LGBTQ behavior on display or tell a joke about it without me knowing it is coming and thus having the option to watch or not watch ahead of time. It is being forced on people at work and everywhere throughout our culture. As a Christian, it should be offensive based on the Bible. That means that Christians are now living in a toxic hostile environment. That it is being forced is harassment to a person that truly believes in Jesus Christ and the Bible. The old saying goes that "one cannot have their cake and eat it too." Likewise, we cannot have our Christianity and believe in homosexuality, too. We can and must speak out about this sin that will change society for all of us, all over the world. Some may say that people who believe the LGBTQ lifestyle is wrong are just haters.

Haters

Every human being has the right to be heard. The LGBTQ community believes that for many years they were not heard. Nobody wanted to give them a chance to speak, and they lived in what was referred to as being "in the closet." If a person was LGBTQ, most often they did not reveal it for fear of reprisals. Now, however, the community is no longer in the closet. The lifestyle has become a part of our genre, and gay marriage has been legalized in many states. Now, in a few short years, the LGBTQ lifestyle is talked about and promoted in terms of fairness and diversity for everyone. Now, in a few short years, a negative label has been applied to those that do not agree with the LGBTQ lifestyle.

> Homophobia: irrational fear of, aversion to, or discrimination against homosexuality or homosexuals[14]
>
> Heterosexism: discrimination or prejudice against homosexuals on the assumption that heterosexuality is the normal sexual orientation[15]

There is a need to set the record straight for all those that would say Christians are homophobic haters so that they can dismiss this entire chapter. Based on the preceding definitions, there is no reason for a Christian to fear the LGBTQ community. One can hate a sin and still love the sinner. Jesus demonstrated this precept many times. One example is when Jesus did not condemn the woman caught in adultery.

> They say unto him, Master, this woman was taken in adultery, in the very act. Now Moses in the law commanded us, that such should be stoned: but what sayest thou? This they said, tempting him, that they might have to accuse him. But Jesus stooped down, and with his finger wrote on the ground, as though he heard them not. So when they continued asking him, he lifted up himself, and said unto them, He that is without sin among you, let him first cast a stone at her. And again he stooped down, and wrote on the ground. And they which heard it, being convicted by their own conscience, went out one by one, beginning at the eldest, even unto the last: and Jesus was left alone, and the woman standing in the midst. When Jesus had lifted up himself, and saw none but the woman, he said unto her, Woman, where are those thine accusers? hath no man condemned thee? She said, No man, Lord. And Jesus said unto her, Neither do I condemn thee: go, and sin no more. (John 8:4–11 KJV)

This is a clear demonstration of the separation of the sin and the sinner. Even though Jesus allowed her to escape her accusers, He instructed her to go and sin no more. He loved her, but He did not condone the sin. Christians would have to hate everybody if they hated any one person for sinning because we have all sinned.

The LGBTQ community is a big proponent of diversity. Actually, "diversity" can be looked at on both sides. The LGBTQ community wants humanity to be diverse and accept their lifestyle. Those that do not are called homophobic. On the other hand, Christians can ask society now to be diverse and to accept their Christian beliefs and say the LGBTQ lifestyle is sinful and an abomination against God. That would make those that do not believe what the Bible has to say about it *"Christianphobic."* Likewise, those people who do not believe what the Bible has to say are suffering from *"Christianphobia."* This way of thinking displays the error in labeling someone just because they disagree with you. Christians should not hate, fear, or discriminate any of God's other human creation. We may disagree, but name-calling and smearing someone with a derogatory term is a distraction from the real issue. The real issue is sin and Satan. Diversity to support the LGBTQ community is no more or less important than diversity to support Christianity and freedom of religion. This chapter does not mean Christians are haters. It means Christians believe in their Bible and Jesus Christ.

God's Moral Law Versus Man's Legal Rights

- God's moral law

God's laws for man are very specific. Even though the grace of Jesus has saved us from our sins because humankind was not able to keep the law, we are still required to do the will of God. The Bible says, "Behold, to obey is better than sacrifice, and to heed than the fat of rams" (1 Samuel 15:22). Concerning the LGBTQ lifestyle, the Bible says:

> And God said, Let us make man in our image, after our likeness: and let them have dominion over the fish of the sea, and over the fowl of the air, and over the cattle, and over all the earth, and over every creeping thing that creepeth upon the earth. So God created man in his own image, in the image of God created he him; male and female created he them. And God blessed them, and God said unto them, Be fruitful, and multiply, and replenish the earth, and subdue it: and have dominion over the fish of the sea, and over the fowl of the air, and over every living thing that moveth upon the earth. (Genesis 1:26–28 KJV)

This is very clear. Often people comment about the Bible not being clear about certain subjects. This is not one of those situations. God intentionally made two sexes. With a command to be fruitful (have sex) and multiply. This is the first evidence in the Bible to explain at least one reason for the two sexes. Two people of the same sex cannot be fruitful. The only way a person could not agree with this point is to tell Christians they must scratch out these verses from their sacred text.

Leviticus 18 discusses many sexual sins including incest, adultery, and bestiality. Then in verse 22, it specifically speaks about homosexuality.

> Moreover thou shalt not lie carnally with thy neighbor's wife, to defile thyself with her. And thou shalt not let any of thy seed pass through the fire to Molech, neither shalt thou profane the name of thy God: I am the LORD. Thou shalt not lie with mankind, as with womankind: it is abomination. Neither shalt thou lie with any beast to defile thyself therewith: neither shall any woman stand before a beast to lie down thereto: it is confusion. (Leviticus 18:20–23 KJV)

Here once again, the Bible is clear. Men and women are not interchangeable when it comes to who a person can be intimate with. In the Hebrew language, *abomination* means something disgusting, abhorrent, loathsome, or detestable.[16]

In the twenty-first century, without a foundation built on the Bible, many people are doing what is right in their own mind. However, as Christians we must consider this in the context of God's creation and what God said would be going on at this time in the church age. Concerning the bisexual, lesbian, gay, pansexual, transgender, and queer community, the Bible says:

> Because that, when they knew God, they glorified him not as God, neither were thankful; but became vain in their imaginations, and their foolish heart was darkened. Professing themselves to be wise, they became fools, And changed the glory of the uncorruptible God into an

> image made like to corruptible man, and to birds, and four-footed beasts, and creeping things. Wherefore God also gave them up to uncleanness through the lusts of their own hearts, to dishonor their own bodies between themselves: Who changed the truth of God into a lie, and worshipped and served the creature more than the Creator, who is blessed forever. Amen. For this cause God gave them up unto vile affections: for even their women did change the natural use into that which is against nature: And likewise also the men, leaving the natural use of the woman, burned in their lust one toward another; men with men working that which is unseemly, and receiving in themselves that recompence of their error which was meet. (Romans 1:21–27 KJV)

Verse 24 says that God has basically done what many parents do with a hardheaded child that will not listen. At some point a parent might say, "Okay, go ahead with your hardheaded self and see what happens." Verses 24–25 make it clear that the LGBTQ lifestyle is about "lust" not "love." In verse 25, worshipping the creature means that the "fleshly lust" is what drives some to do things with their bodies that the Creator did not design. This text is very clear. Verses 26–27 are a New Testament rebuke of homosexuality.

- Sodom and Gomorrah

  > But before they lay down, the men of the city, even the men of Sodom, compassed the house round, both old and young, all the people from every quarter: And they called unto Lot, and said unto him, Where are the men which came in to thee this night? bring them out unto us, that we may know them. And Lot went out at the door unto them, and shut the door after him, And said, I pray you, brethren, do not so wickedly. Behold now, I have two daughters which have not known man; let me, I pray you, bring them out unto you, and do ye to them as is good in

your eyes: only unto these men do nothing; for therefore came they under the shadow of my roof. And they said, Stand back. And they said again, This one fellow came in to sojourn, and he will needs be a judge: now will we deal worse with thee, than with them. And they pressed sore upon the man, even Lot, and came near to break the door. But the men put forth their hand, and pulled Lot into the house to them, and shut to the door. And they smote the men that were at the door of the house with blindness, both small and great: so that they wearied themselves to find the door. (Genesis 19:4–11 KJV)

Clearly the men of Sodom in this text were interested in homosexual activity. Lot put a stop to that behavior and was almost attacked himself. In verse 24, Sodom and Gomorrah are destroyed, when the Lord "rained brimstone and fire from the Lord out of the heavens" (Genesis 19:24), because "the outcry against them is great, and because their sin is very grave" (Genesis 18:20).

- Man's legal rights

God's moral law is clear on the LGBTQ lifestyle. However, humanity's government, laws, policies, and procedures and their effect on society are another issue. Legally, slaves were property and counted as three-fifths of a person for tax purposes. Legally for many years, women could not vote in America. Legally, man's law says it is okay to cut a baby out of a woman's stomach, which Jesus would never do. All these things represent the dichotomy between God's moral law and humanity's legal laws. Throughout our American history, the two may not support the same belief. It may be legal to do something under human law that does not represent the will of God. Fortunately, in America we have the right to discuss issues openly even though some will continue to be debated. American people are not forced to believe in the Bible, so, yes, that makes the LGBTQ lifestyle debatable to some. Does everyone deserve the same legal rights under human law? Yes. Should legal discrimination be allowed by human law anywhere, at any time, against anyone. No. Thus, the dichotomy is laid bare. The LGBTQ lifestyle is a debatable moral issue. Legally, by human laws everyone should be treated fairly.

Love

I love you—Christians loving others. Let's get this straight. Every Christian should be able to look at every human being on this planet and say, "I love you," and mean it from every fiber in their body. As a Christian, I am compelled by God to love everyone, and there are no exceptions. The Bible tells Christians they should be careful about whom they might hang out with, be yoked with, and listen to, but it never gives me permission not to love them. (See chapter 4: "I Repent for Not Practicing True Love.") Therefore, I am not given the option to love some and hate others. Should people of the same sex love one another in a godly way. Yes, absolutely.

Love who I want to—LGBTQ community choosing who to have sex with. Some say that people should be able to love whomever they choose to. This is a distorted use of the word *love*. As stated in the previous paragraph, the Bible says we should love "everybody." Furthermore, just because a person loves somebody does not mean they should have sex with them. A person may love his or her grandmother, grandfather, mother, father, brother, sister, son, daughter, nieces, nephews, or neighbors; however, that does not mean he or she should have sex with them. The LGBTQ lifestyle is truly an issue about who a person has sex with—not whom they love.

> Love suffers long and is kind; love does not envy; love does not parade itself, is not puffed up; does not behave rudely, does not seek its own, is not provoked, thinks no evil; does not rejoice in iniquity, but rejoices in the truth; bears all things, believes all things, hopes all things, endures all things. Love never fails. But whether there are prophecies, they will fail; whether there are tongues, they will cease; whether there is knowledge, it will vanish away. (1 Corinthians 13:4–8 NKJV)

This is what the Bible gives us as a definition of love. This has nothing to do with whom a person chooses to have sex with.

> This is my commandment, That ye love one another, as I have loved you. Greater love hath no man than this, that a man lay down his life for his friends. (John 15:12–13 KJV)

In this text, Jesus is describing what He is about to do. He is explaining that His going to the cross as a sacrifice is an act of love. This is another definition of love that has nothing to do with choosing whom to have sex with. Therefore, using love as a reason for who one has as a partner is not a valid argument. Love and lust are two entirely different things.

Other Text

Leviticus chapter 20 is chocked full of what the Hebrew children were supposed to do and not do. Many of them are about sexual sins. Sins like adultery with your neighbor's wife, adultery with your father's wife, sex with your daughter-in-law, and a man marrying a woman and her mother are all forbidden under the penalty of death. Also, in that group is:

> If a man also lie with mankind, as he lieth with a woman, both of them have committed an abomination: they shall surely be put to death; their blood shall be upon them. (Leviticus 20:13 KJV)

Of course, even though this verse points out that homosexuality is wrong, we thank God for the blood of Jesus and instead of us putting anybody to death, we will surely let God do the judging on judgment day for all these acts in chapter 20. Homosexuality is the only sin in this group of sins that our culture has deemed acceptable as a way of life.

In 1 Corinthians 6:9–10, the Bible makes it plain about who will not enter the kingdom of heaven. Among those mentioned are fornicators, adulterers, and homosexuals. These groups are listed along with the unrighteous.

Jesus coming to earth helped to clear up what God meant about several issues. The Sermon on the Mount, Matthew 5–7, is full of the statement, "You have heard that it has been said, but I say to you …." In each of these statements Jesus is making sure the interpretation and implications of the stated issues from the Old Testament are clear to His audience. Even though our culture is not administering the death penalty for homosexuality and these other sexual sins, what we do know is that they are very serious to God.

Jesus Speaks on Male and Female Marriage

> And he answered and said unto them, Have ye not read, that he which made them at the beginning made them male and female, And said, For this cause shall a man leave father and mother, and shall cleave to his wife: and they twain shall be one flesh? Wherefore they are no more twain, but one flesh. What therefore God hath joined together, let not man put asunder. (Matthew 19:4–6 KJV)

In this text, when Jesus says, "Have you not read," He is referring to Genesis 1:27, in the Old Testament. Thus validating Old Testament Torah writings when it comes to marriage and God's creation of male and female.

Conclusion

There is a way that seems right to a person, but the final result leads to death, according to Proverbs 14:12. For Christians, the Bible is our Word and Jesus is our Rock. Using that as a foundation, no option exists about how to view the LGBTQ community. We cannot do what seems right in our own eyes. We must follow the word of God. Keeping in mind that those that practice the lifestyle are still children of God, they should be loved. It is not our place to judge and condemn anyone. What is clear based on the text shared is that the Bible considers the lifestyle to be a sin and therefore against the will of God and wrong.

Conversely, we Christians should not be condemned for our belief in the word of God. Diversity should also mean being diverse enough to allow me to believe and practice my religious beliefs.

Some believe that you can evolve to a new acceptance of homosexuality in the twenty-first century. However, my God does not evolve. The Bible tells me He is the same yesterday, today, and tomorrow. The Bible is clear on this sexual sin. The laws of humanity may not choose to discriminate, but there is a higher moral law that Christians should live by, and we all need to speak up and stand up against all sin in our culture.

Therefore, Lord, I repent for accepting the LGBTQ lifestyle as a God-approved way of life. I am Christian, and I must speak up. Lord, please forgive me, and help me to do better.

Chapter 17

I REPENT FOR NOT SPEAKING UP ABOUT SIN AND EVIL

It is always the other person. "It's someone else's duty or responsibility." "I'm not going to get involved." "I don't have time." "I don't want to hurt anybody's feelings." "I can't do anything about it." "That's just the way things are." Excuses, excuses, excuses are the only reason that things are happening in the world today that seem so far from how God told us to live. The Bible speaks clearly about what sin is. The Bible speaks clearly about what sin does. We will look at our twenty-first century culture, why some people might not speak up and some biblical reasons why we should speak up.

Sin and Evil

Sin in the Old and New Testament means missing the mark. In biblical terms, that would be missing the standard established by God. It is an offense against God. Sin is a moral deviation from God's desired plan and purpose. Evil things in the Old Testament refer to things that are bad, wicked, hurtful, troubling, and harmful. Likewise, in the New Testament, evil refers to things such as toil, vicious, malice, derelict, and mischief. All these Greek and Hebrew definitions for both sin and evil obviously spell bad news for humanity as individuals and as a society. Nothing good results from sin and evil.

The sobering irony about evil is that while we are on the journey called life, the Bible says the heart of man has evil thoughts from his youth (Genesis

8:21). The Bible also says we have all sinned in some way and come far short of the glory of God (Romans 3:23). So, why not just accept it? Why not just acquiesce and give up and go quietly along with Satan and his demons? Should we not stir anything up and just roll over and play dead when we as Christians see things that are not pleasing to God? In too many ways, unfortunately, it seems that is exactly what many people are doing in the twenty-first century.

Twenty-First Century

Why are we living in such an evil culture and not doing our part to speak up? Think of all the things going on in our culture that are hurtful to people: opioid epidemic, mass shootings, random shootings, gangs, child abuse, sex trafficking, bullying, terrorism, suicides, sexual harassment, racism, homosexuality, promiscuity, and adultery to name a few. Sin today is so ubiquitous that many people do not even notice the problem. Yes, the Bible speaks against these sins. But where is the Christian outrage? We should be speaking up because it is affecting our world and because it is our duty as Christians to speak up.

Is promiscuity okay now because we live in the twenty-first century? Is promiscuity okay even though the word *virgin* or *virginity* is used over sixty times in the Bible? Is promiscuity okay even though the Bible uses an analogy of a bride for New Jerusalem coming down from God out of heaven (Revelation 2:2)? Where are the Christians shouting loudly against adultery today? Adultery is one of the original Ten Commandments, but we seem not to be outraged about it anymore. Where are the Christians shouting loudly against homosexuality today? It is still a sin, according to the Bible. (See the previous chapter on the LGBTQ lifestyle.) When is the last time you have seen a group of Christians (Black, White, Latino, Asian, Native American, African, etc.) stand up together against racism as Christians? Why is it that all Christian groups do not stand together? Why are minorities the largest group to celebrate Black History Month? Does that mean White Christians do not or should not care? Where is the outrage?

> He that saith he is in the light, and hateth his brother, is in darkness even until now. He that loveth his brother abideth in the light, and there is none occasion of stumbling in him. But he that hateth his brother is in darkness, and walketh in darkness, and knoweth not whither he goeth, because that darkness hath blinded his eyes. (1 John 2:9–11 KJV)

Yes, when we are personally affected, people often make that particular issue a cause to combat for the rest of their lives. Nobody seems to be bothered unless the sin comes to their neighborhood and knocks on their door. Truthfully though, in reality, any sin is not against any particular individual or group. Sins and iniquity committed knowingly are a statement against God.

Other Sins

Numerous other sins could be mentioned here that are being overlooked today. This chapter, however, is just about the silence.

Adultery	Fornication	Uncleanness	Lewdness
Idolatry	Sorcery	Hatred	Contentions
Jealousies	Outbursts of wrath	Selfish ambitions	Dissensions
Heresies	Envy	Murder	Drunkenness
Revelries	Lovers of self	Lovers of money	Boasters
Pride	Blasphemers	Disobedience to parents	Unthankful
Unholy	Unloving	Unforgiving	Slanderers
Without self-control	Brutal	Despisers of good	Traitors
Headstrong	Homosexuality	Lovers of pleasure	Idolatry
Effeminate	Theft	Covetousness	Extortioners
Murder	Lying	Wickedness	Lasciviousness
Haughty			

To see these sins and others listed in the Bible, refer to Galatians 5:18–21, 2 Timothy 3:2–7, Romans 1:29–31, 1 Corinthians 6:9–10, Matthew 15:19, and Mark 7:21–22. When has the average person spoken up about this list of sins as something God does not like? How many of these sins are brushed off or looked at as no big deal in our culture?

Reasons for Not Speaking Up

We should all be shocked and appalled when we witness sin and evil, anywhere. However, many people come up with all sorts of reasons for not speaking up.

- Nonbelief

Some people do not believe that doing things God's way is important. Some do not believe in God. For some the Bible is just a literature book. That is fine if that is what they choose. However, this book about repenting is not written to nonbelievers. This book is written to those who have accepted Christ and have believed at one time or another. If you have believed, then you should repent for allowing sin, evil, and iniquity in your presence and not speaking up.

- Fear and shame

What will people say if I speak up? Will I be ostracized by my friends and acquaintances? "For whosoever shall be ashamed of me and of my words, of him shall the Son of man be ashamed, when he shall come in his own glory, and in his Father's, and of the holy angels" (Luke 9:26). Perhaps someone will hate me for standing up for God. Perhaps someone will even want to kill me.

> And I say unto you my friends, Be not afraid of them that kill the body, and after that have no more that they can do. But I will forewarn you whom ye shall fear: Fear him, which after he hath killed hath power to cast into hell; yea, I say unto you, Fear him. (Luke 12:4–5 KJV)

- Unaware of the long-term potential repercussions (don't take it seriously)

Elie Wiesel, in his book *Night*[17] talked about the first days when German soldiers came into their Jewish village before the Holocaust. The Jewish men were systematically gathered and taken out of town, a few at a time. Day after day, week after week, the strongest people were taken from the villages. Even though they were warned of the atrocities that were taking place, nobody believed they needed to react, and therefore the plague on the Jewish community continued. Once the men were gone, there was nobody left in the village that could really resist the roundup. Finally, the rest of the people in town were taken out of town and put on trains without speaking up and fighting back, until their town was emptied, and it was too late. Those that made it were taken to concentration camps. Nobody took the warning seriously.

Satan has a way of lulling us to sleep as things happen. It's like we are being cooked in a slow cooker. When we do not consider the long-term repercussions, then Satan continues to pile on one atrocity after another. That is what happens when no action is taken. This is what happens when nobody speaks up.

Reasons Christians Should Speak Up

- It is a war

Many today seem to have gone to sleep on the truth that we are in a war with Satan. Going to sleep in the middle of a war could prove fatal. The Bible refers to our condition in warrior terms.

> Finally, my brethren, be strong in the Lord, and in the power of his might. Put on the whole armor of God, that ye may be able to stand against the wiles of the devil. For we wrestle not against flesh and blood, but against principalities, against powers, against the rulers of the darkness of this world, against spiritual wickedness in

> high places. Wherefore take unto you the whole armor of God, that ye may be able to withstand in the evil day, and having done all, to stand. Stand therefore, having your loins girt about with truth, and having on the breastplate of righteousness; And your feet shod with the preparation of the gospel of peace; Above all, taking the shield of faith, wherewith ye shall be able to quench all the fiery darts of the wicked. And take the helmet of salvation, and the sword of the Spirit, which is the word of God. (Ephesians 6:10–17 KJV)

That does not sound like Christians should be lying down to everything that comes our way and not speaking up. If you as a Christian don't speak up, the sin will find its way back to your doorstep, family, or community.

- We are salt and light

It is our duty to speak up as Christians. It is our duty to stand up and show up.

> Ye are the salt of the earth: but if the salt have lost his savor, wherewith shall it be salted? it is thenceforth good for nothing, but to be cast out, and to be trodden under foot of men. Ye are the light of the world. A city that is set on an hill cannot be hid. Neither do men light a candle, and put it under a bushel, but on a candlestick; and it giveth light unto all that are in the house. (Matthew 5:13–15 KJV)

God is telling us to speak up, tell the truth, and be visible. We are called to tell the world what thus saith the Lord.

Sin Is Sin and Evil Is Evil

We need to put all this sin into context and call it what it is. Sin is sin, and evil is evil. You can love every sinner and hate the sin. A person can love another person that does something evil without condoning the evil action. If we as Christians believe in the Word written in God's Bible, we must make a decision and speak up about what is not in keeping with His beliefs. Everybody else seems to have a voice. Christians also need a voice outside of our four walls on Sunday morning or Saturday evening or whenever we choose to get together for worship services. That voice is the voice of all Christians.

Therefore, Lord, I repent for not speaking up about sinful and evil things going on in this world as often as I should. I cannot sit idly by and do nothing. I cannot just say that's the way things are. Lord, please forgive me, and help me to do better.

Chapter 18

I REPENT FOR CLERGY: PASTOR, BISHOP, PRIEST, PROPHET, EVANGELIST, AND ELDER ABUSE

For the purpose of this chapter, all pastors, bishops, priests, prophets, evangelists, and elders will mostly be referred to as clergy. All are our spiritual leaders. God has stated that they should hold a very important place in our society. However, society has changed in their view of clergy. Today, the role of clergy varies a lot, and clergy themselves vary a lot in different settings. Our clergy today are not given the same responsibility that clergy may have had in the past. Those that are deemed closest to God today are not required to go up on mountaintops to seek the Lord on our behalf. Clergy today are not required to sacrifice lambs or bullocks for our salvation. We abuse our clergy by not letting them lead when God gives them direction. We abuse our clergy by putting them on a pedestal and expecting them to perform. We abuse our clergy by talking negatively about them and not praying for them. We abuse our clergy by not honoring them. And frankly, we abuse our clergy with disrespect, by not committing to grow in our own personal relationship with God.

Dwane Massenburg

Changed Position

One reason our perception of clergy has changed is because there are so many voices and so-called authorities about so many different subjects today. Our clergy share society's spotlight of important influential people with a lot of other people. One hundred years ago, the most important people in many communities were the traveling doctor, the storekeeper, and the local clergy. In today's society, important people who we may deem just as worthy of stating right or wrong as a clergy member could include a politician, a professional athlete, a successful businessperson, or a professional entertainer. Think of the entertainers that have spoken out recently on certain societal issues. We have not heard the combined voice of the clergy on some of these important issues. In many cases, society seems to have outgrown what clergy have to say. Society is not asking, "What does the pastor say about it?" On top of that, negative publicity about our clergy today can tend to go viral very quickly. That leads to a loss of respect for clergy that are trying to do a good job and are sincere.

Second, today there are many variations within the clergy ranks. There are many denominational differences, of course. There are megachurch clergy, small church clergy, televangelists, and chaplains. There was a time when you would always see clergy dressed up formally, in public. Now, daily clergy may be seen in various outfits when out in public. Social media has also changed the perception people have about clergy in this way because they are seen portrayed doing everyday things that may have been always true but never seen. The professions of clergy are different. Some are full-time clergy and televangelists, leading megacongregations, while some are bivocational leading small congregations with less than fifty members. Also, one of the large considerations for clergy variation today is more females in clergy positions. One hundred years ago, this was practically unheard of.

The competition for having a meaningful voice in our society and the changes we see in clergy today have all affected the response people have to their clergy. However, to God, the people called to do his work are still called.

Clergy Are Needed

The real question, given the societal changes and variations in clergy themselves, is why do we abuse the good clergy that our society so desperately needs? God is the one that said we need our clergy.

> For whosoever shall call upon the name of the Lord shall be saved. How then shall they call on him in whom they have not believed? and how shall they believe in him of whom they have not heard? and how shall they hear without a preacher? And how shall they preach, except they be sent? as it is written, How beautiful are the feet of them that preach the gospel of peace, and bring glad tidings of good things! (Romans 10:13–15 KJV)

This text lays out the importance of clergy to society. Our American culture is constantly looking for answers to fix things. We always want to know why? We are always trying to understand the meaning behind bad behavior. Christians however, already know. We already understand sin and what it will make a person do. We already understand that the devil will work anyone deeper and deeper into a mess until corruption, confusion, and death are the outcome. The answer is the love of God, the grace of His Son—Jesus Christ—and the communion of the Holy Spirit. That message must be delivered. People need to be made aware of this life-altering good news. Who will deliver the message? Bingo! Hence, the desperate need for clergy in our society. Clergy deliver real answers for real problems. It is God's design that the preached word is what reaches the heart and makes a difference. It is God that called the prophets and the twelve disciples. It is God that has called every true clergy trying their best to deliver His word today. It is God who says in this verse that they are so important that even their feet are beautiful.

Let Them Lead

We abuse our clergy by not letting our clergy lead. Clergy that have demonstrated their love for God, love for their congregations, and have not been in the headlines for doing something outlandish against the will of God, deserve to be respected and followed. No, clergy are not perfect. However, those trying to do the will of God have been called by God. God will direct them on what needs to be done to help the congregation and when it should be done.

> He that descended is the same also that ascended up far above all heavens, that he might fill all things. And he gave some, apostles; and some, prophets; and some, evangelists; and some, pastors and teachers; For the perfecting of the saints, for the work of the ministry, for the edifying of the body of Christ. (Ephesians 4:10–12 KJV)

Therefore, God's assigned clergy should lead congregations on what saith the Lord. Nowhere in the Bible does it suggest deacons, trustees, councils, or boards should say which ministries and efforts should be championed when it comes to reaching people for Christ. Therefore, if deacons, trustees and boards dispute the direction of the clergy, they are "not" doing a biblical, godly thing. They are working against God. Love in the heart of a called clergy will lead them to do what will edify the body of Christ. They should not have to argue with church leaders all along the way for every decision like God had to keep arguing with the Israelites.

Performers

We also abuse our clergy by wanting them to be performers. This is more prevalent in some congregations than others. Every Sunday people tell preachers, "I enjoyed your message." We say this the same way one might say, "I enjoyed that movie," or "I enjoyed that play." This may not sound right, but the preached word is not meant to be enjoyed. It is meant to reach into the souls of men and women and change hearts and minds to follow God. It is meant to be contemplated and pondered over. It is meant to confront us with shortcomings that God wants us to get right. Can and should we enjoy a worship service if we truly love the Lord? Absolutely! Is enjoyment the purpose? Absolutely not! Leaving the service closer to God is the purpose. Therefore, it is shameful to seek a congregation to join simply because of the charisma of the clergy. Or, for that matter, the performance of the choir director and choir. Paul discussed this same issue in his letter to the Corinthians. Early Christians were trying to say one clergy was better than another.

> For ye are yet carnal: for whereas there is among you envying, and strife, and divisions, are ye not carnal, and walk as men? For while one saith, I am of Paul; and another, I am of Apollos; are ye not carnal Who then is Paul, and who is Apollos, but ministers by whom ye believed, even as the Lord gave to every man? I have planted, Apollos watered; but God gave the increase. So then neither is he that planteth any thing, neither he that watereth; but God that giveth the increase. (1 Corinthians 3:3–7 KJV)

Imagine if Jesus came back to earth today to teach and preach "without" the miracles He performed. How many churches today would elect Him as pastor? He would not use rhymes or whooping or big words to entice listeners. I wonder if He would try to sing for the congregation. He would simply preach truth, over and over again. Jesus would certainly not seek the limelight. Would He be elected in your congregation? Would His performance match what you are looking for? Would Jesus dress good enough for your church? Would He look the part? Would this plain preacher without a place to lay His head (foxes have holes, birds have nests, bees have hives, and turtles have shells) be good enough for your congregation to elect Him as the clergy of your congregation?

Speaking Negatively

The Bible say that a person should not tell lies and spread lies about other people. That includes our clergy. Gossiping and saying things we do not know for a fact is especially detrimental when it is done to our clergy. It casts a shadow among nonbelievers that causes them to not respect the office of clergy.

> Do not receive an accusation against an elder except from two or three witnesses. (1 Timothy 5:19 NKJV)

This text means that bad news about clergy should be handled very discretely. God is involved. Even if a clergy person does, without a doubt, do something wrong, it is not a time to gloat and spread gossip. Yes, even clergy "may," in fact, "will," do wrong sometimes. We have all sinned. However, it remains that the office of clergy is ordained by God, and the office should be respected. Do we think we should run around town and gossip everywhere we can about what the clergy did? In fact, is it appropriate to talk about and point fingers at anyone that has fallen short? For that, I believe the confrontation Jesus had with the woman caught in adultery is the best example.

> And the scribes and Pharisees brought unto him a woman taken in adultery; and when they had set her in the midst, They say unto him, Master, this woman was taken in adultery, in the very act. Now Moses in the law commanded us, that such should be stoned: but what sayest thou? This they said, tempting him, that they might have to accuse him. But Jesus stooped down, and with his finger wrote on the ground, as though he heard them not. So when they continued asking him, he lifted up himself, and said unto them, He that is without sin among you, let him first cast a stone at her. (John 8:3–7 KJV)

In this text, the woman caught in adultery is brought publicly by her accusers to receive judgment and perhaps a punishment from Jesus. They were ready to have her publicly belittled, shamed, and put in her place. Imagine how happy the devil is when the opportunity arises to have a clergy member publicly defamed. Jesus, however, waits until the crowd dissipates. Then, He does not condemn the woman but just tells her to stop doing what she is doing from here forward. He tells her this privately. Clergy deserve the same respect. Therefore, anyone that has a desire to gossip about anyone else's wrongdoing, including clergy, should first go get a large mirror and look at themselves and list their own wrongs to put on public display. That is what happened to the scribes and Pharisees in this text. They demonstrated to the entire crowd that they also were not perfect by walking away. Jesus told this woman, caught in sin, to go and sin no more. That is what we should do for everyone caught in sin. We should pray for them and not put them down or run their name through the mud. God will take care of clergy that scatter his sheep. That is not a job for the rest of us imperfect human beings.

Growth Refusal

This is the most deceptive way that many people abuse their clergy. Consider a child that has been told time and time again about not doing something. Yet, they continue to do the very thing their loving parent has asked them not to do. They do it in public. They do it boldly. They do it loudly. In the meantime, their loving parent continues to try to reign them in. Most of us would consider that child to be disrespectful and embarrassing to their loving parent. Now consider your clergy. Those that have been truly called, really do love their congregation. They spend time each week preparing a sermon that they hope, with the help of God, will make a difference in the lives of their members. Yes, that is the job of clergy, but, just like any parent, they do hope day after day that they will see an improvement in behavior. This is why "old church saints," set in their ways, can be the most frustrating and heart-wrenching for clergy. They are left wondering, "Is it me?" "Are they really claiming to be a Christian, the way they act?" The hardheaded behavior of some congregants is disrespectful to their clergy and to God. It leaves the clergy thinking, *When will they ever grow up?*

Honor Them

In our society, I have had church officials and lay members argue with me about the fact that clergy are just men. True enough. This is the same attitude that got people hung up about Jesus, the Son of God. He was 100 percent man. However, He was also 100 percent God. Some may talk sarcastically about clergy as if they are just human. True, they are. But they are much more than that after they are called by God. Miriam and

Aaron decided that they were just as important as Moses. They downplayed that Moses was a chosen vessel. They decided to speak up against Moses. For a moment, they assumed that they knew as much as Moses and that they were just as qualified as Moses to be in charge of Israel. God set the record straight.

> And Miriam and Aaron spake against Moses because of the Ethiopian woman whom he had married: for he had married an Ethiopian woman. And they said, Hath the LORD indeed spoken only by Moses? hath he not spoken also by us? And the LORD heard it. (Now the man Moses was very meek, above all the men which were upon the face of the earth.) And the LORD spake suddenly unto Moses, and unto Aaron, and unto Miriam, Come out ye three unto the tabernacle of the congregation. And they three came out. And the LORD came down in the pillar of the cloud, and stood in the door of the tabernacle, and called Aaron and Miriam: and they both came forth. And he said, Hear now my words: If there be a prophet among you, I the LORD will make myself known unto him in a vision, and will speak unto him in a dream. My servant Moses is not so, who is faithful in all mine house. With him will I speak mouth to mouth, even apparently, and not in dark speeches; and the similitude of the LORD shall he behold: wherefore then were ye not afraid to speak against my servant Moses? (Numbers 12:1–8 KJV)

I do not envy Aaron and Miriam for what happened on this day. Being called out personally and specifically by God to be reprimanded would certainly qualify as not a good day in my book. Since none of us are qualified to know the heart of a person, it is probably better that we honor those that are in position to represent God. God will take care of everything else. Many people have gotten themselves in trouble trying to be play God and keep clergy in check. In fact, we are told in the Bible to honor our clergy.

Let the elders that rule well be counted worthy of double honor, especially they who labor in the word and doctrine. For the scripture saith, thou shalt not muzzle the ox that treadeth out the corn. And, The laborer is worthy of his reward. (1 Timothy 5:17–18 KJV)

Therefore, Lord, I repent for my role in clergy: pastor, bishop, priest, evangelist and elder abuse. If they are called by God, I should respect God's calling. Lord, please forgive me, and help me to do better.

Chapter 19

I REPENT FOR IGNORING WHAT NATURE TEACHES US

Nature is God's creation. It can be argued that many of the ills in our society today are the result of humankind in general becoming more urban and less rural. In rural upbringings, people generally are more in touch with nature. They can appreciate how delicate and intricate nature is. They can appreciate how awesome nature is. They can appreciate all the wonderful lessons that nature can teach us. However, in many ways, in the twenty-first century, humanity along with our pride and arrogance has chosen to ignore nature. God's word tells us to pay attention to nature.

In Romans 1:18–21, God plainly says that His anger is displayed by looking up at the heavens and comparing it to all the ugly unrighteous and unholy things that men do when they are trying to suppress the truth. Everything about God is demonstrated by them because God lays it out for them to see. The animals and plants on the earth reveal that they know God themselves. In fact, all things in nature, those we can see and those we usually cannot see, are clearly seen and evident when we pay attention. This has been true since the earth was formed. Humanity has no excuse. God may be denied, and His awesome, magnificent power may not be given credit for what it is, but it is still obvious. Humanity may not be thankful, but that way of thinking is worthless. Trying to deny God in nature is quite perplexing. It will eventually drive people to a cave of confusion when it comes to understanding other things in the world.

Delicate and Intricate

If you take a close look at nature, you understand how delicate God's design really is. The same God who designed an enormous whale, a huge elephant, and a giant sequoia tree also designed the octopus, snakes that slither, and birds that fly. Think of how delicate and intricate the design of everything is and how it all must work together.

When it comes to delicacy, consider our own bodies. Think of all the working parts that come together to make us who we are. Humanity has made artificial prosthetics for many limbs that work very well, but can you imagine all the intricate details God put into the making of a human hand. Each bone grows in proportion to the proper size. The skin on the knuckles and bending joints is made to stretch. The fingers themselves grow to different lengths to accommodate our use. Fingernails grow to protect the edges. Many muscles and nerves coordinate to allow us to grab, pick up, push, and pull objects. This hand design was valuable for humanity five thousand years ago, and it is still valuable for us today. Even the skin on the inside of the hand is different from the skin on the outside. We can cross our fingers, pluck, rub our hands together, and clap to cause different effects and sounds.

That is an absolute miracle. That could not have happened by accident or evolution. It is too intertwined. It is too much of a system of order. God's design of everything is very delicate and intricate. My wife recently went to the hospital, and the doctors told us there were seven different kinds of white blood cells. That is a lot of detail. I see your glory, Lord.

Awesome

In the Bible, in the book of Job, God reminds us why we need to repent for not paying attention to the awesomeness of God and His creation. In fact, Job himself had to repent for this.

> Then Job answered the LORD, and said, I know that thou canst do every thing, and that no thought can be

withholden from thee. Who is he that hideth counsel without knowledge? therefore have I uttered that I understood not; things too wonderful for me, which I knew not. Hear, I beseech thee, and I will speak: I will demand of thee, and declare thou unto me. I have heard of thee by the hearing of the ear: but now mine eye seeth thee. Wherefore I abhor myself, and repent in dust and ashes. (Job 42:1–6 KJV)

While Job was sick and in despair, he finds himself questioning the sovereignty of Almighty God. God uses His creation to put Job in his place. Another reason why it is so important for us to consider nature is because God uses it to demonstrate Himself to us. God reminds Job of the vastness and awesomeness of His creation. Four chapters (38–41) record God's reprimanding of Job. He asks Job about the foundations of the earth and where they are fastened. He asks about the clouds, the stars, the snow, the wings of a peacock, the feathers of an ostrich, and the strength of a horse. In other words, God reminds Job that His creation is awesome, and we should take notice. Only an awesome God could create such an awesome world.

Nature Can Teach Us

We can also learn a lot if we stop ignoring nature. Take the seasons of the year, for instance. If you are fortunate enough to live in a region of the world that experiences winter, spring, summer, and fall, then you already understand that some things in our lives will be around for a season. Then our life will transition to another season, and we should move on. Consider daytime and nighttime. Before man-made lighting, perhaps we should have learned that our bodies were meant to have a certain amount of rest after the sun sets. The Bible tells us we should learn planning from ants, ingenuity from badgers, teamwork from grasshoppers, and perhaps patience and timing from spiders.

> The ants are a people not strong, yet they prepare their meat in the summer; The conies are but a feeble folk, yet

make they their houses in the rocks; The locusts have no king, yet go they forth all of them by bands; The spider taketh hold with her hands, and is in kings' palaces. (Proverbs 30:25–28 KJV)

Yes, God is in the nature that we walk by every day. His creative design is delicate, intricate, awesome. We can learn a lot for ourselves if we pay attention.

Examples

Fall. I noticed in my own backyard the progression of things that happen in the fall of the year. First, acorns fall and hit the ground. Then, as if they know it is their turn, the leaves fall on top of them. This provides a cover from the cold and later turns into a thin layer of topsoil for the acorn seed to germinate in. Then, in sequence, the fall rains and winter snow come to keep the soil moist. The winter allows time for the acorn to sprout roots that reach deep into the moist soil. By springtime, a perfect environment has been created for the young acorn to break ground as a young oak tree.

This is a perfect demonstration of our Creator's divine order. It is delicate and balanced. God is letting us know that there is a time and season for all things, but they should occur in order. Think of all the things humanity could learn from this one example. Young people could wait until they were married to have sex. Then, having waited and lived through the dating phase perhaps time for a more friendly type of love instead of a sexual relationship would allow more marriages to stay together.

Encore Azaleas. Azaleas are beautiful flowers that usually bloom in the spring. Their small flowers are a sure way to find out if there are any bees or other pollinating insects in your neighborhood because the blooms will be full of them. Usually, healthy bushes are so full of blooms in the spring that you cannot see the branches or underside of the plant when they start to bloom in April.

To my surprise while walking around at a nursery in September one year, another plant had similar blooms that were in full display. The blooms were just as vibrant and slightly larger, but they were just as numerous on the plant as those that bloom in the spring. The bush was called an Encore Azalea. A very fitting name for a plant that looks the same and blooms the same but always is most beautiful about six months later than the regular azalea.

This is such a perfect demonstration of God teaching us that our best time in life may not be when we are in high school. Our best time may be when we are in our forties, fifties, or even seventies. Many renowned entertainers or businesspeople did not truly hit their stride until later in life. There is never a need to give up because you are not a star and retired by the time you are thirty-five. Just keep living. Your time is coming.

Ice storms and snow. In the winter in most parts of our country, there are two main "winter warning" types of precipitation. Those two types are snow and freezing rain. Snow in the Rocky Mountains provides icepack, and the spring runoff provides water for many places in the valleys below all the way until the next snow season begins. On the other hand, ice storms create another, more drastic benefit for humanity. Think of all the landscapers across the country that spend their time pruning and trimming away unwanted branches and underbrush in the fall. That is what God is doing in the winter with an ice storm. Ice builds up slowly on branches and limbs. As the icy mixture continues to fall, the buildup becomes too much for limbs that are weak in any way. Dead limbs get heavier and heavier, and some begin to break away. Weak and decaying limbs give out. All this makes more room for more sunlight to get through in the springtime. That allows for more new healthy limbs to grow later. Also, we should note that this occurs during a season of the year that presents the least damage to the tree. The heavier the ice storm, the more pruning takes place.

God teaches gardeners with winter weather that the correct time of year should be chosen for whatever needs to be pruned. Most pruning for most plants does occur in the wintertime. There is no way the ice pack of snow in the mountains should be ignored as only good for skiing or snowboarding. We can learn from this that there are some things that should be held in reserve when we are blessed in any season. Some of the reserves may be absolutely necessary in another season.

Hurricanes and heavy rains. Nothing is more devasting than a hurricane or monsoon. When they come, entire neighborhoods can be wiped out. Heavy rains during some seasons in certain areas can cause massive flooding that will do the same thing to an area as a hurricane. In one instance the devastation is caused by wind and rain, and in another instance the devastation is caused only by flooding. Despite the devastation, the hurricane season starts during the hottest time of the year in America. Drought conditions often give way to flooding situations in some areas when a hurricane comes up the East Coast or spins in the Gulf of Mexico.

God teaches us when it comes to the drought that He will meet our needs just when it looks like no hope exists. The hurricanes and heavy rains come at a cost to the landscape, but they do break the drought and begin a wetter season going into the fall of the year.

Predators and prey. Throughout the animal kingdom, there are predators and prey. Animals with fangs and claws survive off herbivores. Sometimes larger and more ferocious animals with fangs will also survive off smaller animals even though they also may have fangs and claws. Predators are throughout the animal kingdom including insects, birds, sea life from octopus to whales, and large land animals from bears to lions.

What is one of the key elements we can learn from God concerning the predators and prey of the animal kingdom? The main lesson here is balance. When predators become too dominant and prey become too scarce, then the predators will die off; the balance will be reset, and the cycle will restart.

We all need balance in our lives, and studying any one small portion of the animal kingdom will teach us that too much work while neglecting family is not good. It will teach us that too much money spent on frivolous things at the expense of saving for a house or your child's college may not be the proper balance.

Deciduous trees. Deciduous trees bear leaves that turn colors in the fall and then drop off the tree. In the spring, new leaves seem to magically appear on branches that looked like dead twigs just a few weeks earlier. Looking at the branches and twigs does not give any clue about what is happening inside. It is amazing.

Likewise, preparation when no one else can see your work is a valuable lesson. Many sports figures and famous people are so good when we see them in the limelight. They are so good they make things look easy. However, no one knows all the work, sweat and tears that went into the preparation to make that person a superstar.

Hibernation. Many animals hibernate for the winter. Bears, some squirrels, marmots, and many other small mammals hibernate. Their blood pressure and body temperature drop. They have spent many of the months prior to hibernation planning. They prepare the hibernation location and most store a lot of fat to prepare their bodies to survive during the cold weeks.

Hibernation reminds me of older people telling me when I was young to always save for a rainy day. God's wisdom is displayed in this perfect example of saving for the future. Every year these hibernating animals do the things they need to do to survive a cold, harsh winter. Young people need to take note of this now. All working people need to be aware that retirement is coming. Someday what you store up will take care of you. Otherwise, the cold, harsh winter will be brutal.

Childbirth. Sometimes we humans are so self-conscious that we forget that we are also warm-blooded mammals in the animal kingdom. Our own natural progression is a part of nature that we should pay attention to. Babies come into this world totally helpless. A newborn could not survive a week without some type of constant care. Why did God allow this? Gazelles in the wild can run within a few minutes of birth or they will be captured and eaten. Yet, most early human babies do not learn to walk until about nine months have passed.

What can we learn? Is there a lesson we can learn from why God did it the way He did? Yes. The lesson demonstrates the importance of parenthood. Parents that do not take their role seriously are not studying their infant newborn very closely. God wants us to realize that a child will have to be taught everything to survive. From infant to adult, a child will have to be trained and coached all along the way.

Desert animals. I have driven through the Mojave Desert in California. It is supposed to be the driest desert in North America. Cactus, Joshua trees, and hot, arid temperatures are normal. Yet, life is present throughout the desert. It is amazing. How do animals survive in such a climate? Many of them wait until nighttime to forage for food. They can find what they need to eat and, in the meantime, avoid the intensity of the hot summer sun.

This teaches us that no matter how prepared we are for things that happen in this life, we may still have to wait for everything to work out. Waiting to make our move may be the most prudent thing we can do.

Nature Talking

Growing up in rural Virginia, I would hear my grandparents say a lot of old sayings. My grandmother would say, "Be quiet because the Lord is doing His work," just as a loud clap of thunder was heard in the distance. I learned to respect and revere nature from sayings like this. It has been a great blessing in my life. Nature has a lot to teach us all if we just pay attention.

Therefore, Lord, I repent for ignoring what nature, your divine creation, reveals about you. I will pay closer attention and appreciate your handiwork. Lord, please forgive me, and help me to do better.

Chapter 20

I REPENT FOR NOT PARENTING

There is no excuse for parenting not being number two or three on your life priority list. Number one should be your allegiance to God and His call on your life (see chapter 10: "I Repent for Using God like a Vending Machine"). Number two should be your spouse if you are married (see chapter 35: "I Repent for Not Honoring Marriage"). That means parenting should be number two if you are not married and number three if you are. That is pretty high on the priority list of things that should be important to you in life.

Parenting should come before working two jobs to pay for a big house, making sure your stock account is just right, driving a fancy car, or having the right dishes in your china cabinet. Parenting should come before your efforts to make it big in your career. If you are robbing your children of the time they need to be with you and learn from you, then your priorities should be checked. Parenting is not a perfect science, but it must be attempted with all the vigor, imagination, and ingenuity that we have. Parenting is important. We have examples of biblical parenting, and we also have direct suggestions on how to parent from the Bible.

Not a Perfect Science

So often you hear people say that being a parent does not come with a manual. That is true, if you are not a Christian. It is not true if you are a Christian, even though it may seem that way, because the outcome is not guaranteed. Adam and Eve were the parents of both Cain and Abel. Because we believe the world was much more subdued than it is today, it is reasonable to assume that Adam and Eve were undoubtedly the largest influence over their sons' lives. They grew up in an environment without many distractions as we would consider them today. Yet, one son was a humble believer in God based on his sacrifice. The other son, however, portrayed an attitude of selfishness, enviousness, and cruelty. How did this happen if the parenting that was delivered was the same? Well, the truth of the matter is that good or bad parenting does not guarantee the outcome of children. Children have their own lives to live, and they are born with different personalities, strengths, and weaknesses from day one.

Aaron had Nadab and Abihu. Aaron was a priest for the nation of Israel. Moses was the uncle of Nadab and Abihu. Yet the two sons of Aaron did not follow the way of God.

> And Nadab and Abihu, the sons of Aaron, took either of them his censer, and put fire therein, and put incense thereon, and offered strange fire before the LORD, which he commanded them not. And there went out fire from the LORD, and devoured them, and they died before the LORD. Then Moses said unto Aaron, This is it that the LORD spake, saying, I will be sanctified in them that come nigh me, and before all the people I will be glorified. And Aaron held his peace. (Leviticus 10:1–3 KJV)

Hophni and Phinehas were the sons of Eli. Eli was a priest for the nation of Israel. Even though Israel was God's chosen nation, and Eli was a priest, neither of his sons knew God. They were reared in the right environment with a godly father. However, they stole from people in the community and committed fornication with women at the door of the tabernacle. Their actions were their own choice. Eli admonished them to stop. All this is explained in 1 Samuel 2.

> Now the sons of Eli were corrupt; they did not know the Lord. (1 Samuel 2:12 NKJV)

With all that said, it does not at all excuse the importance of parenting. Once again, it is not an exact science. There are no guarantees. Yet, God and nature have arranged for children to arrive in this world in a very dependent fashion. It is a full-time job, and there are no days off.

The Importance of Parenting

If you love your children, you must ask yourself, who is teaching your children their core values that will follow them throughout life, if you are not? Will you leave it to the gang members and extremists that are constantly looking for somebody to influence and take advantage of? Will you leave it to a babysitter that might not think like you, about major issues? Will you leave it to a cousin that is in the family but thinks very differently from you? Whether a person is a biological or adoptive parent, they have a lot of responsibility. Children have no better guidance than a loving parent that cares.

Children must grow up physically, mentally, and spiritually. The Bible says, "When I was a child, I spoke as a child, I understood as a child, I thought as a child: but when I became a man, I put away childish things" (1 Corinthians 13:11 NKJV). That means that while reaching adulthood, a child must learn to speak, understand, and think like an adult. Who is better than a loving parent to teach a child all this?

Biblical Parenting

Children cannot rear themselves. They do not know enough to accomplish the task. God said "tell your children" many times in the Bible.

God instructs the Hebrews: "And you shall tell your son in that day, saying, this is done because of what the Lord did for me when I came up from Egypt" (Exodus 13:8 NKJV).

David instructs Solomon: Now the days of David drew near that he should die, and he charged Solomon his son, saying. I go the way of all the earth; be strong, therefore, and prove yourself a man (1 Kings 2:1–2 NKJV).

Child-Rearing from the Bible

The Bible gives specific instructions on training children. The Bible is very thorough.

Train your children.

> Train up a child in the way he should go, and when he is old, he will not depart from it. (Proverbs 22:6 KJV)

In other words, teach your children right from wrong. Teach them everything you know by example and by talking.

Discipline your children.

> He who spares his rod hates his son, but he who loves him disciplines him promptly.
>
> (Proverbs 13:24 NKJV)
>
> Foolishness is bound in the heart of a child; but the rod of correction shall drive it far from him. (Proverbs 22:15 KJV)
>
> Withhold not correction from the child, for if thou beatest him with a rod, he will not die. Thou shalt beat him with the rod, and shalt deliver his soul from hell. (Proverbs 23:13–14 KJV)
>
> The rod and reproof give wisdom, but a child left to himself bringeth his mother to shame. (Proverbs 29:15 KJV)

> For whom the Lord loveth he chasteneth, and scourgeth every son whom he receiveth. If ye endure chastening, God dealeth with you as with sons; for what son is he whom the father chasteneth not? But if ye be without chastisement, whereof all are partakers, then are ye bastards, and not sons. Furthermore we have had fathers of our flesh which corrected us, and we gave them reverence: shall we not much rather be in subjection unto the Father of spirits, and live? For they verily for a few days chastened us after their own pleasure; but he for our profit, that we might be partakers of his holiness. Now no chastening for the present seemeth to be joyous, but grievous: nevertheless afterward it yieldeth the peaceable fruit of righteousness unto them which are exercised thereby. (Hebrews 12:6–11 KJV)

In the world we live in today, it seems that some parents think it is bad news to discipline children by popping their hands or spanking their bottoms, but these Bible verses are perfectly clear. One can choose to believe the Bible or all the psychology "experts." Discipline does not mean abuse, by any means. Physical discipline should not be done in anger. These verses explain that physical discipline is just a teaching method.

Many animals in nature use stern and sometimes forceful actions to get young ones to understand that the answer is no. They do not do it in hate or anger but to teach an important lesson. A dog will snap and bite at her puppies when they get old enough, and it is time to teach them that she will stop nursing them.

Physical discipline is "not" the only form of correction, but the Bible suggest that it should not be excluded. Physical discipline used when children are two or three along with a stern word or two may be enough to teach most children to have respect for the stern look or voice which will eliminate the need for the physical discipline. Notice verse 9 in the Hebrews text mentioned. This is far different from the abuse of throwing shoes or pots and pans at children. It is different from the verbal abuse of cursing out a hardheaded teenager. It is also far different from parents trying to be best friends with their kids instead of parents.

Speak kindly to your children.

> Children, obey your parents in all things, for this is well pleasing unto the Lord. Fathers, provoke not your children to anger, lest they be discouraged. (Colossians 3:20–21 KJV)

Apparently, the discipline and teaching we are required to do must come without anger, rudeness, and meanness. It is all about teaching the lesson that needs to be taught at the time, not demonstrating your superior intellect or power.

Give to your children.

> Or what man is there of you, whom if his son ask bread, will he give him a stone? Or if he ask a fish, will he give him a serpent? If ye then, being evil, know how to give good gifts unto your children, how much more shall your Father which is in heaven give good things to them that ask him? (Matthew 7:9–11 KJV)

This text is self-explanatory. Parents must provide for their children. Provision should be made for needs, not every desire the child may have. Financial stewardship should be taught at an early age.

Pray and sacrifice for your children.

> There was a man in the land of Uz, whose name was Job; and that man was perfect and upright, and one that feared God, and eschewed evil. And there were born unto him seven sons and three daughters. His substance also was seven thousand sheep, and three thousand camels, and five hundred yoke of oxen, and five hundred she asses, and a very great household; so that this man was the greatest

of all the men of the east. And his sons went and feasted in their houses, every one his day; and sent and called for their three sisters to eat and to drink with them. And it was so, when the days of their feasting were gone about, that Job sent and sanctified them, and rose up early in the morning, and offered burnt offerings according to the number of them all: for Job said, It may be that my sons have sinned, and cursed God in their hearts. Thus, did Job continually. (Job 1:1–5 KJV)

Be there for your children and believe in the Godly purpose for their life.

Mary was with Jesus from the time He was born, throughout His ministry, and before and after His crucifixion.

And when they were come in, they went up into an upper room, where abode both Peter, and James, and John, and Andrew, Philip, and Thomas, Bartholomew, and Matthew, James the son of Alphaeus, and Simon Zelotes, and Judas the brother of James. These all continued with one accord in prayer and supplication, with the women, and Mary the mother of Jesus, and with his brethren. (Acts 1:13–14 KJV)

Let children get close enough to bother you.

Then were there brought unto him little children, that he should put his hands on them, and pray: and the disciples rebuked them. But Jesus said, Suffer little children, and forbid them not, to come unto me: for of such is the kingdom of heaven. And he laid his hands on them, and departed thence. (Matthew 19:13–15 KJV)

Children can certainly be bothersome when it comes to our busy lives. We all have so much to do. Jesus likewise had a lot to accomplish during His short years of ministry on this earth. However, if He took the time to acknowledge and entertain children with all their childlike behaviors, so should we. Take intimate time to listen and talk to your children. Children need conversation and physical closeness to form their own thoughts, opinions, and relationship acumen. We never know what life lessons a child might learn from a chance interaction with us. That is why they must be present as often as possible.

Therefore, Lord, I repent for not adequately appreciating the awesome task of parenting. I will take my role more seriously. I will be a better parent. Lord, please forgive me, and help me to do better.

Chapter 21

I REPENT FOR WORLDLINESS— FALLING FOR THE HYPE

The first industrial revolution involved the invention of the steam engine. It changed the world. Then came the so-called second industrial revolution wherein everything began to be mechanized and mass production was just starting to become a way of life. Until then humankind was pretty much relegated to an agricultural lifestyle along with a horse and buggy as the normal mode of transportation. In America at the time, a person's biggest concern may have been making sure they did everything possible to have a good crop season while providing for the chickens, a few hogs, and perhaps one milk cow to provide milk. Industrialization and advertising hit the world by storm. In just a few generations, life has transformed from a "survival" focus to an "I want" focus. Along with that came a deep dive into more worldliness and falling for the hype that certain things had to be owned and certain things had to be done to have a fulfilling life. What does God have to say? How does this affect our children? Is there another way for Christians to live?

Now, some people can afford to be more concerned about style, color, shape, size, and lighting instead of where the next meal is coming from. The interesting point about this chapter is how different it is for every individual in America. Many people in America are living below the poverty line. For these people, even though this chapter does not apply in actual practice, it can still be a factor in the form of added stress or depression simply because they are not able to take advantage of all the things they see advertised. It is difficult to imagine someone driven to illegal activities trying to appease an appetite for things the advertisers have encouraged us to expect. The truth is that we can all be affected by falling for the hype that life can only be good if we can live a certain way and afford certain indulgences.

What God tells us to do concerning worldliness

> Do not love the world or the things in the world. If anyone loves the world, the love of the Father is not in him. For all that is in the world: the lust of the flesh, the lust of the eyes, and the pride of life is not of the Father but is of the world. And the world is passing away, and the lust of it; but he who does the will of God abides forever. (1 John 2:15–17 NKJV)

> I beseech you therefore, brethren, by the mercies of God, that you present your bodies a living sacrifice, holy, acceptable to God, which is your reasonable service. And do not be conformed to this world, but be transformed by the renewing of your mind, that you may prove what is that good and acceptable and perfect will of God. (Romans 12:1–2 NKJV)

These two texts demonstrate how God feels about the things people spend so much time, money, and effort trying to acquire in this world. God is more concerned with our souls. These texts tell us specifically not to long for the contraptions that the world says we must have. God says it is all lust and pride. Moreover, God points out that it is all fruitless anyway. Instead, these texts tell us that living for God and controlling our mind against worldly desires is the only thing acceptable to God.

What Is Worldliness?

Being well traveled is *not* worldliness. Being a world-renowned scientist, chef, or social worker is *not* worldliness. Vince Lombardi, a famous football coach who won the first two Super Bowls, is famous for saying, "Winning is not everything, it is the only thing." This may be true in specific situations. For goal-setting purposes in an isolated environment, this quote may apply. For example, if one is on a mission to save his children from an attacking dog, I believe that most people would agree that there is no turning back and no options except to save one's children. At this place and at this time, winning is the only thing. I will give all I have, and I am willing to die trying to save my children. Another example is being on a combat mission in enemy territory. You must have this type of commitment if you and your squadron are going to make it out alive. Success of the mission is the only rational result and must be committed to while disregarding everything else going on in the entire world. At this place and at this time, winning is the only thing.

However, outside of life-and-death situations like these, there are always other people, places, and things that should be considered. Other people are living in dire situations around the world and in your neighborhood. Other people are hungry every night around the world and in your neighborhood. Children are desperate in many places of the world and in your neighborhood. Many social causes may be worth our attention. If one's entire life is so focused on some goal or activity that they cannot see or be concerned about the things of God or other people, they may be living a worldly life. Worldliness is when selfishness takes over one's life, and the biggest concern is to get the biggest, latest gadget. Worldliness is when your main concern becomes, "How can I get in the spotlight?" How can I become the most important, biggest hotshot on the planet? Worldliness is when we are consumed with the selfish pursuit of worldly (man-made) things to brag about.

One may ask, "Am I living a worldly life?" A warning sign to be considered is when your whole life is so focused you can't take time to help someone else that is really hurting. Do you take time for family outings, or are you missing all of them? It may be okay for a specified period, like going to college, but if you have been missing all your family outings for twenty years, some introspection may be warranted. You may indeed be living a worldly life when acquiring and maintaining material things and achieving accolades becomes so important that what is happening to the rest of humanity around you does not matter. You may be living a worldly life when all you think about is you. This is what the Bible is talking about in 2 Timothy, when Paul discusses people who are overly concerned with and in love with things that bring selfish enjoyment and fleshly pleasure to themselves instead of having that kind of enjoyment and passion for God. Paul mentions this right along with other sins such as lying, covetousness, and pride. Paul says these are among the many sins that will be prevalent during the last days of humanity as we know them. We shift into worldly living when we stop spending time thinking about the things of God.

For clarity, I am not suggesting that it is wrong to accomplish a goal, laugh, and have fun. God created us with the ability to laugh, sing, and applaud. There is a time for all different things, activities, and occurrences in our lives, according to Ecclesiastes 3. However, God expects us to have balance. "God is love" (1 John 4:8 KJV). If we love like God loves, then the spirit in us will always remind us of the plight of others. A Christian is always more concerned about others than the false hurdles many people set for themselves seeking selfish pleasure, endless adventure, and costly expenditures regardless of what is happening to other people around them. God is more concerned about people. Advertisers will have us believe that name brand this, designer that, and collector's items on the mantle and in the driveway are a must. Not to mention, some people must have the correct unread books on their bookshelf, just for show.

Children and Worldliness

Children are affected by worldliness in two ways. The first way is when children are neglected by their parents or custodial caregivers simply because they are so enthralled with worldliness that they are too busy to read to the child, bathe the child, feed the child properly, or otherwise spend time with the child. Children need more than new toys. They need our time and attention. They need conversation, training, and teaching. Social Services might refer to this as neglect if they had the chance to observe this behavior. Second, children are affected by worldliness early in their lives by being targets of advertisers and large companies. A lot of advertising is specifically targeted toward children. Hence, during Christmastime there is a rush for the "must have" toy. There is a market for the "must have" clothing. Children are taught early to desire certain items so they can be like their friends and have the same gadgets their friends have. They are taught early to want to dress like their friends. In many respects, this seems like an unfair abuse of innocent naïve minds. However, in our American culture today, it seems difficult to avoid much of this type of conditioning.

What Worldliness Does

When people become worldly, they are like a cheating spouse. Meaning that they become more concerned about things that do not matter than they do about God and the things that should matter. This will ultimately hurt us. Our worldliness even causes fights and wars as we become envious of what we see in the world that we do not have.

> From whence come wars and fightings among you? come they not hence, even of your lusts that war in your members? Ye lust, and have not: ye kill, and desire to have, and cannot obtain: ye fight and war, yet ye have not, because ye ask not. Ye ask, and receive not, because ye ask amiss, that ye may consume it upon your lusts. Ye adulterers and adulteresses, know ye not that the friendship of the world is enmity with God? whosoever therefore will be a friend of the world is the enemy of God. (James 4:1–4 KJV)

This text is very straightforward. Fights among people on the street and even wars between nations occur because worldly lust tells many people that they need more. It points out that pleasure seeking makes us the same as someone that commits adultery. In other words, what the world has to offer has become more important than the God who created everything.

The pleasures of worldliness can make us depressed during slow cycles because they do not last. The thrill is short-lived. God is eternal. He is what is, what was, and what is to come. Humankind, on the other hand, builds things that last for a short season. Going down practically any road, there are abandoned, rundown, and boarded up houses; overgrown by weeds and trees. These are houses that at one time were the pride and joy of some new homeowner. At some point in the past, these houses were brand new, with a brand-new smell and perhaps brand-new paint and brand-new carpet. Now these houses are rotting and decayed, and nobody cares about them anymore. I wonder if the hardworking couple that worked two jobs each when it was first built would think it was all worth it, if they could see the condition of the house today. Suppose instead of working two jobs they had spent more time with their son, established a better relationship with him, and kept him from making the decisions that led him into prison. Suppose they had spent more time comforting their aging parents. Would they now feel more rewarded? Every brand-new car winds up in a junkyard. Every new outfit winds up in the trash. Even if it goes through several hands, it still eventually winds up in the trash. How many extra shifts and stressful nights are spent trying to find a way to pay for these items? The things of this world will fade, and our life can be used up because of it.

In the Bible, Luke 15 tells a story about a son that leaves home to do some worldly living. This son left to live it up in every way possible at the time. He got his inheritance from his father and was off to enjoy himself. However, when the money ran out, there was nowhere left for him to feel enjoyment. He had been used by his friends and acquaintances. When the money ran out, they left him. His peace and joy had left him. He found himself poor and destitute. The writer of Ecclesiastes put it this way:

> Vanity of vanities, saith the Preacher, vanity of vanities; all is vanity. What profit hath a man of all his labor which he taketh under the sun? One generation passeth away, and

another generation cometh: but the earth abideth for ever. (Ecclesiastes 1:2–4 KJV)

Put the world and the things therein in prospective. Don't waste all your precious moments, days, weeks, and years on things that will decay. Learn to find peace and solace in your life without being caught up in everything being sold or what your friends say is important. The pleasure is short-lived. Some rich people and movie stars are known to commit suicide when the thrill is over. Put your heart into something that will last.

Worldliness makes us compromise our standards. Trying not to make waves, people often "go along" just to "get along." It is easy for us to find ourselves laughing at things that Jesus would not laugh at. Some often pay for tickets to see things that the Spirit of God tells us we should not see. Some participate in things that God the Father has already revealed to us are wrong.

> Who knowing the righteous judgement of God, that those who practice such things are deserving of death, not only do the same but also approve of those who practice them." (Romans 1:32 NKJV)

This text explains that the pull of the world can lead us to relinquish our walk with God. When we participate in these things with others, we not only do damage to ourselves; we also do damage to society. The pats on the back and the purchasing of the tickets supports and encourages much of the ungodly behavior to continue. We are helping to perpetuate the grasp that the devil has on our lives.

How Do We Fall into Worldliness?

There are basically two ways we can fall into worldliness. It can happen fast, or it can happen slow. When it happens fast, people who otherwise would normally think twice about a person or situation find themselves suddenly torn with decisions or circumstances that are thrust upon them quickly. When it happens slow, people often start doing something that begins innocently and twenty years later wonder how their situation turned out to be like it is.

Winning the lottery, getting a huge professional athletic contract, or inheriting a large sum of money are all ways that people could suddenly find themselves in a place where they could make financial decisions far beyond what they would normally be able to do. Suddenly, they may have access to worldly things that just yesterday they could not have afforded. Suddenly, a person has no financial limits and can indulge in the lust of the eyes, the lust of the flesh, and the pride of life. This could quickly spiral out of control and lead to worldly living.

Another way Satan gets us into worldly endeavors is by getting us into bad habits a little at a time. One inch at a time is all it takes to wind up on the wrong side of the road. Come watch this, come do that, come taste this, you ought to try that, is all it takes. A look, a whiff of, a hint of whatever, sometimes is all it takes. The first time someone gave you a compliment on your new car, did it give you so much pride about its look that you can't go to worship service because you must wax it every Sunday? Are you spending money on a new outfit every week at the expense of money you could be saving for your child's college education? Habits that began a little at a time can have disastrous effects down the road.

Worldliness can be a fast or slow killer of our relationship with the Lord, no matter where we are in our walk. Worldliness is a distraction. Jesus describes it in His parable of the sower.

> Now he who received seed among the thorns is he who hears the word, and the cares of this world and the deceitfulness of riches choke the word, and he becomes unfruitful. (Matthew 13:22 NKJV)

Instead of Worldliness

> By faith Moses, when he was come to years, refused to be called the son of Pharaoh's daughter; Choosing rather to

> suffer affliction with the people of God, than to enjoy the pleasures of sin for a season; Esteeming the reproach of Christ greater riches than the treasures in Egypt: for he had respect unto the recompence of the reward. (Hebrews 11:24–26 KJV)

Moses had a better idea. In America today, Pharaoh's house would be like growing up in the White House with all the trappings, privileges, and Secret Service escorts that go with it. Growing up there would assure that one would attend the best schools, eat the finest foods, and have access to the best medical care. No niceties would be withheld. Moses walked away from all that and went to live with his people on the farm, in rural America, or in the projects. He turned his back on everything the world had to offer. He chose to consider the life of the disadvantaged and the poor. In the process, God used him mightily. God wants our mind on Him as we go through the day. That would be best for all humankind.

> If ye then be risen with Christ, seek those things which are above, where Christ sitteth on the right hand of God. Set your affection on things above, not on things on the earth. For ye are dead, and your life is hid with Christ in God. (Colossians 3:1–3 KJV)

All of us that claim to be Christians now, were not born Christians. We all had our time in the world when the trappings and commercials told us how to live and what should be important to us. However, now, Jesus has come into our life. He healed many blind people when He was here walking the earth, and He is still allowing us to see now. As new creatures in Christ, Christians should now see the error of their ways prior to being baptized. Our daily longing should be to get closer to God instead of continuing to seek after worldly lust.

Therefore, Lord, I repent for thinking and acting too worldly. I repent for falling for the hype and letting it distract me from my relationship with You. Lord, please forgive me, and help me to do better.

Chapter 22

I REPENT FOR NOT REALLY KNOWING WHAT JESUS DID FOR ME

People say often that Jesus Christ died for our sins, and He certainly did. However, Jesus the Christ did so much more for us. If we don't pay attention, we will miss all the powerful, wonderful things His life meant to us as people created by Him. He lived for us. He became us. He died for us, and He is still to this very day working on our behalf.

Imaginary Scenario

Imagine a ten-year-old boy playing with Play Doh. He decides to make cities with his Play Doh, so he makes stick people of all kinds. Later that week something magical happens. With superpowers, he makes his stick people come alive. However, they refuse to get along. They fight and take advantage of each other. They form groups and start fighting other groups. The little boy keeps making more stick people of all kinds, but they start to destroy each other. Finally, using more superpowers, the little boy asks his father for permission to shrink himself and become one of the stick men just so he could teach his stick people how and why they should get along. Granted the permission, the little boy becomes one of his stick men. He walks among them and talks with them. He tells them he enjoys them.

He tells them he loves them, and they should get along. He tries to share all he can, but he cannot stay with his stick people forever. The little boy goes back to his original size and resumes making more stick people. He cares for them as much as he can.

In this imaginary scenario, we see the absolute awesomeness of what God has done for us via the man Jesus Christ. Many scholars believe that the incarnation of Jesus Christ is the greatest miracle in the entire Bible. How does God, the creator of all the universe, condense himself into one single human body, temporarily confined by all the laws of physics, biology, chemistry, and other currently known sciences? It is almost beyond our ability to imagine. Yet, that is exactly who Jesus Christ represents for us.

From the Beginning

Jesus was there at the beginning of the existence of humanity. In this text He is referred to as the "Word."

> In the beginning was the Word, and the Word was with God, and the Word was God. The same was in the beginning with God. All things were made by him; and without him was not any thing made that was made. In him was life; and the life was the light of men. (John 1:1–4 KJV)

Furthermore, John 1:10 goes on to explain all three aspects of who Jesus was to mankind. Jesus lived in this world as a man. He lived, walked, and breathed like every other man that has ever walked the earth. Jesus had His part in making the world. This means that even before He was incarnate as humanity knew Him, He already existed. Lastly, this verse explains that even though people did know Jesus as a human being, they did not know that He was in fact God walking among them while He was here. That is why the climax reached in Matthew 16:13 is so important when Jesus questioned His disciples about who He really was. He was making sure that at the very least, His twelve disciples were sure about it. This was a critical moment in Jesus's ministry because from then on, the theme of the gospels seems to turn toward His passion week in Jerusalem. No longer is He just introducing Himself to the world and working miracles so people would pay attention. He was now free to work toward fulfilling the purpose of being the sacrificial lamb for all humanity for all time.

We know Jesus Christ lived in the New Testament, but a Christophany is when Jesus appeared in the Old Testament. Throughout the Old Testament Christophany examples include:

- Genesis 32

Jacob wrestles with a man all night. The man told Jacob that his name would change from Israel to Jacob. However, the man would not tell Jacob his own name. Eventually, in verse 30, Jacob explains that he has seen God and renames the physical location of their meeting place to Peniel because he states that he has seen God.

- Joshua 5

In this chapter, Joshua is confronted by a man with a sword. Joshua later realizes whom he is talking with when he confronts the man. He tells Joshua that where he is standing is holy ground, just as God the Father did when He told Moses the same thing on top of a mountain, in front of a burning bush. Joshua later worships the man, proving that he realizes that the person he is speaking with is God Himself.

- Other Old Testament examples

Many Bible scholars argue that other examples where the Bible says something about God appearing or an angel of the Lord appearing are all examples of Christophanies.

Jesus and the Trinity

Jesus was a part of the triune God that created us, (See "the Godhead" section in chapter 6). He loved us so much that He came down to our level just so we could live an abundant life. It was all for us. He loves us. He is the potter; we are the clay. He is the living, breathing image of God the Father, for us.

> He is the image of the invisible God, the firstborn over all creation. (Colossians 1:15 NKJV)

Jesus is God. Water can exist in many forms and yet maintain the same chemical makeup. We ourselves are body, soul, and spirit. We, therefore, should be able to comprehend, then, that the triune God is able to have a part of Himself that is visible and walks and talks, just like us. Jesus Christ is that person.

Jesus My All

The question is not really, "What did Jesus do for humanity?" The question really is, "What is it that Jesus did not do for humanity?" He has done everything. Below is a list of some of the things He has done or continues to do for us.

- He lived for us:
  - fulfilled prophecy for us (Luke 18:31, Matthew 26:54)
  - was manifested with a purpose to destroy the works of the devil (1 John 3:8)
  - He taught us (Matthew 5–7; Matthew, Mark, Luke and John)
  - made me a fisherman (Matthew 4:19)
  - hungry for us (Matthew 4:2)
  - brought us a sword (Matthew 10:32–38)
  - is the Way for us (John 14:6)
  - is Bread for us (John 6:35)
  - is the Light for us (John 8:12)
  - is the Door for us (John 10:9)
  - is the Good Shepherd for us (John 10:11)
  - is the Resurrection for us (John 11:25)
  - is the True Vine for us (John 15:5)

- o showed us righteous indignation (Matthew 21:12–13)
- o thirsty for us (John 19:28)
- o tired for us (Matthew 8:24)
- o made us His friends (John 15:14–15)
- o felt pain for us; laughed at, scourged and spit on (Luke 18:32–33)
- o lonely while suffering for us (Mark 14:37, 41)
- o sweated blood (sick and sorrowful for us) (Mark 14:34–36, Matthew 26:38)
- o betrayed by friends for us (Matthew 26:56, 69–75)
- o was humble for us (Matthew 26:52–53, Mark 14:61, John 19:10–11)
- o was committed (came to die for us) (John 12:27)

To expound on some of these, Jesus was the fulfilment of prophecy. There are several references in the Old Testament about a Messiah coming. His multifaceted purpose including specifically destroying the effects of the sin the devil had caused and to take away his ultimate negative impact on humanity, which is death. When Jesus rose from the dead, He proved that death was no longer the final say about the end of our lives.

To the generations of all humanity, incarnate Jesus became the greatest teacher of all time. He taught us by His words and by allowing us to observe His walk, His attitude, His love for those close to Him, His love for strangers, and His love for children. He taught us everything that the laws in the Old Testament could not explain. He taught us how to react to our emotions and our pain. He taught us how to react calmly and peacefully when we are abandoned and neglected.

Incarnate God (namely Jesus Christ) taught us how to endure and still stay focused. He was tired, felt pain, and was abused for us until He allowed humanity to nail Him on a cross, but He did not lose focus. It was so stressful, the Bible says, that He sweated blood, and yet, He did not lose focus.

Jesus announced to His disciples that because of Him we are no longer just servants doing what we are told, not understanding why. The life and death of Jesus allows us to be friends with Him. That should not be taken lightly. Especially when we consider that when Jesus says something, He is talking in absolutes. He is not a friend like we may think of some friends today. Some so-called friends are friends on the surface. They act like friends if things are going well. They are our friends as long as money is flowing, and things are easy. They are our friends if we stay healthy and are not a burden. However, when Jesus is your friend that means you have a friend for life. There will be no selfishness in Jesus. He will always be doing things on your behalf. No matter what you have done, He is still your friend. No matter where you go, He will already be there as your friend. No matter how you have messed up, He will still be your friend. When you need Him to help you make a decision, He will be your friend if you let Him. No matter when you call on Him, morning or night, He will be your friend. If you are sitting on the couch right now wondering what television show you should watch, you can imagine Jesus sitting right their beside you. Once you get to know Him, He will help you decide what to watch and what not to watch. He is truly there all the time. That is a real friend.

Jesus the Son pointed us to God the Father by being the way, the door, and the vine. He showed us the grace of God by being the Good Shepherd. He also made sure we understood our relationship to the Triune God by calling us His friend.

Jesus Christ gave each of us a purpose for living. He told us that everything we do is not as important as reaching out to others about God by calling us all fishermen. We all should be sharing the gospel.

- He died and rose for us:

    o He saved us (Matthew 18:11)
    o He provided us grace (2 Corinthians 13:14)
    o He died for our sins (cast them in sea of forgetfulness) (1 Corinthians 15:3, Colossians 2:15, Romans 5:6)
    o He rose for us (justified me) (Colossians 2:11–14, Romans 4:25)
    o became circumcision (allows me to receive Holy Spirit and put off sin) (Colossians 2:11)

- He is the victory for us (1 Corinthians 15:57)
- freed me from the law of sin and death (Romans 8:1–2)
- made me a child of God (John 1:12)
- made me an heir of God (Romans 8:17, Galatians 4:7)
- He gives me hope (1 Corinthians 15:13–19)
- is a quickening Spirit for us (1 Corinthians 15:45–47)
- brother for us (Mark 3:34)
- intercedes for us (Romans 8:34)
- heads the church for us (Colossians 1:18)
- represents everything we need (Colossians 1:19, 2:9)

When Jesus died on the cross and rose again, there are so many other things that were accomplished. The moment He died, all of humanity that believe in Him was saved. He instantly became the sacrificial lamb that died for our sins. The victory for all that believe was instant. When Jesus died, my relationship with God the Father was renewed, and I have a renewed Spirit within. I am no longer blocked in my relationship with God the Father because Jesus's death took away all my sin.

Futuristically, the instant Jesus died, there was real hope in this life for all Christians because we were no longer held accountable to a strict standard of laws we could not meet. We were freed from the law of sin and death. Even now Jesus is on the right hand of God the Father, petitioning and interceding on our behalf.

I Am

Because Jesus is God, He is a part of the "I Am." God told Moses to tell Pharaoh that, "I Am" sent you. I believe God was telling His creation throughout eternity that whatever you need or whatever you are looking for or whatever you are trying to get to, I Am it. Jesus is everything to us. That He lived among us does not diminish His deity. He took all the laws that Satan wants to condemn us with and nailed them to the cross. He restored our relationship with God the Father. Thank you, Jesus, for all that You did and are doing.

> In whom we have redemption through His blood, the forgiveness of sins. (Colossians 1:14 NKJV)
>
> And you, who once were alienated and enemies in your mind by wicked works, yet now He has reconciled in the body of His flesh through death, to present you holy, and blameless, and above reproach in His sight. (Colossians 1:21–22 NKJV)

Therefore, Lord, I repent for not really appreciating all that Jesus the Christ did for me. Lord, please forgive me, and help me to do better.

Chapter 23

I REPENT FOR TRYING TO WIN AT ALL COST

Winning is okay. Children win a science contest, and we praise them and talk about how proud we are of them. Athletes win a race, and the crowd cheers. Sports teams win a trophy, and everybody becomes a fan. In most Little League ball, kids are taught to be good sports when they participate in competition. Some young children are taught to share from the time they are toddlers. An attempt is made by most good parents to teach their children to be polite: yes ma'am, no sir, please, and thank you. However, many children are not taught, and some choose not to adhere to those good manners. Therefore, they arrive at adulthood assuming it is okay to lie, cheat, steal, be rude, and have total disregard for other people and their belongings. That is winning at all cost. When all other morals and Christian behavior are thrown out the window, then the assumed attitude is to win at all cost. It is okay to win, but there is a line that should not be crossed morally as Christians for the sake of winning. God will promote anyone to win when it is their time. Committing sinful behavior to win the trophy or get the award is not what Christ would do. God is always more interested in the person. This is an ancient issue. What is the sin that makes some people behave this way, and what does God have to say about it?

Cain and Abel

Unfortunately, winning at all cost is not new. None of us were born during the Stone Age but it is easy to imagine that competition has been around since the dawn of man. One could say that it obviously started when Cain thought he was somehow in second place to his brother, Abel. Therefore, he slew his brother Abel in Genesis 4. Cain decided not to go back and rethink what he could do the next time. The quickest way to being in first place was to simply kill the competition. That is winning at all cost. Why would someone adopt this attitude?

Why

The feelings that drive us to do things have been described and explained by many psychologists and psychiatrists. The things that truly motivate us come from inside. Somehow, the current state of the person is not sufficient, and they want something else. They want to change their personal situation by changing themselves, some things, or many things around them. What causes this dissatisfaction may occur quickly or over time. It is impossible to tell since it happens internally.

There is an entire science about this matter that we are not qualified to explain, nor can we take the time to explain here. However, we can discuss the next consideration, which is, "What happens when Christian values or good manners, as discussed above, are disregarded while trying to win? Anything that drives a person this far is a sin. There is no time when sin will be justified by God. His word will not condone it.

Pride and envy. Having a feeling of self-worth is important. It helps a person get up and stay focused. Children learn this at an early age when parents tell them they have done something well. However, misalignment can occur when a child or an adult begins to believe that he or she is the only person that has a right to win. Sometimes people have an ego that will not let them settle for anything less than a win. When someone's ego begins to lead them to a point where they no longer want anyone else to win, then they may have crossed into sinful behavior. Their pride may lead them to do unethical things to assure that they win. After the fact, their envy may lead them to act like Cain.

In a hurry. According to the Bible, we are taught to wait on God to deliver for us. Sarah learned this lesson the hard way when she summoned Hagar to have a child with her husband, Abraham. All she had to do was wait. Instead, even though she lived through it, there was unnecessary drama in her and Abraham's life, for the rest of their life. Refusing to wait on God resulted in adultery, hatred, and envy.

Many people experience this. Often, we see people in our society that are rising in knowledge, experience, and popularity. They are ready to achieve the promotion. They are ready to achieve even more notoriety. However, just when it seems like everything is going their way, news will break about steps they took to get ahead that would have come their way anyway if they had been patient. Trying to win too fast has caused them to lose overall.

The glory. The applause of the crowd encourages many people to do things they would normally not do. What will you do to be in the limelight? Is the notion of being famous particularly appealing? Many public personalities believe that any publicity is good publicity. They are only concerned with having their name in the news so that they will be more well-known. The appeal of riches and a lavish lifestyle emboldens them to do anything, say anything, and act in any way just to win the prize. Often, when they have sold out on all their morals, it is sad to see some of these same people suffering from depression or become suicidal because they do not know who they are anymore.

Below me. Unfortunately, some people have a superiority complex. They need to win to keep others in their place. Without much thought, there are people who believe that winning at life means that all others they know must be below them. They believe others have to have a lower I.Q., a lower status, a lower education, or a lower accumulation of assets. Therefore, their goal is to win at all cost, so they can be on top to feel good about themselves.

When people believe others are below them, they will step on them. They will show ruthless disregard for others. Other people's feelings do not matter. They will behave in such a way that ethics, morals, and people's lives do not matter. An example of the manifestation of this type of attitude is when you see corporate giants make a profit by doing things that harm other human beings. Whether it is polluting water, polluting the air, forced child labor, or unsafe working conditions, all these acts reveal a CEO or board of decision-makers that are more interested in winning more accolades and profits for shareholders than they are in loving God's other lowly human beings that are being victimized.

Greed. Poor people want to be rich, and rich people want to be richer. People have killed people for a few thousand or even as little as a few hundred dollars. Poor people kill for money, and rich people kill for money. That means the amount of money is not the determining factor. The main issue is greed. When wanting more money causes a person to set aside Christian values, then he or she is trying to win at all cost.

God's Involvement

The first error in this thinking is that people fail to acknowledge that it is God Almighty who determines who "quote, unquote," wins, in this life. God is in control. Consider these verses.

> The Lord kills and makes alive; He brings down to the grave and brings up. The Lord makes poor and makes rich; He brings low and lifts up. He raises the poor from the dust and lifts the beggar from the ash heap, to set them among princes and make them inherit the throne of glory. For the pillars of the earth are the Lord's and He has set the world upon them. He will guard the feet of His saints, but the wicked shall be silent in darkness. For by strength no man shall prevail. (1 Samuel 2:6–8 NKJV)

> I returned and saw under the sun that the race is not to the swift, nor the battle to the strong, nor bread to the wise, nor riches to men of understanding, nor favor to men of skill; but time and chance happen to them all. (Ecclesiastes 9:11 NKJV)

Have you ever considered the happenstance that has surrounded your life? Being in the right place at the right time may be a coincidence, or it may be the divine providence of God. Meeting the right person that can open doors for you may be a coincidence, or it may be the divine providence of God. Your soul was born in a certain family. Your soul was born in a certain year, in a certain month, on a certain day. You went to a certain school. Who placed all the other people that played with you on your championship team? Was all of that you deciding how you were going to win, or did God orchestrate it? How did you meet your spouse? Did God assist with how the chance encounter took place? What if your spouse had lived two states away?

For some people, winning arguments is more important than getting to the right answer. The chief priest and elders debated with Jesus in the temple to win the argument, disregarding the truth of God that was being delivered. All they cared about was winning. That is why they did not answer.

> And when he was come into the temple, the chief priests and the elders of the people came unto him as he was teaching, and said, By what authority doest thou these things? and who gave thee this authority? And Jesus answered and said unto them, I also will ask you one thing, which if ye tell me, I in like wise will tell you by what authority I do these things. The baptism of John, whence was it? from heaven, or of men? And they reasoned with themselves, saying, If we shall say, From heaven; he will say unto us, Why did ye not then believe him? But if we shall say, Of men; we fear the people; for all hold John as a prophet. And they answered Jesus, and said, We cannot tell. And he said unto them, Neither tell I you by what authority I do these things. (Matthew 21:23–27 KJV)

Some people will even stoop to trying to use God Almighty to get ahead. To them, God becomes like a job, or a trade, or a commodity they can offer to others for some benefit to get ahead in life.

> Perverse disputings of men of corrupt minds, and destitute of the truth, supposing that gain is godliness: from such withdraw thyself. But godliness with contentment is great gain. For we brought nothing into this world, and it is certain we can carry nothing out. (1 Timothy 6:5–7 KJV)

Some seem to think that to win at this life they must accumulate the largest pile of assets. An old saying is that "whoever dies with the most toys, wins." Jesus addresses this and points out that our lives amount to much more than the number, amount, or size of the things we own.

> For whoever desires to save his life will lose it, but whoever loses his life for My sake and the gospel's will save it. For what will it profit a man if he gains the whole world, and loses his own soul? Or what will a man give in exchange for his soul? (Mark 8:35–37 NKJV)

Who Loses?

There is no free ride in God's kingdom. Sin has a cost. Sin always leads to death. There will always be a victim on the other side of the person who is trying to win at all cost. There will always be someone taken advantage of on the other side of the person trying to win at all cost. Someone will be hurt. In fact, since the Bible says that sin can be passed down to the third and fourth generation, that means when somebody is hurt today, the repercussions may last several lifetimes.

Okay to Win

Do not misunderstand this chapter. Winning is not necessarily a bad thing. However, winning at all cost, to the detriment of other people, who are also created, formed, and loved by God is wrong. Winning at all cost regardless of the laws, principles, and guidance He has laid out for us is not being like Christ. Paul said instead of being concerned about winning, a Christian should learn to be content.

> Not that I speak in regard to need, for I have learned in whatever state I am, to be content. I know how to be abased, and I know how to abound. Everywhere and in all things, I have learned both to be full and to be hungry, both to abound and to suffer need. I can do all things through Christ who strengthens me. (Philippians 4:11–13 NKJV)

This life is very brief. The older one gets, the faster time seems to go by. The question becomes how you will you spend your time in this life. What happens when there is a fork in the road and a winning opportunity diverges from a family or social need. Sometimes the choice must be made. There are many winners in our lives that may have had to settle on another path because of a circumstance that would not let them move when opportunity came knocking. That does not mean they should be deemed a lesser person. It means they made a different choice. God may deem their choice to be more important than focusing on the opportunity to win a trophy from man. Suppose you have a sick parent at home when you could be practicing on the tennis court. Suppose your child has an ailment that requires constant care just when a challenge is going on at the office that you know is your specialty and you could win any competition concerning it. It certainly is not a bad thing to support your child. In fact, turning your back on your child to win any competition is not what Christ would do. Priorities must be made in each life. Winning is good, but it is not the only thing.

All Christians must weigh every issue for themselves as they make decisions. The main thing is that no one should assume God does not know your motives. He knows. You will win if it is your time. Play hard and work hard, and God will make a way. Lying, cheating, stealing, and being corrupt is not required nor desired to be a winner.

Therefore, Lord, I repent for trying to win at all cost in the wrong way. Lord, please forgive me, and help me to do better.

Chapter 24

I Repent for Trying to Find Answers in All the Wrong Places

This is a strange chapter because it depends on one's perspective. The title states there are wrong places to find answers, which implies that there is a right place to find answers. Comments in the preface of this book allow me to state that there is only one place to find right answers to the most important questions in our lives. That would, of course, be the Holy Bible. Jesus Christ is the author, and God the Father is the Creator. Many people spend a lot of time trying to find answers in other ways. Often people spend much of their whole lives trying to find something to please their soul. There are many pagan religions. There are also other things we do that are attempts to find solace, such as: visit fortune tellers, practice astrology, practice the spiritual part of yoga, worship our job, worship our vehicle, worship our spouse, worship our children, etc., etc., etc.

Other Things

The Philistines were a major enemy of Israel. Their armies had gathered to attack Saul. Saul and King Achish were committed to work together against the Philistines. However, Saul had a problem. His spiritual mentor had recently died. Samuel was buried in Ramah, and all Israel cried for him. So, that left Saul without a spiritual guide, which he felt that he needed when he saw the size of the Philistine army. Based on the scripture, he was very afraid. Saul petitioned God and wanted an answer via dreams, prophets, or any means. However, God would not answer Saul because the kingdom was going to be taken from him. Saul had disobeyed God. Out of fear, Saul took matters into his own hands and resorted to his own wisdom. He sought a spiritual medium from Endor, whom he had previously thrown out of the country (1 Samuel 28:7). This did not end well for Saul. He and his sons were killed shortly thereafter.

Many of us have made the same mistake. Whenever we do wrong, we still think we can command God to answer us and make lemonade out of our lemons. Many believe we should be able to demand when it is time for God to step in, no matter how much we have butchered our relationship with Him. Then, whenever God does not move fast enough for us, we create our own answer.

> Woe to those who go down to Egypt for help, and rely on horses, who trust in chariots because they are many, and in horsemen because they are very strong, but who do not look to the Holy One of Israel, nor seek the Lord. (Isaiah 31:1 NKJV)

This verse mocks the futility of humanity looking in other places for help. Going to Egypt is saying they are seeking help from other men and women, known to be nonfollowers of the God of Abraham, Isaac, and Jacob. All humanity needs to look around. Everyone has issues and problems. Yet, we seek marital advice from our friends who are having their own marital problems or are divorced themselves. We seek child-rearing advice from our peers who have children the same age as ours and have not seen the true outcome of what their own child-rearing techniques will deliver. Or we may seek child-rearing advice from someone that does not even have children themselves, which means they have zero hands-on experience. Consider the source of where the so-called experts on different topics are getting their information. In other words, consider who it was that taught your teacher. Were they godly people with God-fearing ideals? If not, the Bible tells us that we should not seek their council.

Further in this text, horses, chariots, and strong horsemen are mentioned. When this scripture was written, horses, chariots, and strong horsemen represented a strong and powerful military force. That meant that a nation was not only strong but wealthy. This is like America today boasting about atomic bombs, stealth bombers, nuclear submarines, supersonic laser-guided missiles, and sophisticated aircraft carriers.

Instead of bragging, we should put our power into perspective. We cannot stop other countries that dislike us from acquiring much of the same military power. Other countries now that do not like America have nuclear weapons. So, with this kind of lethal destruction around the globe, is it a time to brag or to pray? That is exactly what happened to David in 1 Samuel 28. He thought his army was big and bad until he looked across the way and found out there were other similar armies with equal force.

Before bragging, we should also keep in mind that doing God's will and staying in relationship with Him is much more important than the size of our army. God is the source. As powerful as our army may be, we have found that we cannot even stop a simple virus from invading our shores and killing hundreds of thousands of Americans. We need God because we cannot stop the fires in the West from burning millions of acres. We need God because we cannot stop the violence in our cities. For numerous other reasons, it is evident that trying to find solutions from any other source besides God is temporary at best and fruitless in most cases.

Some may say that seeking outside help is the same thing that people do when they seek council from a clergy person. They say it is the same as trying to get inspiration from a pastor's sermon. It is not the same because most honest clergy will tell you right away that they are not the source of their own inspiration and dialogue. Pastors invite you to become knowledgeable about what he or she is preaching about for yourself. Practically all churches have Bible study or Sunday school times wherein they are attempting to teach you so that you can work out your own solutions along with God. Pastors, like others that people seek for council, truly do have their own issues, but they will let you know that they are only the messenger. The answer that they give to your problems and issues is coming from God's Bible.

Sometimes people look for meaning in this life from sources that are not godly, only to find in the end that they are not fulfilling. Jesus tells us about a son who squanders his inheritance thinking that he knew more about what was important in life than he could learn continuing to work with his father.

> And the younger of them said to his father, Father, give me the portion of goods that falleth to me. And he divided unto them his living. And not many days after the younger son gathered all together, and took his journey into a far country, and there wasted his substance with riotous living. And when he had spent all, there arose a mighty famine in that land; and he began to be in want. And he went and joined himself to a citizen of that country; and he sent him into his fields to feed swine. And he would fain have filled his belly with the husks that the swine did eat: and no man gave unto him. (Luke 15:12–16 KJV)

This youngest son was trying to find answers. He thought the answer to life was a party and a good time. He believed it so strongly that he could not wait for his father to die and leave his inheritance. He was ready to live the "high life," and he wanted it now. Not only did he want it right now; he left home to get it. If a person has had the opportunity to grow up or at some time in his or her life to be in the presence of a believer, he or she should be very cautious about leaving that presence. That presence is a covering. That covering is a protection from God. When people leave that presence before God's time, they are taking on all the responsibility for making sure they themselves stay protected by God, the Holy Spirit, and His angels. This son left home without realizing that his father had been providing much more than just a roof over his head and food for him to eat. His father had provided wisdom, patience, a work ethic, and a living example of how to live one's life.

He may have had what he called a good time for a few days. However, the good time vanished. Those that may have befriended him for a few days vanished. His fancy ride and good clothes became worn after just a few days. When the money ran out, so did the good times.

Many people look for answers to life via personal human relationships. Some become workaholics and make their jobs their sole reason for being. Does this really work? What happens after thirty years of working to build skyscrapers, or plumbing, or working in a factory? Does it make you feel whole? Do you have a family to share your accomplishments with? Do you feel empty inside because something seems to be missing? If money and fame were all it took to soothe my soul, why do so many with wealth and fame seek comfort in a bottle, pills, or a needle? Why do so many rich and famous people still commit suicide? The answer to all these questions is because besides a relationship with our Maker, there is no peace for our soul. Jesus it the only answer for everyone in our world today. It does not matter how rich or poor a person is, he or she still needs God. It does not matter it a person came from High Street, in a mansion, the Royal Palace in England, or the projects in your closest city, everyone needs the atonement that Jesus gave us on the cross.

The Bible states:

> And God spoke these words, saying: I am the Lord your God, who brought you out of the land of Egypt, out of the house of bondage. You shall have no other gods before Me. (Exodus 20:1–3 NKJV)

Think of all the ways our society does not respect this verse. We have made gods out of movie stars, politicians, and professional athletes in our society. It is okay to appreciate someone's performance on the stage or playing field, but when we try to mimic everything they do, we have made a god out of them. An overindulgence in dressing like them and looking like them and acting like them is a problem. Some people are having surgery on their body so that they can look like a movie star or someone they deem as important. That is making a god out of them. Children and their parents spend money they cannot afford to wear clothing or shoes with some athlete's name on them. That is making a god out of them.

Even some clergy in our society are overly idolized. This is evident when "unrepentant" clergy beat their wives, abuse their children, commit adultery with a church member, and marry another congregant without skipping a beat. Do clergy fall short, make mistakes, and sin? Certainly, they do. Are they allowed to serve God again? Certainly, they are. The Bible is full of these examples. The key word in this paragraph so far is *unrepentant*. Anyone that follows an unrepentant, larger than life person doing things that are not biblical may have made a god out of that person. The Bible says that those who remain unrepentant and scatter the sheep of God will have a price to pay.

> I am the Lord, and there is no other. There is no God besides me. I will gird you, though you have not known Me. That they may know from the rising of the sun to its setting, that there is none besides Me. I am the Lord, and there is no other. Isaiah 45:5–6 (NKJV)

Here we see the Bible stating that even looking for another god is futile. This verse makes it impossible to say other religions and other gods are okay. However, it does not mean we as Christians have the right to tear down, defame, and ostracize other religions because we too were captives in Egypt. We too have fallen short and remain blessed by God with much grace to see the light of His Son Jesus Christ.

> But these two things shall come to you in a moment, in one day. The loss of children, and widowhood. They shall come upon you in their fullness because of the multitude of your sorceries, for the great abundance of your enchantments. For you have trusted in your wickedness; you have said, "No one sees me." Your wisdom and your knowledge have

warped you; and you have said in your heart, "I am, and there is no one else besides me." Therefore evil shall come upon you. You shall not know from where it arises. And trouble shall fall upon you; you will not be able to put it off. And desolation shall come upon you suddenly, which you shall not know. Stand now with your enchantments and the multitude or your sorceries, in which you have labored from your youth. Perhaps you will be able to profit. Perhaps you will prevail. You are wearied in the multitude of you counsels. Let now the astrologers, the stargazers, and the monthly prognosticators stand up and save you from what shall come upon you. Behold, they shall be as stubble. The fire shall burn them; they shall not deliver themselves from the power of the flame; it shall not be a coal to be warmed by, or a fire to sit before! Thus shall they be to you with whom you have labored. Your merchants from your youth; they shall wander each one to his quarter. No one shall save you. (Isaiah 47:9–15 NKJV)

It is clear here that the Bible is pointing out the result of trying to replace God and find answers in the wrong places. Nothing will work. The texts shared here list other gods, images and likenesses, idols, sorceries, spiritual mediums, enchantments, wickedness, your own wisdom, your own knowledge, counsels, astrologers, stargazers, prognosticators, and merchants as solutions some people are using to find answers in this life. However, the bottom line is that we all have to decide for ourselves. Therefore, faith is required to be a Christian. Either you believe He is the one and only and act accordingly, or you do not. No matter who a person might talk to or consult, it cannot replace the wisdom of God. No matter how wise a person may think they are, it cannot replace God. Fortune tellers will not be able to help anyone find answers that God cannot share with them. Yet, some people continually try everything but God. Seeking God first for answers is the most important decision a person could ever make.

Jesus Leaves No Doubt That He Is the One and Only Way to God with All the Answers We Need

Verily, verily, I say unto you, He that entereth not by the door into the sheepfold, but climbeth up some other way, the same is a thief and a robber. But he that entereth in by the door is the shepherd of the sheep. To him the porter openeth; and the sheep hear his voice: and he calleth his own sheep by name, and leadeth them out. And when he putteth forth his own sheep, he goeth before them, and the sheep follow him: for they know his voice. And a stranger will they not follow, but will flee from him: for they know not the voice of strangers. This parable spake Jesus unto them: but they understood not what things they were which he spake unto them. Then said Jesus unto them again, Verily, verily, I say unto you, I am the door of the sheep. All that ever came before me are thieves and robbers: but the sheep did not hear them. I am the door: by me if any man enter in, he shall be saved, and shall go in and out, and find pasture. (John 10:1–9 KJV)

Thomas saith unto him, Lord, we know not whither thou goest; and how can we know the way? Jesus saith unto him, I am the way, the truth, and the life: no man cometh unto the Father, but by me. (John 14:5–6 KJV)

I am the true vine, and my Father is the husbandman. Every branch in me that beareth not fruit he taketh away: and every branch that beareth fruit, he purgeth it, that it may bring forth more fruit. Now ye are clean through the word which I have spoken unto you. Abide in me, and I in you. As the branch cannot bear fruit of itself, except it abide in the vine; no more can ye, except ye abide in me. (John 15:1–4 KJV)

Jesus declares that He is the door, the way, and the vine that can lead anyone in the right direction. He is saying that if a person wants answers, then He is the way to find them. Sadly, in our culture, sometimes it feels like you are asking a child to take a bad-tasting medicine just by mentioning the name of Jesus.

Joshua had to make the same choice that we have to make when we are looking for answers. He was leading his people and he wanted it to be clear where he stood. He told them they had the same choice. Where can I find answers? Which god should I believe in? His response in Joshua 24 says a person can look back at other things people have tried. Perhaps your parents were in a gang, and they taught you everything about selling drugs. Is that the answer and wisdom that is best to apply to your life? Joshua also told his people that you can look around at what other people are trying now. Consider the liars and schemers that will do anything to get ahead regardless of who may get hurt. Is that your answer for peace, prosperity, and self-worth in this life? Joshua declared that he would get his answers for life from God. He and his family would trust God above anything else.

The quest for knowledge and answers is nothing new. We are all enthralled by watching contestants on game shows win thousands of dollars by answering trivia questions about all sorts of subjects. We see people in the limelight that look so happy and on top of everything, but we really do not know what is going on behind closed doors. We do not know until the news comes out about the mental issues, drug abuse, divorce, drinking problem, or suicide. Then, the entertainment shows portray it as such a surprising tragedy. The truth is that no amount of money can stop a liar from being a liar. No amount of education can stop an abuser from being an abuser. No policies and laws have stopped poverty from being a part of our everyday lives in every state in America. We have been looking for answers in all the wrong places. Trying to climb the ladder in life and fix ourselves has made us lose ourselves. A change of heart toward Jesus Christ is the answer we all need.

Therefore, Lord, I repent for trying to find answers in all the wrong places. You are the only one that can satisfy my soul. Lord, please forgive me, and help me to do better.

Chapter 25

I REPENT FOR GIVING LIP SERVICE TO MY BELIEF, WORK, AND FAITH IN GOD

Lip service to God implies that there is more talk about one's commitment than there is action to prove that a person is serious. Lip service is like a tree having a lot of blooms but never bearing any fruit. It reflects our belief in God because maybe we do not really believe. Lip service shows up in the work we do for Christ and the faith we have in the outcome. Where do we stand as twenty-first century Christians? Is church an activity like going to see a movie? Are we committed to God or to our lifestyle? Are we faking our Christianity? Is our heart, mind, and soul into it? Is Christianity a daily walk or a part-time celebration? Some seem to think it is okay to be a Sunday morning and Easter Sunday Christian.

Old Analogy

There is an old joke about the difference in the commitment level of a chicken and a hog, when it comes to you and I having a good country breakfast. We all know the hog is more committed because he or she must die to provide us with meat for breakfast. The chicken, on the other hand, can claim some commitment, while only laying an egg. The chicken's life is not required for it to claim, "I am committed." Now, if you have a chicken leg to eat with those eggs, there is definitely more of a commitment from the chicken too.

Compare that analogy with many that claim to be Christians today. There are people who are not committed at all that can walk around the farm and not give anything toward breakfast. Some churchgoers come and go into a worship building each week. They give minimally, do not join any ministry, and do not come back to any special evening services. Yet, if someone on the street asked if they go to church and if they are a Christian, they readily answer affirmatively. For the purposes of this chapter, that would be considered lip service. There is no demonstrated commitment to God at all. While no one can judge what is in someone's heart, the fruit that is being demonstrated implies no commitment. Then, consider the chicken laying an egg type of Christian. Every Sunday they come in and do their part. They may even be a big contributor relative to other members of the congregation. However, they may not be big contributors relative to their financial well-being. These may be the type of Christian parents that drop their children off at church but do not go to church themselves. There is evidence of some commitment as long as it does not impose on personal desires to do other things or be in other places.

Twenty-First Century Christian

The question is how committed are we to our Christianity in the twenty-first century. Most of us are not sacrificing on a mission field. Most of us go to a worship service once per week, put whatever we want to in the offering plate, perhaps clap, analyze our fellow churchgoers for faults and inconsistencies, critique the speaker, critique the choir, and go home until next week. Then we will do the same thing all over again. Yes, during our worship services we are great Christians. We quote a few scriptures. We even make side comments like, "Lord have mercy," when something happens, or, "Thank you, Jesus," when we get a raise or win something. Compare that with the commitment the disciples portrayed in the book of Acts during the early church age.

What does it take to be a serious Christian? Perhaps one may say you should go to somebody's congregation every week. Let's say you do. Let's say you spend approximately two hours per trip. That would mean you are dedicating fifty-two weeks times two hours per week or 104 hours per year toward being a good Christian. God, however, blesses us with 365 days times twenty-four hours, or 8,760 hours per year. That means if we go to a worship service every week for two hours, we are giving God less than 2 percent of our time during the year. Is that enough time to consider yourself a Christian who is on fire for God? What type of service are you performing outside of the congregational walls?

Part-Time Christianity

Can we be a serious Christian, "sometime"? Is it okay to go to our worship service and still tell "little white lies" on Tuesday? Is it okay to be a Christian in some environments and not in others? The list of sins and moral missteps that could be asked about here is too long. Consult Romans 1:29–31, Galatians 5:18–21, and 2 Timothy 3:2–7 for a list wherein we could ask, is it okay to commit one of these sins a week? How about two? Would that be considered only giving lip service to our Christianity? Some will say you are being too dogmatic. We cannot be perfect! Well, Jesus said in Matthew 5:48 that perfection is the goal. Perfect in the Greek translation that is used in the referenced verse means complete, or of full age, or mature. The Bible, while acknowledging that we can never say that we do not sin, is also stressing that when we come to a new understanding about God and the scripture, we should be honest with ourselves and grow as we learn. Otherwise, when we realize that the Bible plainly tells us to do one thing, but we refuse and do another, then we are only providing lip service to our Christianity. We are literally lying to God. James said:

> Wherefore lay apart all filthiness and superfluity of naughtiness, and receive with meekness the engrafted word, which is able to save your souls. But be ye doers of the word, and not hearers only, deceiving your own selves. For if any be a hearer of the word, and not a doer, he is

> like unto a man beholding his natural face in a glass: For he beholdeth himself, and goeth his way, and straightway forgetteth what manner of man he was. But whoso looketh into the perfect law of liberty, and continueth therein, he being not a forgetful hearer, but a doer of the work, this man shall be blessed in his deed. If any man among you seem to be religious, and bridleth not his tongue, but deceiveth his own heart, this man's religion is vain. Pure religion and undefiled before God and the Father is this, To visit the fatherless and widows in their affliction, and to keep himself unspotted from the world. (James 1:21–27 KJV)

This text was not meant only for priests, bishops, pastors, elders, and church leaders. It was meant for all of us. We are all encouraged here to get serious with God and our Christianity and stop just giving lip service to what we believe in. We cannot just be a hearer worship service after worship service while continuing to act like a demon straight from hell.

Faking My Christianity

Another way one could say a person was giving lip service to Christianity is if they were after it for a purpose other than love, grace, mercy, and salvation. No scripture exemplifies this better than Acts 8:9–22. Simon the Sorcerer wanted the power of the Holy Spirit only so he could make money.

> But there was a certain man, called Simon, which beforetime in the same city used sorcery, and bewitched the people of Samaria, giving out that himself was some great one: To whom they all gave heed, from the least to the greatest, saying, This man is the great power of God. And to him they had regard, because that of long time he had bewitched them with sorceries. But when they believed Philip preaching the things concerning the kingdom of God, and the name of Jesus Christ, they were baptized, both men and women. Then Simon himself

> believed also: and when he was baptized, he continued with Philip, and wondered, beholding the miracles and signs which were done. Now when the apostles which were at Jerusalem heard that Samaria had received the word of God, they sent unto them Peter and John: Who, when they were come down, prayed for them, that they might receive the Holy Ghost: (For as yet he was fallen upon none of them: only they were baptized in the name of the Lord Jesus.) Then laid they their hands on them, and they received the Holy Ghost. And when Simon saw that through laying on of the apostles' hands the Holy Ghost was given, he offered them money, Saying, Give me also this power, that on whomsoever I lay hands, he may receive the Holy Ghost. But Peter said unto him, Thy money perish with thee, because thou hast thought that the gift of God may be purchased with money. Thou hast neither part nor lot in this matter: for thy heart is not right in the sight of God. Repent therefore of this thy wickedness, and pray God, if perhaps the thought of thine heart may be forgiven thee. (Acts 8:9–22 KJV)

Simon was all about looking Christian without caring about being Christian. Sometimes people can get themselves caught up in the practices of Christianity. Holding a certain office in your congregation may allow you to be in the limelight. Performing a certain duty may allow others to recognize your gift and treat you with high esteem. This was Simon's problem. He saw what Peter was able to do, and he wanted the glory without understanding the purpose and the sacrifice. The Bible warns us about being lukewarm. As you can see here, Simon was rebuked by Peter and told to repent for his desire to buy the power of Christianity. It cannot be bought. The Bible commands that we be zealous.

> And unto the angel of the church of the Laodiceans write; These things saith the Amen, the faithful and true witness, the beginning of the creation of God; I know thy works, that thou art neither cold nor hot: I would thou wert cold

> or hot. So then because thou art lukewarm, and neither cold nor hot, I will spue thee out of my mouth. Because thou sayest, I am rich, and increased with goods, and have need of nothing; and knowest not that thou art wretched, and miserable, and poor, and blind, and naked: I counsel thee to buy of me gold tried in the fire, that thou mayest be rich; and white raiment, that thou mayest be clothed, and that the shame of thy nakedness do not appear; and anoint thine eyes with eyesalve, that thou mayest see. As many as I love, I rebuke and chasten: be zealous therefore, and repent. (Revelation 3:14–19 KJV)

So, what is a lukewarm Christian? A lukewarm Christian is a person that is just giving lip service to their Christianity so they can look like they are serious when truthfully, in their heart, they are not. As this text says, they are not too hot and not too cold. In other words, nothing moves them. Seeing poor children on the street does not move them with compassion. A lukewarm person is more likely to blame the child for how they look or how they may be acting; not acknowledging that many of these children may look like they look and act like they act because they do not have a parent at home for guidance. A lukewarm Christian will laugh at a misogynistic or racist joke if they are not a part of that group because being on one accord with the joke teller is more important to them than standing up for righteousness, like Jesus would do. Just laughing is easier. A lukewarm Christian will attend church service on Sunday and listen to the preacher preach about love and marriage while continuing a long adulterous relationship with someone in the same congregation the following week. A lukewarm Christian is a person that will accept an award for being a fine, upstanding pillar of the community while at the same time continuing to embezzle funds from their place of employment. Lukewarm means lip service is applied, to look the part of a loving Christian, but in reality knowing that it is not real in their heart.

In this text, clearly God does not like lukewarm, lip service Christians. The text says God would rather a choice be made. Make a decision to be hot or cold. Providing lip service with a lukewarm attitude does not do any good for humanity overall. It is fake. and sooner or later, it will be exposed.

Many Americans may be in a position, as the text says, to feel as though they can ignore God because they are wealthy. Maybe it has been a long time since money and finances have been a problem in their family. Maybe they can afford the best schools and best doctors, so God is not important anymore. Perhaps they feel like lip service is all they need to do so that for appearance's sake they look like they are doing everything right and living a godly life. Perhaps they are even the largest giver in the congregation. However, according to this text, lip service at the very least is unproductive and sets a very bad example. God is not impressed.

There's Plenty to Do

There is plenty to do when your heart, mind, and soul is into loving, praising, and worshipping God. Jesus told Peter, if you love me, feed my sheep. Feed, feed, feed, He said. That means getting busy providing what the sheep need. Some sheep may need physical food for their body. Feed them. Some people may need fellowship and comfort for their soul. Feed them. Some people may need help with spiritual food they do not understand. Feed them. There are children everywhere that need guidance. Feed them. The work is endless. Look around your neighborhood. There are needs everywhere.

When your heart, mind, and soul are into something, it becomes a part of you. When your heart is into something, you are passionate about it. When your mind is into something, you are always thinking about it. When your soul is engaged, that means your imagination and conscience can almost feel and see God. When you heart, mind, and soul are focused on God, you will want to do His will, not because you have to but because you want to.

> The things which you learned and received and heard and saw in me, these do, and the God of peace will be with you. (Philippians 4:9 NKJV)

Christians should be busy "doing." Loving God and loving His other human creation (your brothers and sisters in Christ) means the things to do will never end. Love is a motivator. It will help your soul see the needs of other people. If we are true Christians, our faith should show up in our works. There is plenty of work to do.

> Then He said to His disciples, "The harvest truly is plentiful, but the laborers are few. Therefore, pray the Lord of the harvest to send out laborers into His Harvest." (Matthew 9:37–38 NKJV)

This text makes it clear that there is more work than workers. Every Christian should feel challenged by this text. The world cannot afford for us to be lazy Christians. To be great Christians, we must serve. Jesus explained in the gospels that great Christians must be great servants. You cannot be a great Christian by giving the biggest offering, or singing the loudest, or shouting the most often. God knows our hearts. Even the preacher and choir director, with all the gifts God gave them, must do what they do with a servant's heart, to be great. Whatever is done must be done with God and others in mind. We all know Paul was a busy man for the gospel. Paul says we Christians should be busy like him. When sporting teams make it to their championship game, you often hear the players say, "I left everything on the field." That means they gave 110 percent effort. Jesus deserves that, also.

> Jesus said to him, "You shall love the Lord your God with all your heart, with all your soul and with all your mind." This is the first and great commandment. (Matthew 22:37–38 NKJV)

After this text, the Bible says that all the prophets and all the law are hanging on it. That means that every Old Testament law is somehow grounded in loving God and loving your fellow person. It means that every word and every action ever done by any prophet somehow has a foundation of love for God or love for your fellow brothers and sisters. Loving them cannot be a passive action because so many needs are out there. Loving them will not allow any serious Christian to only give lip service to the cause. Someone can fake being a Christian and go home and sit on the couch and act like others are not hurting. Someone can fake being a Christian and always turn a blind eye to inhumane treatment of others, but a real Christian cannot do this. The belief, work, and faith that motivate any Christian to get busy for God are all intertwined in these two verses.

Therefore, Lord, I repent for giving lip service to my belief, work, and faith in You, God. Help me to get busy in the kingdom. Lord, please forgive me, and help me to do better.

Chapter 26

I REPENT FOR BELIEVING I SERVE A ONE-DIMENSIONAL GOD

Seeing God as one-dimensional implies that He is only good at one thing. It implies that He can only be one way. It implies that He can only act one way. This is so untrue. This is a primary example of why we are so different from Him. God cannot be put into a box. That is a mistake we make trying to manage and compartmentalize His existence in a form we can understand. Instead, we need to humble ourselves and face our own limitations.

God in a Box

Oftentimes we act like God is our child, and we can manipulate Him however we want Him to be. Some act like we can direct Him wherever we need Him to go. Sometimes we act like God must behave a certain way. When we treat God like a one-dimensional being, we confine Him to a box. We humans like to put things in a box because it helps us to understand it. We like to think everything is relative to something else. However, God is not. Nothing compares to God, so by faith we need to accept His awesomeness. God alone is self-existent. He is a God, which is, which was, and which is to come. God is immutable and impeccable. God is omnipotent, omnipresent, and omniscient. The Bible tells us how ridiculous it is to attempt to fit God inside one of our church congregations, our nations, or our little earth. Humanity needs to take a back seat to the Sovereignty of God.

> And now I pray Oh God of Israel, let Your word come true, which You have spoken to Your servant David my father. But will God indeed dwell on the earth? Behold, heaven and the heaven of heavens cannot contain You. How much less this temple. (1 Kings 8:26–27 NKJV)

Solomon states his understanding of who God is in this prayer. He is saying that while we may like to claim Him in our congregation, in our country, and on our earth, God is way too big to fit in our box. He is exponentially larger than that. He cannot be contained. Solomon, known as the wisest man that ever lived, was aware of that.

> Thus says the Lord, "Heaven is My throne, and the earth is My footstool. Where is the house that you will build Me? And where is the place of My rest? For all those things My hand has made, and all those things exist," says the Lord. "But on this one will I look: On him who is poor and of a contrite spirit, and who trembles at My word." (Isaiah 66:1–2 NKJV)

One of the worst battles a pastor has when taking over an existing congregation is trying to help people understand that the house of God should, in fact, be deemed God's house. It does not matter if your grandfather was the person that donated the land. It does not matter if your uncle was the chairman of the deacon board for twenty years. It does not matter if you are the chairman of the trustee board, lifelong choir director, or head usher. Any building that is erected and used for praise and worship services should be viewed as God's house. The reason why it should be deemed as God's house by the worshippers. They of all people should realize that everything that the building is made of came from God. God blesses us to build our sanctuaries. He provided us with our earth, and heaven is where He resides. It is too much for anyone to assume they own God in any one place.

The richest landowner in the world and all the goods he may possess mean nothing to God. The reason why is because all of it officially resides on God's property. In reality, at best we are all renters. We hold a spot for a while. It feels like we are dominating. We feel like we will be around forever and that we will pass on what we have to our heirs to own forever. None of this is true. God is the only eternal being. The great kings of history have proven that dynasties do not last forever. Even nations are nothing compared to God. A nation is like a grain of sand on a large beach to God. The kings, presidents, or emperors mean nothing to God. God cannot be compared to them, and they should not be compared to God. We cannot put God in the same box that we put our earthly leaders in. They do not hang out at the same club. To imply that is like saying the meanest two or three dogs in a kennel own a chain of kennels. This is not the case. Like the pieces on a chess board, God has designed the board, moves any piece where He wants them, and can wipe the board clean and start over any time He desires.

> God who made the world and everything in it, since He is Lord of heaven and earth, does not dwell in temples made with hands. Nor is He worshiped with men's hands, as though He needed anything, since He gives to all life, breath, and all things. (Acts 17:24–25 NKJV)

This a New Testament confirmation that God cannot be put into a box. The verse starts by reminding us of the expanse of God. It may be impossible for our human minds to really grasp an entity that created much more than our minds and inventions can successfully wrap our hands around.

> We cannot contain God, but many try to understand God by assuming they should be able to put a boundary around infinity.

Then verse 25 goes on to point out that God does not need us. He does not need our temple. He does not need our hands. In fact, He does not really need our worship. Instead, the opposite is true. We need God for life, breath, and everything else. Therefore, it is so ridiculous for us to imagine that we can put God in a box. The created cannot do that to their Creator.

Dwane Massenburg

The Mistake: How Many See Their One-Dimensional God

Going to the church building. Sunday morning for most denominations, Saturday morning for Seventh Day Adventist or whatever day is specified for your normal praise and worship service is often perceived as the manifestation of who God is. In other words, songs, preached word, fellowship time, and perhaps a feast represents who God is to many people. God becomes what we do at the church building to have a good time. This is why so many people flock to fellowship in congregations where the pastor is dynamic, the choir is electrifying, and the crowd is sizable. Many mistakenly believe that if they are attending a regular church service, then they are, by definition, good Christians—never mind how they may be acting during the rest of the week.

Creator. Yes, God is the creator of everything we know and understand. He has created everything made of matter, atoms, and cells. Yes, God has synchronized everything to work in our bodies as it does: the blood plays a role, the kidneys play a role, the lungs play a role, the feet play a role, the skin plays a role, *et cetera, et cetera, et cetera.* He put everything in motion like the rotation of the earth and the rotation of the earth around the sun. All the things we have learned about chemistry, physics, biology, botany, and any other science were all created by God. He did create, and He is still creating. However, to see Him as just a creator is to deny so many other aspects of who God is. He is still intimately working in our lives today.

Savior, provider, healer, and way maker. Savior in this section is not referring to our eternal Savior. For this section, savior is only referring to being saved from an accident, mishap, evil people, or anything else someone would normally like to avoid.

Yes, for Christians, God does act as our savior and provider, but God is not Santa Claus. God is our healer, and He will make a way for us when things get desperate in our lives but He is not Santa Claus. Think about how we act in our society. When our commercialized Christmas is approaching, we threaten children with the notion that they better be good or else Santa will bring them a bag of coal. We tell them that they will not get anything good for Christmas. Then, we relent and always deliver any toys we are able to deliver to any mean, evil-acting, brat child we know. I am not aware of anyone that can afford it who practices the Christmas tradition that has ever not delivered on Christmas Day. The threat to withhold is a farce. God is not a Santa Claus who will always deliver our goodies regardless of our behavior.

Similarly, and sadly, many people believe that God is only a bearer of good gifts. God is can save us in catastrophes, provide for us in times of need, and heal our aches, pains, and illnesses. God is able to make a way out of what looks impossible, but it is not just because we ask. Consider our president. Everyone does not have access to the president. A person cannot attack the president's motorcade one day and then next week expect to be allowed to go in and have a conversation with Him. Many believe they can treat and acknowledge God any way they want to, and He will still be a bearer of only good gifts. This is absolutely not true. Refer to the following chart. God is patient with our hardheadedness, but He does not play when it comes to discipline.

Heaven bound. Many believe God can only keep His good promises. Many mistakenly believe that everyone that has claimed to accept Christ will wake up in heaven. Many believe that no matter what we say, no matter how we act, and no matter what we do, we are all destined for heaven to be angels looking down on the rest of humanity. This is absolutely not true. The Bible tells us that there will be a lake of fire that many will be cast into. This will be God's choosing.

One thing we must keep in mind about people being heaven bound is that it is God's doing, and we cannot judge other people. We do not know what is in someone's heart. That is between them and God. Bible scholars discuss what is known as "eternal salvation" of a believer. Basically, it means that once you confess Christ the very first time, you are forever saved from that point on in this life and throughout eternity. There are many verses that support this belief. On the other hand, Jesus at one point tells those doing good that He never knew them. In other words, maybe on the day they confessed their belief and got baptized, it was all fake. Maybe, they just felt like it was time for them to do it because it was politically correct, their friends did it, or it would make Mama happy. We do not know, and we cannot judge. We can only know what is in our own hearts. We can only know our own truthful honest relationship with Almighty God. If we are being fake with God, He knows, and we are not heaven bound just because we have put on a good show.

Taskmaster. Many people only see God as a brutal, ruthless taskmaster. They only see God as a dictator who is mean that is holding them back and will not allow them to have any fun. The most interesting point about this belief is that God is so wonderful that He has given us the perfect way to understand Him via our own existence. Think about our society. There are helicopter parents, and there are lax parents. There are parents that are not even involved with their children's lives. There are parents that do not allow their children to grow up by always making decisions for them. There are parents that keep their kids under strict authority. Truthfully, there are times in the life of a child when a little bit of each type of parent may be best.

Likewise, all these parenting styles demonstrate the many aspects of how God interacts with us. Our relationship is the same. God is a loving parent, and we are His children. Sometimes God may be perceived as a taskmaster because He needs to teach us to behave and listen. Good parents will do this for their children. We deserve it as children because we have misbehaved. It is only for our good if we receive discipline in love. Unfortunately, many people who have not permitted themselves to truly know and understand God are only seeing this one side of Him, if they consider Him to be a taskmaster.

WHY AMERICA NEEDS TO REPENT

Some multidimensional manifestations of our God

The same God that:	Is the same God that:
made the elephant	made the ant
created heaven and earth	destroyed every living thing with a flood
made a single zygote, or cell in our bodies	made the entire multiorgan, multifunctioning entire human body
loves David as a man after God's own heart	will chastise David and let him choose between three punishments. (2 Samuel 24)
opened up the ground and swallowed up Korah's rebellion (Numbers 16)	gave Peter another chance and made sure he was invited. (Mark 16:7)
predestined Jeremiah to be an ordained prophet (Jeremiah 1:5)	gave free will to Ananias and Sapphira, his wife, to choose their destiny (Acts 5:1–11)
is love (1 John but	will make us pay for our evil (Galatians 6:7)
provides a way to salvation (Romans 10:9–10)	will allow sinners and unbelievers to die a second death (Revelation 21:7–8)

No one can pinpoint God. No one can define God. Who can know God? Who can see God? Our God is three in one.

> This is He who came by water and blood, Jesus Christ; not only by water, but by water and blood. And it is the Spirit who bears witness, because the Spirit is truth. For there are three that bear witness in heaven: the Father, the Word, and the Holy Spirit; and these three are one. And there are three that bear witness on earth: the Spirit, the water and the blood; and these three agree as one. (1 John 5:6–8 NKJV)

> The grace of the Lord Jesus Christ, and the love of God, and the communion of the Holy Spirit be with you all. Amen. (2 Corinthians 13:14 NKJV)

Humility

When we understand that God is multidimensional beyond our imagination and comprehension, then we are at the point where Jesus was talking about when He tried to explain to us in Luke 18:17 that the only way we can really ever get to understand who God is, is to first view Him like a toddler looks longingly and lovingly at his or her parents. In other words, because God is Who He is, a person must have childlike faith to accept Him. Children look up and are amazed at all they see and do. They are awestruck easily. We must be in awe of God and not try to put Him in a box. He is not one-dimensional. There are too many facets for us to understand. All humanity should feel the same way when we stop and contemplate the glory of God. Then perhaps, God will continue to have mercy on us. Just like a child we should pray:

"God you are so much bigger than me, I cannot begin to understand the vastness of your being. I apologize for the times I have assumed that I know what you know and that I can understand the complexities of your allowances. I am not capable of making the decisions you make. I cannot understand the decisions that you make. Amen."

Therefore, Lord, I repent for acting like you are one dimensional, and I know everything about you. I really do not have a clue. Help me to humble myself before you. Lord, please forgive me, and help me to do better.

Chapter 27

I Repent for Not Setting the Atmosphere

Jesus Could Tell

The atmosphere or environment in which we live, work, and move in is so important to our everyday lives. It sets the tone. It encourages other things to happen or not to happen. It is powerful. We see this in our country. We see this in our neighborhoods, and we see it in our homes. The atmosphere is very important in our ability to live Christian lives. Jesus Christ Himself dealt with this.

> Now it came to pass, when Jesus had finished these parables, that He departed from there. When He had come to His own country, He taught them in their synagogue, so that they were astonished and said, "Where did this Man get this wisdom and these mighty works? Is this not the carpenter's son? Is not His mother called Mary? And His brothers James, Joses, Simon, and Judas? And His sisters, are they not all with us? Where then did this Man get all these things?" So they were offended at Him. But Jesus said to them, "A prophet is not without honor except in his own country and in his own house." Now He did not do many mighty works there because of their unbelief. (Matthew 13:53–58 NKJV).

This is one of the most important texts in all the Bible about the importance of setting the atmosphere. Just think about it. Here we see God in the flesh, limiting Himself in His earthly work due to the unbelief of other people. Their atmosphere was so negative and vitriolic that even God Himself backed off from working miracles in their presence. The atmosphere can affect us whether it is positive or negative. Think about how the atmosphere impacts our lives.

Our Country

We were drawn together for a moment after the September 11, 2001, attacks on the World Trade Center in New York. For a moment we collectively felt like we were one America. We were all attacked. We were all unified in wanting to know what happened. We were also mostly unified in feeling a need for God and prayers. Then, as always, time passed. Now our political leaders seem more like the text mentioned wherein no one wants to even hear the other person talk. Absolutely everything that comes from the other side is nullified before the words get out of their mouth. All actions are 100 percent right or 100 percent left. The atmosphere is so contentious that one could cut it with a knife. How can we govern with an atmosphere like this? Where will this atmosphere lead us? Storming the Capitol Building may be just a start. There is a way to fix it. It starts with respecting and loving each other, as corny as that may seem.

Anything that is intent on divisiveness will always divide and destroy. Divisive talk shows, newscasts, or political rhetoric where people get paid to fan the drumbeats of ill will do not help to bring us together. The Bible says that it is a soft answer that will keep us from unnecessary anger. That is how we discuss and reason together.

Our Neighborhoods

Do you know your neighbors? Do you recognize their children? Would Jesus know them if He resided on your street? These are questions we can ask ourselves when thinking about the atmosphere of our neighborhood.

Whether you live in a cul-de-sac, in a large city, an apartment, or on a country road, we all have neighbors. We all have people who live close to us that may not be family. We should care about them. They should know that we care about them. This does not mean that we must call them every week or have barbecues with them every summer. It does, however, mean a lot of little things.

A good neighborhood atmosphere may be one wherein a smile or wave is normal when passing someone coming out of their driveway. It may mean taking care of your lawn if you are the only one that does not. It may mean being considerate of a foreign neighbor that just moved in. It may mean being willing to help your neighbor clean up after a storm. This book cannot tell anyone specifically what it takes to create a good neighborly atmosphere because every situation is different. However, it starts with considering what your neighbors may want out of you as a neighbor. Consider their point of view. Maybe you will not be able to fulfill each task, but at least you will know that you sought to understand everything you might be doing to create any negative tension. That is what a true Christian would be concerned with.

Our Home

The atmosphere of a married home starts when a person is dating. A person should realize that their future spouse has been in training for what a home atmosphere should be like during all their childhood years. Growing up in the home of a happily married couple where the parents respected each other is one type of training. Growing up in a household where verbal and physical abuse were common is another type of training. No matter how cute your prospective spouse is, they have been trained. Consider the atmosphere they will be expecting years down the road after the wedding and honeymoon are fading memories.

Now, we must consider other households. A single person, a single parent, an elderly household where both parties are retired, or any number of households in America, all have one thing in common. They all have a normal. Households that are in transition from homeless to home ownership may not be able to set their own atmosphere while they are in transition. Households that are in the process of moving from one location to another may not be able to establish a home atmosphere during the transition. So, for the sake of this paragraph we are referring to families of any type that have a place to go to bed each night that they call home. Care should be taken because it will affect the relationships you have with everyone that enters the doorway, including your children.

It Is Important

Think of all the wonderful benefits when the atmosphere is positive. In the early church in the book of Acts, chapters 3–5, the atmosphere was positive. Jesus had been crucified. However, His disciples were fully aware that He had returned alive. Therefore, there was no more sadness. They had hope, and they had purpose. Miracles were performed, and people were joining the church in droves. It was a great, positive atmosphere, and everybody benefitted.

When a young man wants to pop the question to his longtime girlfriend, he should have plans. He might take her to an upscale restaurant instead of a fast-food restaurant, if he can afford better. If he can afford it, most likely he will take her to a place with candles on the tables, tablecloths, soft live music, chandeliers, a nice entryway, and a maître d' on staff. No one would have to tell you this was an elegant restaurant. Anyone would be able to tell because of the atmosphere.

Likewise, in America, on a Friday night, if I tell you that I am taking you to a place where there is going to be a band, cheerleaders, event parking, lots of teenagers, cool evenings, stadium lights, a crowd, and good smells from a concession stand, you could probably easily guess that I am taking you to a high school football game. If I tell you the atmosphere, your mind will tell you what to expect, how to dress, what the crowd may be like, and how you will probably react to the event. If you like football, you will probably be excited. Your mouth will water thinking about the hot dogs and drinks you might purchase. Speaking of that, you will probably also think about how much money you have, since you know the food will be expensive.

All these thoughts would influence your attitude in your expectation of the event. If you do not like football, your attitude will be negative, and you might even be thinking about how you can get out of going to the game.

So it is with everything we do in our lives. We surround ourselves with things that we might want to do or that will entertain us if we are planning a long trip in the car. What atmosphere are you expecting when you go to work tomorrow? How about at your next religious worship service? What is the atmosphere of your marriage? What is the atmosphere on your street, in your community, state, and country? Is the atmosphere positive or negative? Is the atmosphere something you look forward to, or is it something you dread? Do you travel mostly in healing environments or hurting environments?

> Then His disciples came and said to Him, "Do You know that the Pharisees were offended when they heard this saying?" But He answered and said, "Every plant which My heavenly Father has not planted will be uprooted. Let them alone. They are blind leaders of the blind. And if the blind leads the blind, both will fall into a ditch." (Matthew 15:12–14 NKJV)

This shows how important it is to choose an atmosphere wisely. The atmosphere should not include people who are blind to God and His word. People who are blind to God will lead someone into a ditch.

Create It

God's word suggests that we can often set or at the very least influence our atmosphere. We should avoid negative atmospheres, if possible. Negative atmospheres tend to rub off on us. Even if a people are not conscious of a simple picture on the wall portraying something sinful, their subconscious may be planting a seed of the act or deed. The Bible says, in Psalm 1, that a person is blessed by not being around people who would present a negative, ungodly atmosphere. Do not sit around with negative people. It is better to be alone. We also should not want to follow negative people.

To create a positive atmosphere, think of all the things you can do to create a more welcoming, pleasing, enriching, humbling Christian experience everywhere you go. What could you do at work? What could you do at home? What could you do in your neighborhood?

Consider the example of the Old Testament tabernacle. Everyone was not invited inside. Everything inside was placed there purposefully. Everything inside reflected God. There are many references to incense in the tabernacle of the children of Israel (Exodus 35:15, 39:38, 40:5; Leviticus 4:7; Numbers 4:16 and 16:18). It is described as a sweet odor in the tabernacle. Aromas can help to set the atmosphere. Could deliberately located signs help change an atmosphere that you frequent? What sounds and background noises can you control? Are they helping your Christian atmosphere or hurting it?

Songs can change an atmosphere. This is a good reason for children to be in the choir at church. They will learn songs that will stay with them for the rest of their lives. They will learn songs that they can use to encourage themselves in high school when a parent is not with them. They will learn songs that will come to mind when the devil tries to tempt and discourage them in college. Singing songs and humming spiritual songs to yourself can keep a person in the right atmosphere.

If the things that interest a person are good, healthy, and positive for their well-being then pictures of those things could hang on the wall. Plug in air fresheners with pleasant aromas that could greet you at the door after a hard day's work. A habit of always greeting your loved ones at the door before they have a chance to put down their books or briefcase will certainly encourage all those in the family to look forward to coming home. Even when it is not reciprocated, this is an example of a more mature Christian attempting to control the atmosphere.

Turn off some things sometimes. People have been known to say, "I just had it on for noise." Gospel or instrumental soothing music may be okay for this, but do we really need to have the television on all the time? Words, language, and circumstances plant seeds in our subconscious mind. The truth is, we are not always paying attention to the message behind the comedy or the movie. Consider the things being learned from watching soap operas day after day. Is sin being normalized? Two or three years from now, things will come out of a person's mouth and he or she will wonder where it came from. That is because the seeds planted have suddenly sprung up.

Holiday celebrations have been turned into commercial bonanzas. It is amazing to think of how commercial the day celebrated as the birth of Jesus Christ has become. It is hard to picture Jesus delivering the Sermon on the Mount and excusing Himself to run out and pick up Christmas gifts that have nothing to do with Him. It is also difficult to imagine Jesus hiding Easter eggs to celebrate His resurrection. However one may feel about the cultural celebration of these holidays, our job as Christians is to set the right atmosphere for our family and our children. Every opportunity to teach and acknowledge God must be taken. Otherwise, the world will set the atmosphere and try to convince everyone what it is all about.

Hesitating

Following Christ is never a job for the faint of heart. Attempting to create a Christian atmosphere everywhere one frequents will create tension. Some will not like it. Some will criticize whenever we do not live up to the atmosphere we are portraying. We cannot hesitate because of others' criticism and disdain. The purpose for creating a Christian atmosphere is so we and everyone around us can be more like Jesus. We have not arrived; we are all sinners, but we must press on by setting the atmosphere to enhance our sanctification.

My Mind

We all must ask ourselves, "What is going on in my own head?" People cannot control what is going on around them if they do not control their own thoughts. One of Satan's favorite playgrounds is our mind. As Christians, we should always be controlling our own internal atmosphere, and others should be able to see it in us. This is what non-Christians cannot appreciate about the Christian life. Everything about the Christian life allows us to live in an atmosphere of hope and faith regardless of our present external circumstances. How else could Stephen, a chosen man of God, confidently speak before a council when he was lied on and falsely accused. Stephen's accusers were in an atmosphere of hatred, disdain, and misunderstanding. Stephen was right there in their hateful presence, but they could not change his internal atmosphere. Stephen wholeheartedly believed in Jesus Christ, so he was able to maintain an internal attitude and atmosphere of hope, glory, and forgiveness.

> When they heard these things they were cut to the heart, and they gnashed at him with their teeth. But, he, being full of the Holy Spirit, gazed into heaven and saw the glory of God, and Jesus standing at the right hand of God, and said, "Look! I see the heavens opened and the Son of Man standing at the right hand of God!" Then they cried out with a loud voice, stopped their ears, and ran at him with one accord; and they cast him out of the city and stoned him. And the witnesses laid down their clothes at the feet of a young man named Saul. And they stoned Stephen as he was calling on God and saying, "Lord Jesus, receive my spirit." Then he knelt down and cried out with a loud voice, "Lord, do not charge them with this sin." And when he had said this, he fell asleep. (Acts 7:54–60 NKJV)

Stephen was no doubt at peace with his situation. Even in the face of being stoned to death, he was forgiving. People often give Jesus credit for being on the cross and asking for forgiveness from God the Father for the very people who were crucifying Him. Then, people will say that Jesus could do that because He was God. Well, Stephen was just a regular human being like everyone else that has walked this earth, besides Jesus Christ Himself. Stephen was sold out for God. Asking for forgiveness from God the Father for those that were stoning him is a true sign of controlling your internal atmosphere, no matter what!

Therefore, Lord, I repent for not always controlling my atmosphere. Lord, please forgive me, and help me to do better.

Chapter 28

I REPENT FOR ARGUING AND DEBATING

Listed with the Worst Sins

In Romans 1:16, Paul announces that he is "not ashamed of the gospel of Christ for it is the power of God." He then, like a parent scolding their child, seems to take his unashamed attitude and begins to point his finger at all humanity and tell us the sinful things we do that are not godlike. In his discourse, he mentions things like idol worship, homosexuality, fornication, wickedness, pride, murder, and backbiting. It is a long list. To my surprise when I was investigating this chapter one day, I noticed that some versions of the Bible also included "debate" in this list. Some versions of the Bible use the word "strife." In the Greek, the translation of the word used is *eris*[18]. It means a quarrel, strife, or contention. The main emphasis on the word implies a rivalry. This is a very important point when it comes to Christians getting along because a rivalry means two opposing sides. Second Corinthians also mentions debates or outbursts of wrath.

> Again, do you think that we excuse ourselves to you? We speak before God in Christ. But we do all things, beloved, for your edification. For I fear lest, when I come, I shall not find you such as I wish, and that I shall be found by you such as you do not wish; lest there be contentions, jealousies, outbursts of wrath, selfish

ambitions, backbitings, whisperings, conceits, tumults. (2 Corinthians 12:19–20 NKJV)

There Is a Way

Christians can disagree. Two people trying to make it down the side of a mountain can both look down the mountain and discuss, from the same vantage point, with the same goal, which way is the best way to arrive safely at the bottom of the mountain. Which way is best to go down? Sometimes they will agree and choose a direction. Sometimes, only if time permits, they may have to take longer to convince the other person why their way is the best way. Sometimes, the two people may have to agree to go down the hill using separate paths and meet at the bottom. When this option is chosen, the two parties should still be able to leave in good spirits, when they go in separate directions, and look forward to meeting the other person at the bottom of the mountain. No animosity should exist because they have the same goal. What is important here is that their discussions can be and should be cordial. It is not a rivalry. It is not a contest. The goal is for both to arrive safely, period. The goal is not, who wins!

> "Come now, and let us reason together," says the Lord. Though your sins are like scarlet, they shall be as white as snow. Though they are red like crimson, they shall be as wool. (Isaiah 1:18 NKJV)

The word *reason* in this text is the Hebrew word *yakach*[19]. It means to decide, prove, or convince. So, the onus is on the knowledgeable to convince the less knowledgeable about whatever needs to be done. If time permits, the discussion should continue until both parties see the same decision as the best alternative. That does not make it a rivalry. It is a teaching and learning situation. Both parties should see it as such since both parties should have the same goal. It does not have to become a personal attack. Jesus uses another Greek word, *dialogizomai*[20], for the word *reason* with similar meaning in Matthew.

> And they reasoned among themselves, saying, "It is because we have taken no bread." But Jesus, being aware of it, said to them, "O you of little faith, why do you reason among yourselves because you have brought no bread? Do you not understand, or remember the five loaves of the five thousand and how many baskets you took up?" (Matthew 16:7-9 NKJV)

However, what if you are not having a discussion with a fellow Christian, with the same goal, with ample time to carry out a lengthy discussion. I keep mentioning time because it is crucial. What if there is no time for a lengthy discussion? There is not always time, before a decision must be made. That brings us to the main issue at hand. What if I am not aware of a person's Christianity? What if we may not have the same goals? What if I am in line at a grocery checkout line and get in a debate with the clerk? Now the disagreement can turn into a matter of, "who wins." Time and the person one is disagreeing with may take all the Christianity a person can muster. Either way, the Bible recommends a quick resolution. Matthew 5:25 says, "Agree with your adversary quickly, while you are on the way with him, lest your adversary deliver you to the judge, the judge hand you over to the officer, and you be thrown into prison." In other words, humility and composure are suggested ways for a Christian to settle a disagreement. While this may not be easy, it is a stark contrast to the hundreds of people who wind up hurt, killed, or imprisoned each year after some minor debate leads to raised tempers.

Respect

Is there ever a time when arguing and debating is not appropriate at all? Is there ever a time when a person should maintain silence? The answer may be more a matter of respect and method. Consider the corporate board room or any conversation with your boss. Unless you have just been assured that you have won the lottery, or you already have another job lined up, more than likely, you are not going to be rude to your boss even though you may disagree. Also, given short notice, you will more than likely jump to the task at hand if your boss runs in and needs you to do something in a hurry. How many times have you had to do something at work without understanding why it needed to be done at the time? If you have been working long enough, the answer is probably several, if not many times. This is because we have respect for our boss. We understand that he has the power to change out income and affect our household. Therefore, we allow our boss to make decisions and dictate what needs to be done and when things need to get done. We stop talking and roll with the situation. It is a matter of respect. This same respect is deserved at other times.

Well, fellow Christian, do you have respect for God? If you do have respect for God, you should respect His word. Do you have more respect for your boss than you do for your spouse? Do you have more respect for your boss than you do for your parents? Do you have more respect for the judge in a human courtroom than you do for Christian pastors and leaders? God has said in His word that all these roles mentioned deserve our respect.

I may get a lot of blowback from this in the twenty-first century, so I am just going to put the verses here and let any dissenters disagree with God. Look at all the verses that are in our Bible that state how we should have respect for certain others. Do not read these verses too fast because one set of verses may contain more than one person or persons that should be respected, submitted to, or honored. Does that mean there are times when we should be quiet and accept what we are being told without debate? You be the judge.

> Honor your father and your mother, that your days may be long upon the land which the Lord your God is giving you. (Exodus 20:12 NKJV)

> "A son honors his father, and a servant his master. If then I am the Father, where is My honor? And if I am a Master, where is My reverence?," says the Lord of hosts to you priests who despise My name. Yet you say, "In what have we despised Your name?" (Malachi 1:6 NKJV)

Submitting to one another in the fear of God. Wives, submit to your own husbands, as to the Lord, For the husband is head of the wife, as also Christ is head of the church; and He is the Savior of the body. (Ephesians 5:21–23 NKJV)

Likewise you younger people, submit yourselves to your elders. Yes, all of you be submissive to one another, and be clothed with humility, for God resists the proud, but gives grace to the humble. (1 Peter 5:5 NKJV)

Children, obey your parents in the Lord: for this is right. Honour thy father and mother; which is the first commandment with promise; That it may be well with thee, and thou mayest live long on the earth. And, ye fathers, provoke not your children to wrath: but bring them up in the nurture and admonition of the Lord. Servants, be obedient to them that are your masters according to the flesh, with fear and trembling, in singleness of your heart, as unto Christ; Not with eyeservice, as menpleasers; but as the servants of Christ, doing the will of God from the heart; With good will doing service, as to the Lord, and not to men: Knowing that whatsoever good thing any man doeth, the same shall he receive of the Lord, whether he be bond or free. And, ye masters, do the same things unto them, forbearing threatening: knowing that your Master also is in heaven; neither is there respect of persons with him. (Ephesians 6:1–9 KJV)

Let every soul be subject to the governing authorities. For there is no authority except from God, and the authorities that exist are appointed by God. Therefore whoever resists the authority resists the ordinance of God, and those who resist will bring judgment on themselves. For rulers are not a terror to good works, but to evil. Do you want to be unafraid of the authority? Do what is good, and you will

> have praise from the same. For he is God's minister to you for good. But if you do evil, be afraid; for he does not bear the sword in vain; for he is God's minister, and avenger to execute wrath on him who practices evil. Therefore you must subject, not only because of wrath but also for conscience sake. For because of this you also pay taxes, for they are God's ministers attending continually to this very thing. Render therefore to all their due: taxes to whom taxes are due, customs to whom customs, fear to whom fear, honor to whom honor. (Romans 13:1–7 NKJV)

Let me be clear. In these verses, God should be respected and honored, Jesus should be respected and honored, husbands should be respected and honored, mothers and fathers should be respected and honored, bosses should be respected and honored, pastors and ministers should be respected and honored, and elders should be respected and honored. Even government officials should be respected and honored. Also, we should walk in humility before all men. So once again we must ask ourselves whom are we arguing with and whom are we talking back to? We should be quiet sometimes and allow God to work things out in His way. God recommends an order for a reason.

Does that mean we should never speak up when we disagree? No. The next question is how we should respond when we do disagree. That is easy. We should not respond with anger and malice.

> A soft answer turns away wrath, but a harsh word stirs up anger. The tongue of the wise uses knowledge rightly, but the mouth of fools pours forth foolishness. (Proverbs 15:1–2 NKJV)

> So then, my beloved brethren, let every man be swift to hear, slow to speak, slow to wrath; for the wrath of man does not produce the righteousness of God. (James 1:19 NKJV)

Imagine how many relationships, marriages, childhood mistakes, political turmoil, and lives could be saved if we stopped so much arguing and did a lot more listening. It would certainly be wonderful if our Congress and Senate could learn to reason together and listen to one another without calling each other names. Imagine the progress we could make if we just learned how to respond when we disagree.

Therefore, Lord, I repent for arguing and debating too much, and often in the wrong way. Lord, please forgive me, and help me to do better.

Chapter 29

I REPENT FOR NOT GIVING STRONG SUPPORT FOR THE DISADVANTAGED AND PERSECUTED

In this chapter we are talking about more than just poor people. While Jesus Christ was on this earth as a man, He took up for those that were in a disadvantaged position. In His very first sermon in Matthew chapter 5, He exhorts that the poor in spirit, those that mourn, the meek, and the persecuted will all be enriched and comforted in His kingdom. America constantly chastises other countries for their "human rights" atrocities. Instead, we also need to consider what we do to support the disadvantaged, downtrodden, and persecuted in our own community. Some might say, "It is worse over there." Well, that might be because you are not personally living through the bad situation yourself. A disadvantage is a disadvantage, no matter where it is. Imagine someone living year after year needing dental work and suffering through the pain but not having dental insurance. Should they feel better because they know there are people who can afford dental insurance? Should a person that is medically blind feel better because he or she cannot see our American skyscrapers versus the Australian Outback or the Great Wall of China. Those people are still disadvantaged. Being surrounded by other people who are not feeling the pain a person feels does not change or fix the desperate situation that person is going through. History says that many people came to this country because of persecution. Even today people are flooding our borders because of what they feel is persecution in their home countries. By the same token, many people who have already been Americans for a long time are still living disadvantaged and persecuted lives. Who is disadvantaged? Who is persecuted? Do we care enough to do anything about the situation other people are dealing with every day?

Who Is This?

These are people who have the decks stacked against them, so to speak, and are condemned by society to live a subpar life because of their denigrated state. Oftentimes, these people are our neighbors or acquaintances. Unfortunately, so often, we never seem to get involved until the tragedy lands in our neighborhood or under our roof.

Some people in America are still being persecuted and ostracized even in the twenty-first century. Persecution occurs because of what people believe. Persecution occurs because of where people live or have lived. Persecution occurs because of a race or skin color. Some people are persecuted because of their size or weight. Some people are persecuted just because they are shy. Persecuted people need unconventional help, just like those that are disadvantaged.

Think about some of the people in our society that are disadvantaged, downtrodden or persecuted. For years in our American society, people who have some types of mental issue have been set aside or put into mental institutions. The Americans with Disabilities Act has taken care of many people who suffer from various types of disability. Our welfare system takes care of many that are in need. Consider people living in a community with a bad water supply or living near a toxic landfill. Consider people whose lives are abruptly changed due to a drunk driver. Consider people who buy a house one year, and then the husband and wife both are laid off when the largest corporation in town shuts down abruptly. Property values would plummet, and the family would suddenly be destitute. When you are riding down a street or country road and assuming that some people choose to live in squalor or with unkept yards, ask yourself what might have caused it.

Unfortunately, instead of asking what caused it, many people simply pass by. We are apathetic about a situation until it hits home. The biblical book of James says that we should not wait to help all these disadvantaged and persecuted people. Playing as if they are not there is just purposely turning a blind eye to the situation. Not doing anything is a dereliction of our Christian duty to love one another. The need is everywhere.

Many children are in foster homes waiting to be adopted. These children have tremendous needs. Our courts have systems and protocols set up for children that are delinquent from school. The attempt is to try to be proactive and keep them from getting into trouble later. Consider children that have incarcerated parents or parents on drugs. Where are these children supposed to get help if both parents have issues? They can very easily fall through the cracks. When you hear about a thirteen-year-old child who acts out in school for no apparent reason, we should ask ourselves what is behind the behavior. We have become sensitized to bullying in our society because it seems that after many school shooting investigations, the police have discovered that the shooters had been bullied themselves. However, nobody cared about these downtrodden, persecuted individuals until their plight began to have repercussions that could affect their own children.

Caring Enough

How is it we never seem to get involved until the tragedy lands on our doorstep? People in our society are screaming for help, and others often pass by and ignore once, twice, three times, and more. Many people in our society are too busy planning the next birthday party, or wedding, or graduation, or bridal shower, or retirement to take the time to help others really in need, right next door. I once preached a sermon called "How Deep Is Your Love?" Surface love is superficial. The word *love* is said often, but real love for any of these disadvantaged people would cause action to occur. Suppose you child or grandchild's name was in one of the categories mentioned above. Most would agree that having your own child or grandchild involved would make action happen quicker. Why? Is there a limit on our love for others?

Thank God for the biblical story of Naomi and Ruth. Naomi had it going on for a while. She was newly married and newly relocated at the beginning of the story. I am sure many in her local family were looking up to her. She soon had two sons, which was very important in that culture. Imagine someone in our culture today being in Naomi's situation. Most of our society would see Naomi as a young intelligent person compared perhaps to someone that just stayed at home and found a job. Relocating from home somehow makes one seem more in-the-know.

However, things quickly took a turn for the worse when Naomi's husband died, followed about ten years later by the death of her two sons. All Naomi had left were her two daughters-in-law. She was a realist and suggested the three should split up, when one of the greatest pronunciations in all of history is recorded.

> Turn back, my daughters, go; for I am too old to have a husband. If I should say I have hope, if I should have a husband tonight and should also bear sons, would you wait for them till they were grown? Would you restrain yourselves from having husbands? No, my daughters; for it grieves me very much for your sakes that the hand of the Lord has gone out against me! Then they lifted up their voices and wept again; and Orpah kissed her mother-in-law, but Ruth clung to her. And she said, "Look, your sister-in-law has gone back to her people and to her gods; return after your sister-in-law." But, Ruth said "Entreat me not to leave you, or to turn back from following after you; for wherever you go, I will go; and wherever you lodge, I will lodge; your people shall be my people, and your God, my God. Where you die, I will die, and there will I be buried. The Lord do so to me, and more also, if anything but death parts you and me. (Ruth 1:12–17 NKJV)

There are several things to learn from this story, but one of the main takeaways is that Ruth cared enough about her mother-in-law not to abandon her after suffering such losses. This is everything a Christian attitude should be about. They are both poor and destitute. Ruth is totally unselfish here. She cares more about Naomi's plight than she does about her own. Naomi is in bad shape. In her culture, women were second-class citizens without a man. There were no Social Security, Medicaid, or Medicare systems to help a person in old age. Ruth could have walked away. She was still young enough to start anew. She could have thought it would be easier to find a new husband without the baggage of an old mother-in-law in her background reminding everyone that she had been married before every time they saw her. Ruth could be young and single, living a young and single lifestyle. She could have put the blame for a decision to leave on Naomi, saying, "Well, she told me to do it." Instead, it appears she cares more about the plight of Naomi than she does herself. She cares and takes action by vowing to stay with Naomi. Naomi was a prime example of the disadvantaged we are discussing in this chapter, but she was not left abandoned.

> Be kindly affectionate to one another with brotherly love, in honor giving preference to one another, not lagging in diligence, fervent in spirit, serving the Lord; rejoicing in hope, patient in tribulation, continuing steadfastly in prayer, distributing to the needs of the saints, given to hospitality. (Romans 12:10–13 NKJV)

This scripture describes the attitude we should have for everyone but specifically for those that could be considered beneath you. We should love them and honor them. That means we do what we can to make everyone feel important. Giving preference to them implies that if two people share a box of doughnuts, and only one is left, the person that sees the doughnut is more inclined to insist the other person have the doughnut, instead of gobbling it down themselves. This verse also points out what is meant by "strong support."

Dwane Massenburg

Willing to Take Strong Corrective Action

When you really care about the plight of another person, it is not enough to simply say you care. You must do something. It must be real and substantial. Every year we feel good about ourselves when we make sure kids have toys under the tree for Christmas. Then we drive by them the other 364 days of the year when they are hungry and cold. Who goes over their homework with them and encourages them to do better? Who takes them to a ball game? Who is there for them in their time of need when a drug dealer approaches them with an opportunity for easy money? Who really cares? Not being there all the time to fill every need means either we do not care enough, we are ignoring their reality, or we are doing the insufficient good things we do, more for our own accolades than true concern for the situation. Many of our neighbors are hurting right now. Our American economy ebbs and flows. Many get stuck in a rut, and it takes a long time to get out of it.

> What does it profit, my brethren, if someone says he has faith but does not have works? Can faith save him? If a brother or sister is naked and destitute of daily food, and one of you says to them, "Depart in peace, be warmed and filled," but you do not give them the things which are needed for the body, what does it profit? Thus also faith by itself, if it does not have works, is dead. (James 2:14–17 NKJV)

Talking about caring is not enough. The Bible says love thy neighbor. The Bible does not say love thy pets, but Americans spend billions of dollars each year on pets while children are not getting all their needs met. Some people in nursing homes go for weeks without a visit from anyone to share their love. People who claim to be Christians are often too busy for that but spend two to three weeks every year going on vacation. They also take time to go to a church building each week so they can maintain their Christian image. That is not strong corrective action on behalf of so many human beings in need.

Why America Needs to Repent

Two people who did not take firm action in a time of need in the Bible are Reuban and Judah, the brothers of Joseph. Joseph had eleven brothers that were not happy with him because of a dream he had. Nine of Joseph's brothers wanted to kill him. Joseph had a real need for some saving help. He needed someone that had real compassion despite a disagreement. He was persecuted by his own brothers. Yes, Christians should realize that when people are in desperate need, we should help them regardless of our personal disagreements with them. Nine brothers wanted to kill Joseph. Reuben stood up for Joseph but only halfheartedly. Nobody wants to be thrown into a pit and left for dead, but that is what Reuben suggested. This was not good caring action for someone that needed saving. Reuben should have suggested that the nine brothers forget about their hatred and treat Joseph like a true brother and child of God. Likewise, Judah suggested that they sell Joseph into slavery. He is just like Reuben—not really thinking about the loving and fair thing to do for Joseph, their own brother. Reuben and Judah really made suggestions in fear of their other nine brothers. Or, they could have made their suggestions just to get along with their other nine brothers. How often do we not help the disadvantaged, downtrodden, and persecuted, just because of how it looks to our friends and family? Perhaps we fear for our own safety?

> But Reuben heard it, and he delivered him out of their hands, and said, "Let us not kill him." And Reuben said to them, "Shed no innocent blood, but cast him into this pit which is in the wilderness, and do not lay a hand on him" that he might deliver him out of their hands, and bring him back to his father. So it came to pass, when Joseph had come to his brothers, that they stripped Joseph of his tunic, the tunic of many colors that was on him. Then they took him and cast him into a pit. And the pit was empty; there was no water in it. And they sat down to eat a meal. Then they lifted their eyes and looked, and there was a company of Ishmaelites, coming from Gilead with their camels, bearing spices, balm, and myrrh. On their way to carry them down to Egypt. So Judah said to his brothers, "What profit is there if we kill our brother

> and conceal his blood? Come and let us sell him to the Ishmaelites, and let not our hand be upon him, for he is our brother and our flesh." And his brothers listened. Then Midianite traders passed by; so the brothers pulled Joseph up and lifted him out of the pit, and sold him to the Ishmaelites for twenty shekels of silver, and they took Joseph to Egypt. (Genesis 37:21–28 NKJV)

This is horrible, but it is a good example of half-hearted care. Reuben and Judah are perfect examples of so-called Christians that allow wrong to be done right under their noses. Their heart was tugging at them enough to know that something else should be done, but instead of a full rescue, they went along with wrong. This is like being an accessory to a crime that causes pain to someone when you could have stopped it. There are people all around us that need a complete rescue instead of a partial handout. It takes deep love to feel the pain of someone that is living in a bad situation. What does God say when we help a little bit but leave downtrodden, disadvantaged, and persecuted people in their predicament? God did everything for us. He did not hold back. He demonstrated complete love. Perhaps some people do not follow through with complete love because it is not convenient.

It Is a Sacrifice

When you love and care about the person in pain that is suffering and going through difficulties, it is not always convenient, popular, or easy. The good Samaritan in Jesus's parable, (Luke 10:30–37), was inconvenienced and had to use his funds to help. Jesus's command in verse 37 is for us to "go and do likewise." During the civil rights movement in the 1960s, Birmingham pastors were admonished because they could not discern what it felt like to live on the other side of the situation. Every week, these pastors and their congregants prayed to God and sang about His love while practicing pride and self-righteous behavior toward other human beings. Our decision to take care of the disadvantaged, downtrodden, and persecuted should never be about ourselves. This is what Jesus told us clearly concerning how we should treat each other.

> Therefore, whatever you want men to do to you, do also to them, for this is the Law and the Prophets. (Matthew 7:12 NKJV)

We like to call Matthew 7:12 the "Golden Rule," as if man came up with it. In fact, it is Jesus's rule. Paul told us we should assume pain and hurt feelings by observing the recipient's feelings, not our own.

> Rejoice with those who rejoice, and weep with those who weep. Be of the same mind toward one another. Do not set your mind on high things, but associate with the humble. Do not be wise in your own opinion. (Romans 12:15–16 NKJV)

Here again, the Bible is clear that as Christians, we should feel what other people are feeling. Not having our mind on high things means that how other people are feeling should be a priority in our lives. It should not be enough to just drop off toys during the Christmas season. We should not be satisfied as long as other children of God are hurting in any way.

Therefore, Lord, I repent for not giving strong support for the disadvantaged, downtrodden, and persecuted. Lord, please forgive me, and help me to do better.

Chapter 30

I Repent for Not Thanking and Appreciating God for My Trials and Tribulations

When you wake up every morning, your expectations and hope for what you might accomplish or what might be delivered propel you to do what you do and feel how you feel. Perhaps you are expecting to go to work or school today. Your mind is set on all the things you need to do to get there and what will happen when you get there. Perhaps you are hoping to pick up your daughter from the airport this afternoon. If I told you that tomorrow morning, we were going to take a short flight to a beach resort in the middle of June, you would have several specific expectations about tomorrow. You would expect to get up early, you would expect to see airplanes on the runway, lots of luggage, lots of people going through security, airline pilots and flight attendants. You would expect to hear the roar of the jet engines taking off and the pilot on the intercom system. Upon arrival at the beach, you would expect to see lots of people, beach attire, and sand. These expectations would be natural and normal in our society, and you would prepare accordingly.

Expectations influence our beliefs. Then they dictate our feelings. People feel joyous when things go as expected. People feel disappointed, frustrated, and out of sorts when things do not go as expected. Some people suggest that it is best not to have expectations. Thereby eliminating the feeling of disappointment when things do not go as expected. That will not work for a Christian because the Christian life is predicated on hope, faith, and expectations.

> For David says concerning Him: "I forsaw the Lord always before my face, For He is at my right hand, that I may not be shaken. Therefore my heart rejoiced, and my tongue was glad; moreover my flesh also will rest in hope." (Acts 2:25–26 NKJV)

> For I know that this will turn out for my deliverance through your prayer and the supply of the Spirit of Jesus Christ, according to my earnest expectation and hope that in nothing I shall be ashamed, but with all boldness, as always, so now also Christ will be magnified in my body, whether by life or by death. (Philippians 1:19–20 NKJV)

> I have hope in God, which they themselves also accept, that there will be a resurrection of the dead, both of the just and the unjust. (Acts 24:15 NKJV)

When things go well, you may be okay. However, while we live as expectant Christians, and things do not always go our way, does that mean we are doomed to feel anguish and frustration in our everyday lives? When you go out to the car in the morning, and it will not start, are you automatically having a bad day? When you find out your child got into a fight at school, and you have to leave work early, does that mean this has been a bad week? When you find out one of your coworkers has been lying on you to the boss, do you automatically want to give up and find another job? This is where many Christians seem to live. At least, this is how many Christians are constantly talking and acting. They seem to be always sad, upset, and not happy about how life is treating them.

Suppose it is not the things that are happening around you but your expectations of what should be happening around you. You see, if you go to the beach, you should not get all bent out of shape when sand gets between your toes. Therefore, you calmly remove the sand and keep on doing whatever you are doing. You do not display a lot of theatrics and throw a temper tantrum about the sand because you expected it. Now, if you take a three-year-old to the beach, they may cry and pout and throw a tantrum because they may not have matured enough to know that when you say beach, you are also saying sand. Compare that to our Christian walk. Why do we act surprised by trials and tribulation when the Bible tells us to expect tribulation? In fact, it may be good for us.

Problems to Expect

Problems with your family.

> Now brother will deliver up brother to death, and a father his child; and children will rise up against parents and cause them to be put to death. (Matthew 10:21 NKJV)

> Do not think that I came to bring peace on earth. I did not come to bring peace but a sword. For I have come to set a man against his father, a daughter against her mother, and a daughter-in-law against her mother-in-law, and a man's enemies will be those of his own household." Matthew 10:34–36 NKJV)

Problems with Satan.

> And the Lord said to Satan, "From where do you come?" So, Satan answered the Lord and said, "From going to and fro on the earth, and from walking back and forth on it." (Job 1:7 NKJV)

> The thief does not come except to steal, and to kill, and to destroy. I have come that they may have life, and that they may have it more abundantly. (John 10:10 NKJV)

Be sober, be vigilant; because your adversary the devil walks about like a roaring lion, seeking whom he may devour. (1 Peter 5:8 NKJV)

Problems with aging.

For all our days have passed away in Your wrath; we finish our years like a sigh. The days of our lives are seventy years; and if by reason of strength they are eighty years, yet their boast is only labor and sorrow; for it is soon cut off, and we fly away. (Psalm 90:9–10 NKJV)

because "All flesh is as grass, and all the glory of man as the flower of the grass. The grass withers, and its flower falls away. (1 Peter 1:24 NKJV)

Problems with sinful humanity.

Blessed are you when they revile and persecute you, and say all kinds of evil against you falsely for My sake. Rejoice and be exceedingly glad, for great is your reward in heaven, for so they persecuted the prophets who were before you. (Matthew 5:11–12 NKJV)

And ye shall be hated of all men for my name's sake: but he that endureth to the end shall be saved. But when they persecute you in this city, flee ye into another: for verily I say unto you, Ye shall not have gone over the cities of Israel, till the Son of man be come. The disciple is not above his master, nor the servant above his lord. It is enough for the disciple that he be as his master, and the servant as his lord. If they have called the master of the house Beelzebub, how much more shall they call them of his household? (Matthew 10:22–25 KJV)

Do not marvel, my brethren, if the world hates you. (1 John 3:13 NKJV)

How We Should React to Trials and Tribulation

> But I say to you, love your enemies, bless those who curse you, do good to those who hate you, and pray for those who spitefully use you and persecute you. (Matthew 5:44 NKJV)

> See that none render evil for evil unto any man; but ever follow that which is good, both among yourselves, and to all men. Rejoice evermore. Pray without ceasing. In every thing give thanks: for this is the will of God in Christ Jesus concerning you. (1 Thessalonians 5:15–18 KJV)

> Wherein ye greatly rejoice, though now for a season, if need be, ye are in heaviness through manifold temptations: That the trial of your faith, being much more precious than of gold that perisheth, though it be tried with fire, might be found unto praise and honour and glory at the appearing of Jesus Christ. (1 Peter 1:6–7 KJV)

> For this is thankworthy, if a man for conscience toward God endure grief, suffering wrongfully. For what glory is it, if, when ye be buffeted for your faults, ye shall take it patiently? but if, when ye do well, and suffer for it, ye take it patiently, this is acceptable with God. For even hereunto were ye called: because Christ also suffered for us, leaving us an example, that ye should follow his steps. (1 Peter 2:19–21 KJV)

> And who is he that will harm you, if ye be followers of that which is good? But and if ye suffer for righteousness' sake, happy are ye: and be not afraid of their terror, neither be troubled; But sanctify the Lord God in your hearts: and be ready always to give an answer to every man that asketh you a reason of the hope that is in you with meekness and fear: Having a good conscience; that, whereas they speak evil of you, as of evildoers, they may be ashamed

that falsely accuse your good conversation in Christ. For it is better, if the will of God be so, that ye suffer for well doing, than for evil doing. (1 Peter 3:13–17 KJV)

Beloved, think it not strange concerning the fiery trial which is to try you, as though some strange thing happened unto you: But rejoice, inasmuch as ye are partakers of Christ's sufferings; that, when his glory shall be revealed, ye may be glad also with exceeding joy. (1 Peter 4:12–13 KJV)

God Himself May Chastise Us, and He Tells Us It Is Good for Us

As many as I love, I rebuke and chasten. Therefore, be zealous and repent. (Revelation 3:19 NKJV)

The Lord knows the thoughts of man, that they are futile. Blessed is the man whom You instruct, O Lord, and teach out of Your law. (Psalm 94:11–12 NKJV)

And not only so, but we glory in tribulations also: knowing that tribulation worketh patience; And patience, experience; and experience, hope: And hope maketh not ashamed; because the love of God is shed abroad in our hearts by the Holy Ghost which is given unto us. (Romans 5:3–5 KJV)

Ye have not yet resisted unto blood, striving against sin. And ye have forgotten the exhortation which speaketh unto you as unto children, My son, despise not thou the chastening of the Lord, nor faint when thou art rebuked of him: For whom the Lord loveth he chasteneth, and scourgeth every son whom he receiveth. If ye endure chastening, God dealeth with you as with sons; for what son is he whom the father chasteneth not? But if ye be without chastisement, whereof all are partakers, then

> are ye bastards, and not sons. Furthermore we have had fathers of our flesh which corrected us, and we gave them reverence: shall we not much rather be in subjection unto the Father of spirits, and live? For they verily for a few days chastened us after their own pleasure; but he for our profit, that we might be partakers of his holiness. Now no chastening for the present seemeth to be joyous, but grievous: nevertheless afterward it yieldeth the peaceable fruit of righteousness unto them which are exercised thereby. (Hebrews 12:4–11 KJV)

Part of this verse was also included in the chapter on parenting. Here the emphasis is on the fact that you should thank God and appreciate what He is doing for you via His chastisement. Stop expecting your Christian walk to be a bed of roses. Get up in the morning, smiling and asking God to use you to represent Him through some trial or tribulation. Know for sure that the trials are coming, and your attitude and reaction to those trials is in direct proportion to your spiritual maturity to trust God in all situations. Every single day—even those with trials and tribulations—should be viewed through the lens of God and appreciated as opportunities to represent God via our hope, praise, and worship. Great days, good days, bad days, and sad days are all working together for our good.

> A good name is better than precious ointment; and the day of death than the day of one's birth. It is better to go to the house of mourning, than to go to the house of feasting: for that is the end of all men; and the living will lay it to his heart. Sorrow is better than laughter: for by the sadness of the countenance the heart is made better. (Ecclesiastes 7:1–3 KJV)

> This is the day the Lord has made; we will rejoice and be glad in it. (Psalm 118:24 NKJV)

> And we know that all things work together for good to those who love God, to those who are the called according to His purpose. (Romans 8:28 NKJV)

We Do Not Know

Only God knows what will be required of you in this life. You may be required to make a great sacrifice for God. God has a purpose for you, and it may be bigger than having a certain kind of house or driving a certain kind of vehicle. Are you ready? Paul was ready to give the ultimate sacrifice for the name of Jesus Christ, and he considered it a privilege. It was a good day for Paul to represent his Christian walk.

> And when he was come unto us, he took Paul's girdle, and bound his own hands and feet, and said, Thus saith the Holy Ghost, So shall the Jews at Jerusalem bind the man that owneth this girdle, and shall deliver him into the hands of the Gentiles. And when we heard these things, both we, and they of that place, besought him not to go up to Jerusalem. Then Paul answered, What mean ye to weep and to break mine heart? for I am ready not to be bound only, but also to die at Jerusalem for the name of the Lord Jesus. (Acts 21:11–13 KJV)

Therefore, we should see every day as a good day and stop complaining about our minor trials and tribulations. Expect them. Give God some glory the next time something distasteful happens in your life, and be a witness for the goodness of God.

Therefore, Lord, I repent for not thanking and appreciating you for my trials and tribulations. I should expect them. Lord, please forgive me, and help me to do better.

Chapter 31

I REPENT FOR CHILD ABUSE AND NEGLECT

As the old saying goes, "Children are our future." When children are mistreated, it affects both today and tomorrow. Sometimes people forget what it was like to be a young child. Adults laugh and think it is cute when little children say things out of their pure innocence. A five-year-old might cry because they think they will lose their favorite uncle, just because he is getting married. A four-year-old might think it is raining all over the world just because it is raining in her neighborhood. A seven-year-old might still believe in the tooth fairy. We snicker at the innocence and naivete of children. They innocently do not know many things until they reach certain ages or have certain experiences. That is what makes the abuse and neglect of children so atrocious. It is taking advantage of someone that cannot help themselves. A small sapling tree in a forest is very vulnerable. It can be very easily pulled up by the root and killed. It will bend if someone steps on it. It can be wounded for life. Children are like the young sapling in the forest. Abuse and neglect can leave them scarred for life.

Dr. Nadine Burke Harris gave a TED Talk on childhood trauma. She discussed the medical implications of a study known as the Adverse Childhood Experiences Study (ACEs) conducted by Dr. Vince Felitti, at Kaiser Permanente, and Dr. Bob Anda, at the Center for Disease Control (CDC). The study documents the detriment of many things that happen to children, and what long-term effect it has on their health. Childhood trauma they studied included physical/sexual abuse, emotional abuse, physical neglect, emotional neglect, parental mental illness, substance dependence, incarceration, parental separation or divorce, and domestic violence. Ten traumas were listed, and each was considered a point on a scale of ten. They found that the higher your ACE score, the worst long-term effect there would be on the long-term health of the child. A high ACE score (greater than four) dramatically increased the risk of seven out of ten of the leading causes of death. The trauma changes the child's physiology. The brain changes due to the trauma. Dr. Robert Block, the former president of the American Academy of Pediatrics, said, "Adverse Childhood Experiences, are the single greatest unaddressed public health threat facing our nation today."[21]

This evidence demonstrates that how we treat children is crucial. The responsibility does not stop at your own children. Children that are traumatized could grow up to be our neighbors or our child's spouse. Children that are traumatized are more likely to commit suicide or become involved with the criminal justice system. The implications are far-reaching. The children around us that are suffering will be impacted, both physically and psychologically. They are not like adults, who can move away to a better situation. Obviously, a fine line exists between helping and meddling when we see children that we believe may be experiencing abuse or neglect. What should we do as Christians?

Children Are Honored and Respected by God

> And Jesus called a little child unto him, and set him in the midst of them, And said, Verily I say unto you, Except ye be converted, and become as little children, ye shall not enter into the kingdom of heaven. Whosoever therefore shall humble himself as this little child, the same is greatest in the kingdom of heaven. And whoso shall receive one such little child in my name receiveth me. (Matthew 18:2–5 KJV)

In today's America, many children are suffering. "According to United States Department of Health and Human Services tracking, reported rates of neglect in the U.S. are higher than those for other types of child maltreatment. In 2016, reports indicated that there were at least 672,000 maltreated children in the U.S., and 7 children per 1,000 were reported victims of neglect, compared with 1.7 per 1,000 for physical abuse, 0.8 for sexual abuse, and 0.5 for psychological or emotional abuse."[22]

Intentional Abusers

There have been instances where babies were shaken to death by an adult. Sometimes children are beaten to the point where bones are broken. Sometimes in stores, I have heard children cursed at like sailors in a bar by their parents or caretakers. Sometimes I have heard of children that had things thrown at them like shoes, hangers, or pots and pans. Sex trafficking is a form of horrific child abuse. This is intentional, and this is abuse. These things venture into what one would call cruel, mean, and inhumane on the part of the person performing the act against the child. A deliberate harmful act performed against a child is not approved by God.

> But whoever causes one of these little ones who believe in Me to stumble, it would be better for him if a millstone where hung around his neck, and he were thrown into the sea. (Mark 9:42 NKJV)

Let me pause here for clarity. Psychologists will tell you that there are many ways to teach. I agree with them. In my own limited and not statistically significant experience in rearing children, I totally agree that there are different ways to rear, train, and discipline children. There is a gross difference between egregious, angry, physical abuse that is administered for the sole purpose of expressing domination over someone or something that is weaker. Anything done in the form of discipline must be carried out as a teaching moment. The purpose is not to leave scars or incite fear in a young child. The only purpose is to teach. Throwing things at a child like a shoe, pots and pans, or anything you can pick up, is dangerous. It is not teaching. What if the flying object hits the child in the eye. Or what if the child falls down a flight of stairs or bumps his or her head while running from a flying object. Then, you have gone beyond teaching and have damaged your child. That is abuse. On the other hand, there are times, based on the Bible, when physical correction may be one of the many alternatives a parent should use to rear, train, and discipline a child. The child should be disciplined in an age-appropriate, demeanor sensitive way. Many parents try to make their children understand entire sentences or complex thoughts at the age of two or three. At this age, the first word they should be taught is "stop." A three-year-old can be taught the word *stop* with some physical reinforcement. That will teach the child the importance of words and specific sounds and begin to keep the child out of self-inflicted danger. "Stop," before your child touches a hot stove or runs into the street are valuable lessons that can be taught before a child masters the entire English language. Holding a three-year-old's thigh while administering a firm, swift pop on it, while saying, "Stop," at the same time, could be a good lesson. Especially, if the same word, "Stop," is used in other instances when you want a child to abruptly cease and desist whatever he or she is doing or getting ready to do. This is not abuse (see chapter 20: "I Repent for Not Parenting"). The earlier it is taught, the quicker you can teach a child the importance of staying out of harm's way. By teaching the word *stop*, you will begin to decipher the personality of the child based on the demeanor displayed. Many children will very quickly not need any physical reinforcement because they have a personality that responds to just the tone of a parent's voice. This is teaching out of love. This is not abuse out of anger.

Also, for clarity, child labor in the sense of using children as part of a major continuous manufacturing, production, or service operation every day is a form of child abuse. Child labor driven solely by profit motives is wrong. Especially if the work is at the expense of the child going to school to learn other things he or she will need to know in life. This is tricky, because many of us grew up helping our parents in the family business, running errands, performing chores, and handling other parental requests. This is, of course, not child abuse if the motive is teaching and training. God knows motives.

Unintentional Abuse and Abuse by Neglect

Is it neglect when a single parent leaves a fourteen-year-old child at home alone while she works night shift? When two working parents come home after a long day and tell their six-year-old he can go play video games for two hours while they go over to a neighbor's house for conversation and dinner; is that neglect? Is it abusive to tell your eight-year-old who likes to read that you cannot afford for her to buy a particular intriguing book, when you spend thirty dollars per week on getting your nails done? If you do not smoke at work, because it is a smoke-free work zone, but you smoke around your children, inside your own home; is that abuse? Is it abusive to not take your child to the dentist, because you do not have dental insurance? These are hard questions. Were you thinking about your answer to the questions from your point of view or the child's point of view? From the child's point of view, the answers are the same. The child's health, well-being, and physical or mental opportunities to progress are being put on the back burner. To God, children are of the utmost importance. Are you doing all you can for your children? Are you doing all you can for all children? Jesus took time for children. Out of everything He could have been doing, He took time for children.

> Then they brought little children to Him, that He might touch them; but the disciples rebuked those who brought them. But when Jesus saw it, He was greatly displeased and said to them, "Let the little children come to Me, and do not forbid them; for of such is the kingdom of God. (Mark 10:13–14 NKJV)

> And He took them up in His arms, laid His hands on them, and blessed them. (Mark 10:16 NKJV)

Beware

God is watching. God has a purpose and a plan for everyone born. God is watching what is happening to His children. God knows who His children are before they are even born. Consider the story of the birth and childhood of Moses in Exodus. Moses's life was protected by God, before he even knew God. Consider all the young kings that ruled the nation of Israel in 1 Kings and 2 Kings. When God's children are abused and neglected, He knows.

> And there went a man of the house of Levi, and took to wife a daughter of Levi. And the woman conceived, and bare a son: and when she saw him that he was a goodly child, she hid him three months. And when she could not longer hide him, she took for him an ark of bulrushes, and daubed it with slime and with pitch, and put the child therein; and she laid it in the flags by the river's brink. And his sister stood afar off, to wit what would be done to him. And the daughter of Pharaoh came down to wash herself at the river; and her maidens walked along by the river's side; and when she saw the ark among the flags, she sent her maid to fetch it. And when she had opened it, she saw the child: and, behold, the babe wept. And she had compassion on him, and said, This is one of the Hebrews' children. Then said his sister to Pharaoh's daughter, Shall I go and call to thee a nurse of the Hebrew women, that she may nurse the child for thee? And Pharaoh's daughter said to her, Go. And the maid went and called the child's mother. And Pharaoh's daughter said unto her, Take this child away, and nurse it for me, and I will give thee thy wages. And the women took the child, and nursed it. And the child grew, and she brought him unto Pharaoh's daughter, and he became her son. And she called his name Moses: and she said, Because I drew him out of the water. (Exodus 2:1–10 KJV)

> Ye shall not afflict any widow, or fatherless child. If thou afflict them in any wise, and they cry at all unto me, I will surely hear their cry; And my wrath shall wax hot, and I will kill you with the sword; and your wives shall be widows, and your children fatherless. (Exodus 22:22–24 KJV)

God made provision for the baby Moses, and He pays attention to the cries of children. Comfort children if there are some crying around you because God is watching. Be sure not to add to their dismay because God is watching.

Therefore, Lord, I repent for child abuse and neglect. Lord, please forgive me, and help me to do better.

Chapter 32

I Repent for Not Saying No

Saying no takes boldness. It takes guts to stop the process from proceeding; whatever it is. Momentum says, let it go. Then the Holy Spirit does His work and reminds us that it is not right; I should stop it, or I should leave. That is a critical moment. It is life-altering. When the moments are gone, there is often no turning back. Often, there is no way to regroup and resume course. We make choices. The repercussions are most certainly on the way.

So many people are living their lives today with the repercussions of not saying no:

- ✓ I received eight years of prison time for embezzling funds because I had daily, easy access to thousands of dollars. I am going to miss two of my children's graduation ceremonies. I did not say no.
- ✓ My former best friend committed suicide after I turned on her, to be more popular with my new high school cheerleading friends. I could have stopped it, but I did not. I did not say no.
- ✓ I stepped into a car with three other guys, with guns, looking for revenge. We wound up shooting an innocent man; ultimately, I received thirty-five years in state prison. I did not say no.
- ✓ I have a friend with an eating disorder. We picked on her mercilessly. She is in the hospital now, in critical condition, weighing about eighty pounds. I should have spoken up, stopped the picking and tried to help, but I did not say no.

- ✓ For years I have watched pornography almost every day. Now my marriage has fallen apart. The divorce is supposed to be final next week. I did not say no.
- ✓ I was on the board when several of my counterparts formulated a lie to tell the pastor. We drove him away because no one in leadership would back him up. It was a travesty, but I did not speak up against it. Now many of the sheep have scattered, and the church will never be the same. I did not say no.

A long time ago, First Lady Nancy Reagan started a "Just Say No" campaign that was aimed at teaching children to say no to drugs. That was a valid slogan, but it may have been expecting too much because it was aimed at young developing minds. The children may have been dealing with peer pressure and poverty at the same time. Or the young children may have thought that it was an easy way for them to feel like they fit in with more popular kids. To the young children, that may have made drugs seem like the only way out because their minds are immature.

This chapter is not aimed at the immature and vulnerable. This chapter is aimed at the maturing Christian that knows about the love and power of God. This chapter is aimed at the person who, if you are honest with yourself, would admit that there was something in the back of your mind that was telling you not to do it. Something was telling you to leave, stop, or just say no. That something was God Himself, via His Holy Spirit. This chapter is aimed at the person that is ready to take 100 percent responsibility for his or her own actions. We know as Christians that God tells us to make a choice. The Bible has several examples wherein we have been instructed to choose between right and wrong, good and evil, or God and Satan. Each individual must choose for themselves whether it is time to say no and turn around.

If God instructs us to choose, then that means we must have the power to make the choice.

It Is a Choice

The Bible is full of some very bad things: lying, cheating, adultery, murder, and wars. These are all examples of humankind mistreating humankind. This is people treating other people badly. The Bible explains, however, that these things were done as examples for us. Examples are designed for us to observe and learn from. We are not supposed to repeat the bad examples in the Bible after we have a chance to see the horror and devastation they caused. We have a way out. The devil may "show" us what to do, but he does not "make" us do it.

> Now these things were our examples, to the intent we should not lust after evil things, as they also lusted. Neither be ye idolaters, as were some of them; as it is written, The people sat down to eat and drink, and rose up to play. Neither let us commit fornication, as some of them committed, and fell in one day three and twenty thousand. Neither let us tempt Christ, as some of them also tempted, and were destroyed of serpents. Neither murmur ye, as some of them also murmured, and were destroyed of the destroyer. Now all these things happened unto them for examples: and they are written for our admonition, upon whom the ends of the world are come. Wherefore let him that thinketh he standeth take heed lest he fall. There hath no temptation taken you but such as is common to man: but God is faithful, who will not suffer you to be tempted above that ye are able; but will with the temptation also make a way to escape, that ye may be able to bear it. (1 Corinthians 10:6–13 KJV)

All Old Testament occurrences are not there for us to emulate. Much of it is for us to learn from and purposely decide not to do. We are supposed to look at a passage of scripture and allow the Holy Spirit to teach us. Some things we should relish and say yes to. Some things we should disdain and say no, absolutely not. In this text, evil, idol worship, sexual immorality, and complaining are mentioned as things to say no to. Verse 13 states that whatever a person is being tempted with is not new. Therefore, one cannot act like it is the worst situation that has ever happened, and no one else has ever had to deal with it. That is a lie. Anything a person might be going through today has been dealt with before. Some have come out unscathed. Others have come out with repercussions that change their life forever. Which will you be? Will you say no?

In Galatians 5, the Bible teaches us about the fruits of the Spirit and walking in the Spirit. It basically says that at some point as Christians we all should be able to hold our fleshly, sinful desires behind us. With the Holy Spirit, we should be able to subdue all the things that we should say no to.

Confused about Your Choices

Sometimes you agree to do things before you know all the details. Is it a good Christian thing to do? Is it helpful? Is it wholesome? Is it good for me? Is it good for somebody else? Perhaps I should wait and see if what I am getting ready to do lines up with everything else in my life. How does doing this line up with the scriptures I know? How does doing this affect my family, friends, or reputation? Would I want what I am considering doing, on the front page of the local newspaper tomorrow morning? Can I just say no?

> Beloved, do not believe every spirit, but test the spirits, whether they are of God; because many false prophets have gone out into the world. By this you know the Spirit of God: Every spirit that confesses that Jesus Christ has come in the flesh is of God, and every spirit that does not confess that Jesus Christ has come in the flesh is not of God. (1 John 4:1–3 NKJV)

Knowing when to say no is crucial. One should say no as soon as the indwelling Holy Spirit reminds them that something does not feel right. Something does not sound right. Something is wrong. It should not be confusing. Most often, the issue is not confusion because the Holy Spirit is clear. He will always tell us to do what is righteous, pleasing, good, honest, just, pure, and in line with what is good for our fellow human beings. That is not confusing. Often, some people may choose to claim confusion when the real issue is denial. When we fail to humble ourselves before God and are determined to have our own way, we might as well own up to it and say, "I have decided to turn my back on God."

What Makes Us Not Say No?

Sin. When you know it is wrong, God does, too. According to the book of James, in chapter 4, if a person refuses to do things God's way when they clearly understand that God would not or does not like it, then it is simply sin. It is like a child deliberately and unapologetically doing what his or her parent has just said not to do. The child would be saying, by his or her actions, that whatever the parent has requested is unimportant or insignificant. Yet, people often continue doing what they know they should not. Think about the things that might make you continue along a detrimental path. God will not be mocked.

Pride and peer pressure. Pride is a horrible sin. The Bible says seven things are an abomination to God (Proverbs 6:16–18). The list begins with a proud look. In the midst of a situation, when other people are looking, are you too proud to back up, change your mind, and say, no? Not wanting to say no before your friends means their friendship is more important to you than your faith in God.

When people allow peer pressure to cause them to act a certain way, they have essentially put their life in the hands of those peers. They are going along to get along. They may have a great life if their peers are all Christians trying to lead them in the right direction. However, if their peers have dangerous, detrimental, sinful, and illegal things in mind, then those people will fall into destruction at the same time their peers do. It is far better for them to humble themselves, swallow their pride, and back up from whatever or whomever it is that is encouraging them to do wrong. There are prison cells, graveyards, courtrooms, and hospitals for all sizes.

Let your peers go ahead, if that is their choice. Any individual can choose differently.

In other words, pride can often make you do irrational things that can get you into trouble even when you normally would not. This intrinsic danger is known as peer pressure.

Fear. Fear can also make us not say no. Some may feel that something worse will happen if they say no. It is a shame when we see people come forward to be whistleblowers, only to find out that they will be the ones to lose their jobs or be retaliated against. Once a person comes forward with an allegation, the outcome cannot always be guaranteed. Losing a job or a friendship may be a very real consequence of saying no.

In this case, a person must come face-to-face with his or her beliefs. How committed are we to our beliefs? Analyze the fear. Trusting God is an act of faith. God first in a person's life means that saying no to sin or anything wrong is not really an option, regardless of the consequences. Obviously, anyone that must sacrifice today cannot give up any more than the church founders did in the book of Acts.

Not my personality. Perhaps a person has an amiable personality. Perhaps he or she does not like conflict and is easygoing. Amiable personalities were created by God. It is not wrong to be amiable. It is not weak to be amiable. It is God's design.

The same God that created a wolf also created a sheep. People with amiable personalities should align themselves with good shepherds that show the fruit of being strong Christians. That way there will be limited attempts to be steered in the wrong direction. Sometimes, though, even amiable people may have to speak up and say no.

Too late

Perhaps you are too far involved to back out now, so even though you have had a change of heart, you are thinking, "I cannot say no now. I am in too deep." It is never too late to honor one's relationship with God. Even though the devil may have had a person trapped, a new revelation from God means that it is always appropriate to change your mind, say no to continuing, and head in another direction. Resolve the situation now, before it gets even worse.

Scenario 1. Gateway drugs, starter drugs, or recreational drugs are all the same. Drinking is an elusive drug that does not warn you when it is about to take over your life. Your mind is being altered. Slowly at first, for most people, but either way there is not an alarm bell on a particular drink or drug that says, "If you have one more you will reach the point of no return. You will be addicted." That may give pause for at least one last time when a person could decide to cross that threshold. In the meantime, it is never too late to say enough, give it up and say no.

Scenario 2. Promiscuous sex is habit-forming. A discussion could be had about whether it makes a difference if a person has been with three people or seven people. Maybe we should stop at ten. Each adventure adds to the risk of sexually transmitted diseases, broken hearts, and unwanted pregnancies. Each adventure links your soul to a person that may be very distraught when the connection is broken. Is this a guiltless crime? Does God care? It is never too late to stop and say no.

Scenario 3. Lying is a horrible sin, but I must keep it going now because so many people will get hurt. The truth is that they are already going to be hurt because there is no way to erase what was lied about. Therefore, why wait to let the truth come out? The longer the lie is kept a secret, the more pain will be caused. If a friend asks a person to lie because they are friends, one must consider if that is true. Real friends do not ask someone else to do something God does not like. It is never too late to speak up and say no.

The Repercussions

It's all going to work out. I will just try it. No, it's not all going to work out without substantial hard times that could have been avoided if you had chosen to say no and do it God's way.

> Be not deceived, God is not mocked; for whatever a man sows, that he will also reap. For he who sows to his flesh will of the flesh reap corruption, but he who sows to the Spirit will of the Spirit reap everlasting life. (Galatians 6:7–8 NKJV)

Not saying no does not give one a free pass to play sin, for a minute, for free. History is replete with very sad stories that were the result of one-time incidents. One hookup, one theft, one drug usage, one lie, or one extortion have changed people's lives for decades. Sometimes one bypassed opportunity to say no has ended a person or several people's lives.

Therefore, Lord, I repent for not saying no. Lord, please forgive me, and help me to do better.

Chapter 33

I REPENT FOR NOT BELIEVING IN THE POWER OF GOD

People often say everything is relative. That is a true statement when it comes to everything but God. God is God all by Himself and He cannot be compared to anything else humanity is aware of. I know this because of the enormity of His creation. Humanity is insignificant when it comes to God's total creation. God can make miracles happen. They are miracles to us because our limited minds cannot comprehend the power that He has. Praise God; trust His power.

The Enormity of God

We humans arrived with these bodies that are self-contained, with minds that function to maintain our bodies (once we get old enough to think rationally). We are born with blood already in our arteries and veins. We do not have to go to a pumping station. We do not need batteries, no disrespect to pacemaker wearers. How did we get here? Even the atheist must agree that human beings are inhabiting the earth. We are here by some process beyond our comprehension. Were we created here, only for this planet? Or were we transported here from somewhere else? We cannot even imagine. That begs the next question. Who created us? Or who transported us? Now, with that being said, we must ask the next logical question. Where did the creator or transporter come from? This rabbit hole can continue to go deeper and deeper and deeper. I call the creator, God. He is the God of Abraham, Isaac, and Jacob. Using the same power He used to create the universe, He also arranged for a son to be born, named Jesus. If He had the power to create the universe, He has all power. So, in this case, you either believe in God or you do not. You either believe He had a son who lived on the earth as a man, was crucified, and rose again, or you do not. If you believe that, then I cannot fathom any other power God would not have, past, present, or future.

> Thus says the Lord: "Heaven is My throne, and the earth is My footstool. Where is the house that you will build Me? And where is the place of My rest? For all those things My hand has made, and all those things exist," says the Lord. "But on this one will I look: on him who is poor and of a contrite spirit, and who trembles at My word." (Isaiah 66:1–2 NKJV)

The Insignificance of Man

In terms of weight, the average adult human is between one hundred to three hundred pounds, relative to this big earth (too many zeros to put here). In terms of time, the average life expectancy for Americans today is about eighty years. Compare that to the life of some sharks, whales, and tortoises, which live for hundreds of years. Some trees in California are believed to live for thousands of years. The earth itself is anywhere from hundreds of thousands to billions of years old, depending on whose calculation methods you prefer. Our human time is so insignificant.

The imprint of man on the earth, except as a user and exhauster of natural resources, is miniscule. We feel a great sense of accomplishment because we put man on the moon. But it is still God's moon. We are excited because we have submarines that can venture far under the sea. But it is still God's ocean. We are proud because we can perform open heart surgery and kidney transplants. But our bodies are still God's creation. We make nylon for our carpets from hexamethylene diamine and adipic acid, which come from the ground. We make furniture and build houses using God's wood.

We could not survive without the things God provides for us on this earth. God has the power. The last few chapters of the book of Job demonstrate the insignificance of man, relative to the universe. God is all powerful, mankind or womankind is not.

> Then the Lord answered Job out of the whirlwind, and said: Now prepare yourself like a man. I will question you, and you shall answer Me. Would you indeed annul My judgment? Would you condemn Me that you may be justified? Have you an arm like God? Or, can you thunder with a voice like His? (Job 40:6–9 NKJV)

I challenge any human being who claims God is short of power. Can humankind make a leaf come out of a dead-looking oak tree branch in the spring; then, during the summer, grow acorns; tell the acorns when to fall off the tree in the fall, cover the acorns up with leaves so they can germinate in the fall; then, provide winter and spring moisture to produce a new sapling the next spring when the ground warms just enough to allow the seed to open up and grow? Only God has the power over plants and seasons.

> Where wast thou when I laid the foundations of the earth? declare, if thou hast understanding. Who hath laid the measures thereof, if thou knowest? or who hath stretched the line upon it? Whereupon are the foundations thereof fastened? or who laid the corner stone thereof; When the morning stars sang together, and all the sons of God shouted for joy? Or who shut up the sea with doors, when it brake forth, as if it had issued out of the womb? When I made the cloud the garment thereof, and thick darkness a swaddlingband for it. (Job 38:4–9 KJV)

The last few chapters in the book of Job are awesome. They really put in context how humanity compares to God. It points out that there is no comparison. Comparing humanity to God is as absurd as comparing a single Ford car or truck to the Ford Motor Company. The company created the car.

The car will last awhile, but unless it becomes a collector's item stored in a garage, it will eventually be used up, crashed, or otherwise somehow wind up in a junkyard. Meanwhile, the company will still exist and continue to create more cars and trucks. The company creates different kinds of cars and trucks. The car or truck may represent the company, just like the Bible says that we are made in the image of God. However, that does not make the car or truck compare to the company, just as we do not compare to God. This analogy is quite wild, but this is exactly the analogy that God is presenting to Job. All the miracles that are around us every day are His creation.

Everyday Power in Our Lives

We should never underestimate the power God demonstrates over the sheep that hear His voice. Think of the times when you met the right person, in the right place, at the right time. It most likely was not just happenstance. God arranged it. God sent the people there to connect with you. Believing God is a miracle worker should cause us to always look forward to good things that He is working out in our lives.

Consider the life of Joseph. He started off as a favorite son of his father, Jacob. We are not privy to why Jacob was the favorite but it was a huge influence on the direction of his life. Perhaps God was planning something. Joseph dreamed a dream that made his brothers angry and jealous. This caused them to throw him into a pit and sell him into slavery. Eventually, Joseph wound up in prison. That had to be hard to live through, but God had a purpose for Joseph. Imagine if Joseph had been angry and fought back against his brothers to the death. Suppose he carried a grudge and remorse about how his life was turning out and gave up on possibilities. Instead, Joseph lived through the situation and must have maintained a positive attitude because he still wound up being an overseer and prison leader. Also, the people who Joseph kept running into had power to elevate him, and they did.

God intervened in the life of Joseph more directly via a baker and butler that wound up in prison with him. Their dreams were a seed God used to set Joseph free. Joseph the dreamer himself was still interpreting dreams. God sent a dream to Pharaoh, and when Joseph interpreted it, he wound up being the second-in-command of the entire country of Egypt. After all he went through, Joseph was able to redeem himself and save Egypt and his family during a devastating drought.

This same type of maneuvering is occurring in our lives. The power of Almighty God is arranging situations in our lives. We should recognize it and expect it.

The Miracles of God

Think of the discoveries of science that still leave us perplexed about the true mechanism behind it. Consider black holes, zygotes, and DNA. What makes a black hole behave like it does? What creates the gravity? Why do zygotes divide? Why does our DNA line up in the order that it does? Why does our heart beat? I know some will say it beats due to an electrical pulse, but where does the pulse come from? The Bible says that God spoke, and the earth, animals, fish, birds, sun, moon, and stars all came into existence. Many miracles in the Bible cannot be explained except for our belief in God. Some are shown in the next table.

Miracle	Text
The ten plagues of Egypt	Exodus 7–14
Feeding the Israelites with manna	Exodus 16:14–35
Healing powers of a brass serpent	Numbers 21:8–9
Drought, fire from heaven and rain	1 Kings 17:1–19, 18
Raising of the widow's son	1 Kings 17:17–24
An iron ax floats on the water	2 Kings 6:5–7
Daniel is saved from lions	Daniel 6:16–23
Two blind men are cured	Matthew 9:27–31
A huge number of fish caught at Gennesaret	Luke 5:1–11
A man born blind is cured	John 9:1–7
A lame man at the gate of the temple	Act 3:1–26
Peter heals many sick people	Acts 5:12–16
Paul heals several at Malta	Acts 28:8–9

This list illustrates events that are unexplainable occurrences when confined to the limits of the knowledge of humanity. However, even though we cannot explain them, that does not mean they did not happen. We do know that power makes things happen. Power makes things move. Power changes things. Power stops things. Power creates things. When humanity looks at power, we are often referencing the source of the power: electricity, geothermal, a battery, steam, a waterfall, solar, LED (light emitting diode), coal, nuclear, or natural gas. The power of God includes all these sources and many that humanity probably has not even discovered yet. The power of God surpasses all these sources of power. The power of God is supernatural.

So once again we are faced with a dilemma. Either we believe the Bible, or we do not. Many other miracles in the Bible are not mentioned here. I believe they are all true, but for the sanity of the skeptics, what if only half of them were true? What if only a quarter of them were true? Which other parts of your Bible do you want to throw away if you want to throw out the miracles? Every miracle is a wondrous feat that defies all logic and intellect known to humanity. That should be enough to demonstrate the awesome, amazing, wonderful power of God.

Word as Power

The word of God itself is a power source, according to Romans 1:16. This should not be a surprise since Genesis 1 describes God simply speaking to create the earth. The word of God is a power source that brings people to salvation.

That Should Settle It

Nothing is sadder than to watch a sporting event when one team that has fallen behind tucks tail and gives up. You can tell when they give up. Their demeanor changes. Their passion for going after every play changes. Like fans leaving the stadium, you can tell some of the players are just waiting for the clock to run out or the end of the game buzzer to sound. Some are just going through the motions to get to the last hole on the back nine so they can go to the clubhouse and chill. That is the way Christians are when they do not really believe in the power of God. A Christian that understands and believes in the omnipotent power of God should never doubt that God can change any prediction, diagnosis, forecast, or estimate. God can do anything, at any time, with or for anyone. Sometimes we may not understand why God allows things to happen the way they do, but God still maintains the power. Praise His name. Jesus proved that He believed this in the Garden of Gethsemane.

> Then Jesus came with them to a place called Gethsemane, and said to the disciples, "Sit here while I go and pray over there." And He took with Him Peter and the two sons of Zebedee, and He began to be sorrowful and deeply distressed. Then He said to them, "My soul is exceedingly sorrowful, even to death. Stay here and watch with Me." He went a little farther and fell on His face, and prayed, saying, "O My Father, if it is possible, let this cup pass from Me; nevertheless, not as I will, but as You will." (Matthew 26:36–39)

Two things are evident here. First, just because you are a child of God and you have a relationship with Him, that does not mean you will get an easy way out. Second, Jesus acknowledges that God still has the power to change the situation even if He does not.

In the book of Daniel, Shadrach, Meshach, and Abednego said the same thing about God. God is sovereign, and our misunderstanding, misinterpretation, or misrepresentation of that fact does not diminish His power. Even if God chooses not to do something, He still can. His power is unlimited.

Therefore, Lord, I repent for acting like I do not believe in your power. Lord, please forgive me, and help me to do better.

Chapter 34

I REPENT FOR DRINKING, DRUGGING, AND GETTING HIGH

Every day people overdose, are killed by drunk drivers, or commit some heinous act while under the influence of alcohol or drugs. It could very well be your neighbor. Alcohol and drug abuse know no boundaries. The richest families to the poorest may be affected. Any culture, race, or ethnic group may be affected. Yet many arenas in our culture seem not to mind introducing our population to these mind-altering chemicals. Drinks are pulled out at an acceptable office party. We will not debate the medicinal uses of marijuana in this book, but it is now legal in many states. Birthday parties, happy hours, or many types of social gatherings seem to all be a reason in our culture to get a "buzz." Even Saint Patrick's Day (a Christian missionary to Ireland) in today's environment is celebrated as a time to drink. There are many different drugs of choice that may have different effects on the body including addictive capability. Alcohol, heroin, marijuana, cocaine, meth, fentanyl, etc., etc., etc. are all used to alter people's minds. Perhaps it is an attempt to escape reality. Perhaps it is an attempt to help us relax. We will look at the allure of these chemicals. We will also consider what the Bible says about our actions toward them. First, though, we will look at what Jesus did.

We will not discuss any doctor-prescribed or medicinal uses of any drug. No part of this chapter is designed to address people who have been hooked on heroin during the recent opioid epidemic in America. This chapter also does not discuss the addictive properties of any particular alcohol or drug. This chapter, like all the other chapters in this book, is geared toward a behavior that a Christian can repent for and choose another behavior, habit, or practice. It is not designed to suggest remedies to those that may already be chemically (mind altered) addicted.

Jesus and Wine

Jesus is associated with turning water into wine and giving wine to His disciples during the Last Supper. Many say this may present a contradiction.

> And when they wanted wine, the mother of Jesus saith unto him, They have no wine. Jesus saith unto her, Woman, what have I to do with thee? mine hour is not yet come. His mother saith unto the servants, Whatsoever he saith unto you, do it. And there were set there six waterpots of stone, after the manner of the purifying of the Jews, containing two or three firkins apiece. Jesus saith unto them, Fill the waterpots with water. And they filled them up to the brim. And he saith unto them, Draw out now, and bear unto the governor of the feast. And they bare it. When the ruler of the feast had tasted the water that was made wine, and knew not whence it was: (but the servants which drew the water knew;) the governor of the feast called the bridegroom, And saith unto him, Every man at the beginning doth set forth good wine; and when men have well drunk, then that which is worse: but thou hast kept the good wine until now. (John 2:3–10 KJV)

This is the first miracle that Jesus performed in the book of John. Some Bible scholars believe wine was consumed much more frequently in the Jewish culture when the Bible was written. What we do know for sure is that Jesus turned water into wine. He obviously did not count it a sin to consume it, or He would not have allowed Himself to be persuaded to perform the miracle. Yet in many verses in the Bible, it is suggested that people of God should be sober and shy away from "strong" drink. Why would God allow confusion in His Word about drinking alcohol?

Since a person can drink wine and not be drunk, it appears the amount consumed is important. This is similar to other things God has blessed us with that are good in appropriate doses or environments but not good out of design. Things such as the food we eat and sex between a married couple are examples. Food is good and necessary for us to survive, but overindulgence has proven to be harmful to a person's long-term health. Sex between a married couple is designed by God, but outside of the marriage boundary, it is called fornication and adultery in the Bible. Outside of marriage, or as designed, sex is considered a sin. Could wine be one of those things in the Bible that was a part of the Jewish culture at the time; appropriate for weddings or special occasions but not meant to be used like a mixed drink at happy hour. Everyone gets to decide for themselves. That leads us to the question concerning why we indulge in alcohol or drugs.

The Question Is, Why?

Is it okay for me to have a beer? Is it okay for me to have a joint? Is it okay for me to take a hit? The question a person must ask themselves is, Why? What am I trying to accomplish? A person casually participating in this activity knows that it is not like dancing or eating a bag of chips. Everyone knows going into the drinking or drugging that it has the potential to change your brain. Drinking and drugging have an effect on the dopamine reward part of your brain that makes you think you feel good, when in fact other things may be happening to your body. Long-term effects of continuing to drink and use drug will have a long-term effect on your body. Therefore, back to my original question. Why would people want to alter their brains? Why would they want to alter their main computer?

Maybe a person starts drinking and drugging because they want to feel accepted. Everyone else is doing it. To feel like a part of the group, I should do it too. This person should work on his or her self-esteem and learn how to be an individual amid a crowd. Perhaps a person says he or she likes to drink or drug to relax. Aside from diagnosed medical issues, this person may need to analyze the stressors in his or her life and figure out a way to relax without drugs or alcohol. Mindfulness, yoga, or exercising may be an alternative. Maybe a person decides drinking and drugging is necessary to have fun. Does it make them laugh more? Or does it make other people laugh at them more? Is there really fun in acting out of control and unintelligent? Really! Perhaps a person drinks and drugs to get the "buzz"—the altered state. If the buzz is what you are seeking, it is time to be very careful. You may be very close to springing a trap.

> Wine is a mocker, strong drink is a brawler, and whoever is led astray by it is not wise. (Proverbs 20:1 NKJV)

> Who has woe? Who has sorrow? Who has contentions? Who has complaints? Who has wounds without cause? Who has redness of eyes? Those who linger long at the wine. Those who go in search of mixed wine. Do not look on the wine when it is red, when it sparkles in the cup, when it swirls around smoothly. At the last it bites like a serpent, and stings like a viper. Your eyes will see strange things, and your heart will utter perverse things. Yes, you will be like one who lies down in the midst of the sea, or like one who lies at the top of the mast, saying: "They have struck me, but I was not hurt; they have beaten me, but I did not feel it. When shall I awake, that I may seek another drink?" (Proverbs 23:29–35 NKJV)

These verses make it clear that alcohol and drugs are like a mouse trap waiting to spring. They mock you. Looking at the wine swirling in the cup makes a person feel like it is something to be conquered. In the end, the person winds up doing nonsensical things because the ability to think rationally has been lost. The Bible tells us to love our neighbor as we love ourselves. A critical question to ask someone that is casually toying with alcohol and drugs is how much they care about themselves. Do they care enough about themselves to consider the trap waiting to spring?

Recommendations

> Therefore, since Christ suffered for us in the flesh, arm yourselves also with the same mind, for he who has suffered in the flesh has ceased from sin, that he no longer should live the rest of his time in the flesh for the lusts of men, but for the will of God. For we have spent enough of our past lifetime in doing the will of the Gentiles when we walked in lewdness, lusts, drunkenness, revelries, drinking parties, and abominable idolatries. In regard to these, they think it strange that you do not run with them in the same flood of dissipation, speaking evil of you. (1 Peter 4:1–4 NKJV)

Here it seems the Bible is suggesting that if you have been indulging in some things detrimental to your walk with God (including drunkenness, revelries, and drinking parties), it is time to give them up since you are more mature spiritually now. Now is the time for you to repent and choose to do more with the days you are blessed with.

> You are all sons of light and sons of the day. We are not of the night nor of darkness. Therefore let us not sleep, as others do, but let us watch and be sober. For those who sleep, sleep at night, and those who get drunk are drunk at night. But let us who are of the day be sober, putting on the breastplate of faith and love, and as a helmet the hope of salvation. (1 Thessalonians 5:5–8 NKJV)

Here it is suggested that Christians should live a disciplined, watchful life. When Zacharias and Elisabeth were told about the birth of John the Baptist, it was said to them, "For he will be great in the sight of the Lord, and shall drink neither wine nor strong drink" (Luke 1:15 NKJV).

> A bishop then must be blameless, the husband of one wife, temperate, sober-minded, of good behavior, hospitable, able to teach; not given to wine, not violent, not greedy

for money, but gentle, not quarrelsome, not covetous. (1 Timothy 3:2–3 NKJV)

Here it is suggested a bishop (church congregation leader) should be in control of his body and mind and not addicted to wine. The church leader's wife must also be sober. "Even so must their wives be grave, not slanderers, sober, faithful in all things." (1 Timothy 3:11 NKJV). The church leaders are supposed to be sober to be good examples for the congregation. That means if the congregation is learning from their good examples, then they should be sober also. Paul also writes to the church at Ephesus:

> Therefore do not be unwise, but understand what the will of the Lord is. And do not be drunk with wine, in which is dissipation; but be filled with the Spirit, Speaking to one another in psalms and hymns and spiritual songs, singing and making melody in your heart to the Lord. (Ephesians 5:17–19 NKJV)

It's a Social Affair

Since drinking, drugging, and getting high are often done in the presence of others (before addiction sets in), a person may say, "I can handle it. I just do a little bit." That may be a dangerous attitude for two reasons. First, nobody starts off wanting to be a disgusting, loud drunk. The habit changes you once the drug has taken effect. Nobody starts off wanting to steal from their own family or rob a store just to support a drug habit. The drug takes over. That is why everyone should be careful about what they choose to participate in while under the influence of a group mentality. Second, the person that seems to be able to "hold their liquor" or not fall to a drug's influence still has a responsibility.

> Yet for us there is one God, the Father, of whom are all things, and we for Him; and one Lord Jesus Christ, through whom are all things, and through whom we live. However, there is not in everyone that knowledge; for some, with consciousness of the idol, until now eat it

as a thing offered to an idol; and their conscience, being weak, is defiled. But food does not commend us to God; for neither if we eat are we the better, nor if we do not eat are we the worse. But beware lest somehow this liberty of yours become a stumbling block to those who are weak. For if anyone sees you who have knowledge eating in an idol's temple, will not the conscience of him who is weak be emboldened to eat those things offered to idols? And because of your knowledge shall the weak brother perish, for whom Christ died? But when you thus sin against the brethren, and wound their weak conscience, you sin against Christ. Therefore if food makes my brother stumble, I will never again eat meat, lest I make my brother stumble. (1 Corinthians 8:6–13 NKJV)

This text is in the midst of a discussion that Peter and Paul had concerning whether it was okay to eat certain meat. This was a great debate considering the Mosaic laws versus how Jesus's arrival changed many things in our relationship with God the Father. Specifically, this has nothing to do with drinking, drugging, and getting high. Application wise, however, one can see that Paul is pointing out here that we are our brother's keeper. We are held responsible when we lead others to behaviors and habits that their physical bodies may not be able to handle. Everyone should put this on and wear it when we see harm come to our brothers and sisters because of how we may behave.

This human body of flesh is a great gift. God enters our flesh when we are baptized and accept Him as our Lord and Savior. We should cherish His presence. "Do you not know that you are the temple of God and that the Spirit of God dwells in you?" (1 Corinthians 3:16 NKJV).

Therefore, Lord, I repent for drinking, drugging, and getting high. Help me to honor my temple, you are in charge, and I am yours. Lord, please forgive me, and help me to do better.

Chapter 35

I REPENT FOR NOT HONORING MARRIAGE

What is it that makes a marriage? Fairy tales would have us to believe that it takes two people passionately in love with each other. The two get married and live happily ever after. Common-law marriage in some states suggests that just living under the same roof for a while represents a marriage, even without a church ceremony or going to the justice of the peace. Then, there are marriages of convenience that may be political or business arrangements with or without any promise of intimacy or a lasting relationship. The original marriage was arranged by God. Adam and Eve were told to be fruitful and multiply. The marriage institution is important to humanity and should not be dismissed easily nor taken for granted.

The Original Marriage

> And Adam gave names to all cattle, and to the fowl of the air, and to every beast of the field; but for Adam there was not found an help meet for him. And the Lord God caused a deep sleep to fall upon Adam, and he slept: and he took one of his ribs, and closed up the flesh instead thereof; And the rib, which the Lord God had taken from man, made he a woman, and brought her unto the man. And Adam said, This is now bone of my bones, and flesh

of my flesh: she shall be called Woman, because she was taken out of Man. Therefore shall a man leave his father and his mother, and shall cleave unto his wife: and they shall be one flesh. (Genesis 2:20–24 KJV)

Jesus Speaks on Marriage and Divorce

The Pharisees also came unto him, tempting him, and saying unto him, Is it lawful for a man to put away his wife for every cause? And he answered and said unto them, Have ye not read, that he which made them at the beginning made them male and female, And said, For this cause shall a man leave father and mother, and shall cleave to his wife: and they twain shall be one flesh? Wherefore they are no more twain, but one flesh. What therefore God hath joined together, let not man put asunder. They say unto him, Why did Moses then command to give a writing of divorcement, and to put her away? He saith unto them, Moses because of the hardness of your hearts suffered you to put away your wives: but from the beginning it was not so. And I say unto you, Whosoever shall put away his wife, except it be for fornication, and shall marry another, committeth adultery: and whoso marrieth her which is put away doth commit adultery. (Matthew 19:3–9 KJV)

These two verses point out several things. First, marriage is between a male and a female. The two will become one flesh, meaning they grow into one flesh. We are made of body (flesh), soul, and spirit. When we join to become one flesh, our physical bodies join together in a way only God designed. The sexual union between a man and a woman is God's creation. In a marriage relationship, however, we do join in more ways than just our physical bodies.

"Two become one" is very important. Two souls become one soul, meaning that two imaginations become one imagination, two memories start to form one memory, two consciences become one conscience, two affections for things become one affection. This is a unifying of desires and experiences that bind two people together. This means two people share like goals and aspirations and form one strategy to get there.

Two spirits become one spirit, meaning that two individuals praising, worshipping, and giving reverence to God become one family unit praising, worshiping, and giving reverence to God. Two individual spirits with faith in God become one family unit having faith in God.

The "2" become "1"

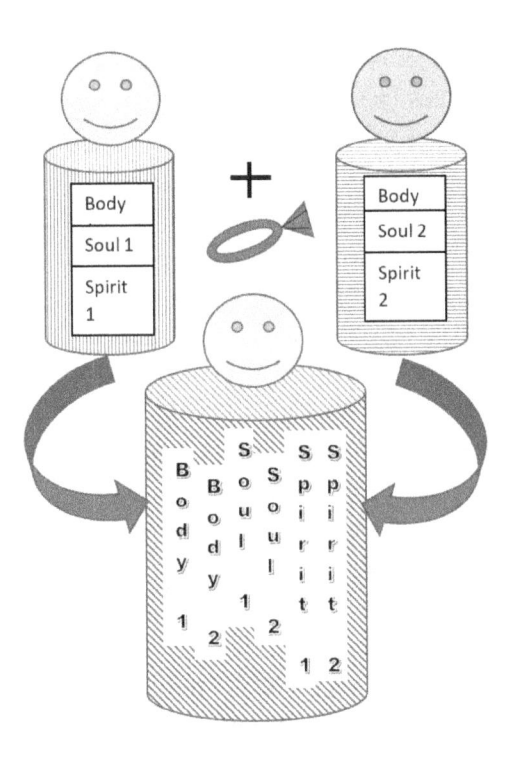

Furthermore, if two become one, two incomes should become one income. Money is one of the top reasons for arguments among couples. God keeps nothing from His bride, the church. Two twenty-four-hour days become one twenty-four-hour block of time that should be divided in a mutually agreeable fashion. It is no longer my time or your time; it is our time. If that is not true, then why get married in the first place? Two sets of friends should become one set of friends. The wife and her girlfriends have no more right to subtract from the new couple's time than the husband and his guys. Your old single friends may not be the best thing to make your new marriage last. The Bible says that two become one. It does not say two plus this or that someone can hang on to.

Second, in Matthew 19:5, shown earlier, Jesus also says, "and man shall leave his mother and father" to be married. The married couple becomes a separate new nucleus for the growth of our communities. That does not mean mother and father are forgotten. It does mean the new couple should have their own responsibilities, work, priorities, and goals. The new couple should be the first priority. Mother and father become secondary relative to the needs and priorities of the new couple. Going over to mother's house every evening may not be the best thing for a new marriage. Telling your mother and father everything about your new marriage is not required, should not be expected, and should not be done.

Why Two? Benefits of Long-Term Marriage

The Bible says that two are better than one. Perhaps God already knew (of course, He did) the struggles it takes to raise children by yourself. It can be done, but two committed parents can shoulder the burden easier.

> Two are better than one, because they have a good reward for their labor. For if they fall, one will lift up his companion. But woe to him who is alone when he falls, for he has no one to help him up. Again, if two lie down together, they will keep warm; but how can one be warm alone? Though one may be overpowered by another, two can withstand him. And a threefold cord is not quickly broken. (Ecclesiastes 4:9–12 NKJV)

A study highlighted in TIME magazine's cover story, "How to Stay Married,"[23] shows that married people have better health, including less likelihood to have things such as heart disease and strokes. Married couples are usually better off financially. It is believed married couples even have better sex lives. Satan's biggest win is to tear up a marriage. When he tears up a marriage, he gets our health, our finances, and our children. So, with the benefits of staying married, why are there so many divorces in our society?

Divorce

Sadly, many sources reveal that divorce statistics for Christian couples are only slightly better than those for nonbelievers. What is going wrong? Our culture today makes it easy to divorce. There is no longer a stigma to divorce. Divorce attorneys advertise best deals and moral support for quick and easy settlements. The attorneys make it sound like there are no long-term repercussions to divorce. They act like once the papers are signed, it is over. That is a big lie. Hurt feelings, missed opportunities, and lost dreams linger for a long time. The outcome of a divorce can last for a lifetime. That is true especially if children are involved. Do not buy into the idea that if I just get away, everything will be better.

Couples often don't reach out for help until they are about ready to walk out of the door on each other. Would you wait until a child has symptoms of starvation before you decided to feed him or her? Well, a new relationship or new marriage is like a new plant that needs a lot of extra water and nourishment to survive. The first five years are extremely critical as new behaviors are learned and new habits are formed. During the first years, you see things about your partner that were not readily evident, when the only time you saw them before was when they were all cleaned up and smelling good for a date. Now, four years later, both of you come home from a hard day at work and must comfort, feed, and entertain the children prior to having time for yourselves. Before you know it, rude talking, ignoring, hollering, door slamming, not smiling, cursing, and throwing things becomes normal. Bad habits are formed, and if they are not squelched, they will kill your relationship. Especially when friends are telling you: "I would not take that," "You need to leave him," or "She is not worth it." These comments come too often in our society instead of

"How about we get together and pray about it." Sometimes intimate details would have to be spoken to a counselor, so pride gets in the way of asking for help. This is what Jesus meant in the text mentioned earlier when He said Moses offered divorce, "because of the hardness of your heart."

Actually, whoever is the most mature Christian has the largest responsibility in a marriage. The most mature Christian should remember when Jesus was asked about forgiveness, He responded by saying a brother should be forgiven, "seventy times seven" (Matthew 18:22). How many times should a spouse be forgiven? A spouse that you fell in love with? A spouse that you said, "I do," to? A spouse that you stood before God and committed to? Think of how many times in the Old Testament God kept forgiving His beloved, chosen Israel.

Ultimately, It Is a Choice

Divorce is not an option; remember it yourself and tell a friend. One cannot choose convenience over commitment. One cannot choose the easy way out over established vows that have been taken. One cannot choose irreconcilable differences. Reconcile them. One cannot choose excuses. One cannot choose to let Satan win the battle and tear up your marriage and your children. Many studies show divorce impacts children in a very negative way. Jesus says in Matthew 19, mentioned earlier, that the only reason for divorce is sexual immorality.

What if your spouse walks away from the marriage and is not willing to try any longer? Even then, as hard as it may seem, the Bible suggests that a person remain married while separated. This is where long patience is required on the part of the most mature Christian.

> And unto the married I command, yet not I, but the Lord, Let not the wife depart from her husband: But and if she depart, let her remain unmarried or be reconciled to her husband: and let not the husband put away his wife. But to the rest speak I, not the Lord: If any brother hath a wife that believeth not, and she be pleased to dwell with him,

let him not put her away. And the woman which hath an husband that believeth not, and if he be pleased to dwell with her, let her not leave him. For the unbelieving husband is sanctified by the wife, and the unbelieving wife is sanctified by the husband: else were your children unclean; but now are they holy. But if the unbelieving depart, let him depart. A brother or a sister is not under bondage in such cases: but God hath called us to peace. For what knowest thou, O wife, whether thou shalt save thy husband? or how knowest thou, O man, whether thou shalt save thy wife? (1 Corinthians 7:10–16 KJV)

Think of how many marriages might get back together in our society if this hard command were followed. God intended for our love and sexual attraction to lead us back to our spouse, not to find someone else in the neighborhood. Amid anger and "I am going to leave her" or "I am going to leave him," God is interested in saving their souls. It is not about you and your hurt and pain. It is about saving their soul, saving the marriage, and notice, even the children are mentioned. What is your interpretation of this text?

Gary Chapman in his best-selling series of books, *The Five Love Languages*[24], mentions what happens after the honeymoon infatuation phase of a relationship is over, and the couple must move on to making real decisions in real time. Every day people have a choice about how to treat their spouse. Divorce should not be an option. Move forward from whatever your situation is today. Make this fourth marriage work, if you have already been divorced three times. Now is the time to get it right. The purpose of this book is not to explain all the nuances concerning staying married. That will take another book all by itself. However, marriage is a very important vow before God, even though to some, our American culture today has made it seem like just a farce that can be entered into and dissolved on a whim.

Therefore, Lord, I repent for my part in not honoring marriage. Lord, please forgive me, and help me to do better.

Chapter 36

I Repent for Not Honoring the Sabbath Day

Honoring the Sabbath is one of the well-known Ten Commandments. What does it mean? Why was it listed as one of the commandments? If it is still relevant, how did we get so far away from following the practice.

Defining Sabbath

In the Bible, as we approach chapter 16 in the book of Exodus, God had just led the Israelites out of Egypt. They learned the meaning of unleavened bread. They were led into the wilderness by a pillar of clouds by day and a pillar of fire by night. They were chased by Pharaoh and his army outside of the Egyptian city limits. And they had taken part in and witnessed the great parting of the Red Sea miracle (Exodus 13–15). Then, in chapter 16, the first time Sabbath is mentioned, God delivers manna to the people to eat. He tells them to gather an extra portion on the sixth day because the seventh day will be set aside as a rest day.

> And it came to pass, that on the sixth day they gathered twice as much bread, two omers for one man: and all the rulers of the congregation came and told Moses. And he said unto them, This is that which the LORD hath said, Tomorrow is the rest of the holy sabbath unto the LORD: bake that which ye will bake to day, and seethe that ye

> will seethe; and that which remaineth over lay up for you to be kept until the morning. And they laid it up till the morning, as Moses bade: and it did not stink, neither was there any worm therein. And Moses said, Eat that today; for today is a sabbath unto the Lord: today ye shall not find it in the field. Six days ye shall gather it; but on the seventh day, which is the sabbath, in it there shall be none. (Exodus 16:22–26 KJV)

The Hebrew word for Sabbath is *Shabbath*[25]. It means intermission. Everybody in the community and family were instructed to honor the Sabbath. No work was to be done. Animals and servants were included in the Sabbath.

> And the Lord spake unto Moses, saying, Speak thou also unto the children of Israel, saying, Verily my sabbaths ye shall keep: for it is a sign between me and you throughout your generations; that ye may know that I am the Lord that doth sanctify you. Ye shall keep the sabbath therefore; for it is holy unto you: every one that defileth it shall surely be put to death: for whosoever doeth any work therein, that soul shall be cut off from among his people. Six days may work be done; but in the seventh is the sabbath of rest, holy to the Lord: whosoever doeth any work in the sabbath day, he shall surely be put to death. Wherefore the children of Israel shall keep the sabbath, to observe the sabbath throughout their generations, for a perpetual covenant. It is a sign between me and the children of Israel for ever: for in six days the Lord made heaven and earth, and on the seventh day he rested, and was refreshed. (Exodus 31:12–17 KJV)

A Sabbath is a constant reminder of a covenant between God and man. This text plainly points out the seriousness God assigns of adhering to the Sabbath day.

In our culture, a bride or groom can always look at their ring finger on their left hand and be reminded of their marriage vows and marriage relationship, whether or not they are in the presence of their spouse. The ring is a sign to stay strong, stay faithful, and stay dedicated to the relationship. The Sabbath should work the same way. It was meant to be a perpetual sign. God designed it to be a constant reminder throughout the life of humankind's busy days that God is still relevant. God is still here. For six days, humankind motivates, strategizes, plans, works, and delivers everything they can to organize and arrange their life situation to be pleasing to them. Then on the seventh day, God had a plan. God's plan was for us to rest, be refreshed, and worship.

The Sabbath was not meant to be a regimented forced duty, but a willing act of love and respect. This is evident from Paul's writing in Colossians.

> Let no one judge you in food or in drink, or regarding a festival or a new moon or sabbaths, which are a shadow of things to come, but the substance is of Christ. Let no one cheat you of your reward, taking delight in false humility and worship of angels, intruding into those things which he has not seen, vainly puffed up by his fleshly mind.
>
> (Colossians 2:16–18 NKJV)

In this text it is clear that Sabbath is not meant to be a regiment wherein some can point the finger and say, you are in line, or you are out of line. It is meant to be a sign of a solemn relationship. It is just a "shadow" of how our relationship should be with Christ. A relationship wherein we want to think of Him, we want to be with Him, we want to worship Him, and we want to praise Him on a regular basis.

Jesus, in the New Testament, clarifies even more that the essence of having a Sabbath is more important than the strict regimen. Jesus points out in Matthew 12 that it is okay to pull corn, save a sheep, and heal on the Sabbath.

And the Pharisees said to Him, "Look, why do they do what is not lawful on the Sabbath?" But He said to them, "Have you never read what David did when he was in need and hungry, he and those with him: how he went into the house of God in the days of Abiathar the high priest, and ate the showbread, which is not lawful to eat except for the priests, and also gave some to those who were with him?" And He said to them, "The Sabbath was made for man, and not man for the Sabbath. Therefore the Son of Man is also Lord of the Sabbath." (Mark 2:24–28 NKJV)

Jesus did not say to forget the Sabbath. He did not say that the Sabbath is no longer important. He said, the Sabbath was made for man. Jesus demonstrated that healing could be done on the Sabbath. That demonstrates a priority that helps humanity but does not take away from our reverence of God because it is the power of God that creates the manifestation of the healing miracle. Jesus also demonstrated that if one is traveling and without food, it is okay to eat on the Sabbath. He and the disciples were hungry in a grain field, and they ate raw grain as they were passing through. No restaurant had to open. No chefs or waitresses had to be hired to work on the Sabbath. They simply ate.

In our everyday life, we make a big deal about births, graduations, weddings, birthdays, and anniversaries. They are times that we set aside for accomplishments and remembrances of things achieved or how far we have come. We celebrate milestones. God gave us six days to work and do what we call making a living. Six days to correspond with creation. Leviticus 23:1–3 says the Sabbath is supposed to be a "Holy Convocation" in honor of God Almighty. A day to worship God for the blessings allowed to come our way throughout the week. God is like any other spousal partner. We are the bride. He is the bridegroom. He is jealous, and He wants our attention, via praise and worship. He wants us to remember Him regularly.

There were different Sabbath observances. In Leviticus 25, God told Moses to instruct the people that when they get to Sinai that even the land should be given a Sabbath. The land was to be planted for six years and then left to itself on the seventh year. Also, there was a feast of trumpets, a day of atonement, and a feast of tabernacles, described in Leviticus 23, wherein certain days were set aside as Sabbath days. No work was to be done.

One of the Big Ten

So far, we have looked at God the Father's instructions saying obey the Sabbath or be put to death, Jesus the Son saying the Sabbath was made for man and not man for the Sabbath, and the book of Colossians saying we should not be judged by our adherence or lack thereof to Sabbaths. What are we to do?

> Do not think that I came to destroy the Law or the Prophets. I did not come to destroy but to fulfill. For assuredly, I say to you, till heaven and earth pass away, one jot or one tittle will by no means pass from the law till all is fulfilled. Whoever therefore breaks one of the least of these commandments, and teaches men so, shall be called least in the kingdom of heaven; but whoever does and teaches them, he shall be called great in the kingdom of heaven. (Matthew 5:17–19 NKJV)

Jesus told His disciples that He did not come to destroy the law but to fulfill it. While He was here, He was the Sabbath. While the bridegroom was here with us, and the disciples had a personal one-on-one relationship with the Son of God, they were able to experience Sabbath, every day. The Word was made flesh and dwelt among us.

The Bible covers the Ten Commandments that Moses brought down from Mount Sinai in Exodus 20:

1. No other gods before me.
2. Do not take the name of the Lord thy God in vain.
3. Make no graven images to worship.
4. Remember the Sabbath Day to keep it holy.

5. Honor they father and mother.
6. Thou shall not steal.
7. Thou shall not kill.
8. Thou shall not bear false witness (lie).
9. Thou shall not commit adultery.
10. Thou shall not covet.

We still believe God is omnipotent. We still believe we should honor and listen to our mother and father. We still believe we should not steal, kill, lie, or commit adultery. We still believe we should not covet. Why should people think remembering the Sabbath is no longer valid? There are over six hundred Mosaic and Levitical laws. The Sabbath was included as part of the Ten Commandments given directly from God.

How We Got Away

Not paying attention to the Sabbath did not start in America. In fact, the prophet Jeremiah continued to rebuke Israel for ignoring the Sabbath.

> Thus says the Lord: "Take heed to yourselves, and bear no burden on the Sabbath day, nor bring it in by the gates of Jerusalem; nor carry a burden out of your houses on the Sabbath day, as I commanded you fathers." But they did not obey nor incline their ear, but made their neck stiff, that they might not hear nor receive instruction. "And it shall be, if you heed Me carefully," says the Lord, "to bring no burden through the gates of this city on the Sabbath day, but hallow the Sabbath day, to do no work in it, then shall enter the gates of this city kings and princes sitting on the throne of David, riding in chariots and on horses, they and their princes, accompanied by the men of Judah and the inhabitants of Jerusalem; and this city shall remain forever. And they shall come from the cities of Judah and from the places around Jerusalem, from the land of Benjamin and from the lowland, from the mountains and from the South, bringing burnt offerings and sacrifices,

grain offerings and incense, bringing sacrifices of praise to the house of the Lord. But if you will not heed Me to hallow the Sabbath day, such as not carrying a burden when entering the gates of Jerusalem on the Sabbath day, then I will kindle a fire in its gates, and it shall devour the palaces of Jerusalem, and it shall not be quenched." (Jeremiah 17:21–27 NKJV)

All through history, humankind has done their part to decide what is important and what is not. In America, "Sunday Blue Laws" were in place in many states and localities in recognition of a traditional Sabbath day. Things such as no retail, no hunting, and no sale of alcohol were common. Some states still have a portion of these laws in place. However, the influence of Christianity has become less prevalent in our American culture.

What It Has Done to Us

Signs of the American cultural transition from the influence of Christianity are things like the removal of prayer in schools, the removal of nativity scenes on government property, and the removal of the Ten Commandments placed in courthouses. All are deemed unconstitutional by the Supreme Court yet at one time they were commonplace across the country. In time we have become a more secular society. In the Bible, the length of the Babylonian captivity is reflected as punishment for ignoring the Sabbath.

> Then they burned the house of God, broke down the wall of Jerusalem, burned all its palaces with fire, and destroyed all its precious possessions. And those who escaped from the sword he carried away to Babylon, where they became servants to him and his sons until the rule of the kingdom of Persia, to fulfill the word of the Lord by the mouth of Jeremiah, until the land had enjoyed her Sabbaths. As long as she lay desolate, she kept Sabbath, to fulfill seventy years. (2 Chronicles 36:19–21 NKJV)

Backtrack to 1930 when the prevalence of a TV in every household was not even a dream. Almost all stores were closed. The dominance of pastimes such as the National Football League, major league baseball, the National Basketball Association, the National Hockey League, or the Professional Golfers Association was nonexistent. Many Americans went to church on Sunday if for no other reason than there was nothing else to do. Families had time for "family time." Businesses were primarily closed on Sunday in America.

Now fast-forward to the twenty-first century. In a recent movie that involved sports being played on Sunday, there was an argument about the impact of changes that may be coming. In the argument, one party was trying to persuade the other to leave things alone, mainly because so much money was involved. Whereas Sunday used to be designated by many Americans as church day or family day, a comment was made during this argument implying that Sunday now belonged to the sports world. The shock of his statement hit me like a ton of bricks. In so many ways, for so many people, his statement was true. A day that had been set aside for resting, praising, and worshiping God has now been taken over by professional sports, 250 TV channels, movie theaters, open businesses, and shopping malls.

In Jesus's parable of the sower, in Matthew 13, He talks about some seed that is planted among thorns. The cares of this world become so intense that they drown out our ability to reflect on and do the will of God. That is what our society has lost for not honoring God's Sabbath day. It hurts us as individuals, as families, and as communities. Our culture would be a lot less stressed if the Sabbath was still honored.

Therefore, Lord, I repent for not honoring your Sabbath day. Lord, please forgive me, and help me to do better.

Chapter 37

I Repent for Wanting to Be Rich and Famous at All Cost

It is not a sin to be rich. King David was what we would call very rich today. King Solomon was also very rich. It is not a sin to be famous. Sarah, Moses, Jeremiah, and Esther were all famous people whose lives are recorded in the Bible. Jesus Christ Himself was famous during the time He lived on this earth. The issue here is why a person wants to be rich and famous in the first place and how they choose to get there. Some are willing to do anything for fame and fortune.

What Is the Allure for Fame and Fortune?

Why do we yearn for this status? To some, rich and famous may mean doing whatever you want to do. Unfortunately, this often proves to be a fantasy because there are degrees of wealth and fame. A person that has a million dollars wants to have two million. A person that has five million dollars wants to have ten million. A person that has fifty million dollars wants to be a billionaire. The toys that go along with each level continue to make what most people would call rich be unhappy. A person that drives a Lincoln wants to drive a Lamborghini. A person that drives a new Lexus wants to drive a new Mercedes. A person that lives in a nice two-story Cape Cod will want a two-story Normandy or Prairie style home. A person with a Normandy will be wishing for a ten-bedroom, eight bath mansion.

> All things are full of labor; man cannot express it. The eye is not satisfied with seeing, nor the ear filled with hearing. That which has been is what will be, that which is done is what will be done, and there is nothing new under the sun. (Ecclesiastes 1:8–9 NKJV)

Having fame and fortune does not mean a person will be satisfied. It seems we can never have enough. Even rich people find themselves not satisfied with what they have.

Another fame and fortune myth is that rich people have no problems. What a joke. This would make sense if one could look at actuarial tables based on wealth and see a correlation. This may be true for very poor people who cannot afford medical treatment. However, once a threshold is reached, rich people die just like poor people. Rich and famous people have health issues just like poor people. The rich and famous take medicine just like everyone else. The rich and famous have water leaks, children that misbehave, marital problems, divorces, and family issues, just like everyone else.

> Because you say, "I am rich, have become wealthy, and have need of nothing," and do not know that you are wretched, miserable, poor, blind, and naked. I counsel you to buy from Me gold refined in the fire, that you may be rich; and white garments, that you may be clothed, that the shame of your nakedness may not be revealed; and anoint your eyes with eye salve, that you may see. (Revelation 3:17–18 NKJV)

This verse makes it plain that rich people do in fact need one thing that everybody else needs. Rich and famous people still need God. So, being honest, being rich and famous may not increase people's life expectancy or get rid of all their problems, but it will allow them to have a jet-set lifestyle, allow them to meet other famous people, and buy many things. One could go to Paris for lunch, take a safari in Australia the next evening and, assuming they could handle the jet lag, be able to have a golf tee time in America this coming weekend. To that I would say, we all need to be mindful of what we do with the days God the Father has blessed us with. Jesus explained it this way.

> And he spake a parable unto them, saying, The ground of a certain rich man brought forth plentifully: And he thought within himself, saying, What shall I do, because I have no room where to bestow my fruits? And he said, This will I do: I will pull down my barns, and build greater; and there will I bestow all my fruits and my goods. And I will say to my soul, Soul, thou hast much goods laid up for many years; take thine ease, eat, drink, and be merry. But God said unto him, Thou fool, this night thy soul shall be required of thee: then whose shall those things be, which thou hast provided? So is he that layeth up treasure for himself, and is not rich toward God. (Luke 12:16–21 KJV)

In this text, God makes a very clear statement about selfishness. The purpose of a person's life must be greater than fame and fortune. Humankind was not put here to just accumulate selfishly. A person should find ways to serve God and God's people if he or she is blessed to achieve abundance. For those that believe in the resurrection of Jesus Christ, it would be a shame to be rich and famous now and not receive greater rewards upon our resurrection. There is more to life than just having a good time and partying. The Ecclesiastical writer is admonishing us about the purpose of our desire for fame and fortune.

> I said in my heart, "Come now, I will test you with mirth; therefore, enjoy pleasure"; but surely, this also was vanity. I said of laughter—"Madness!"; and of mirth, "What does it accomplish?" (Ecclesiastes 2:1–2 NKJV)

> Better is a handful with quietness than both hands full, together with toil and grasping for the wind. Then I returned, and I saw vanity under the sun. There is one

> alone, without companion: he has neither son nor brother. Yet there is no end to all his labors, nor is his eye satisfied with riches. But he never asks, "For whom do I toil and deprive myself of good?" This also is vanity and a grave misfortune. (Ecclesiastes 4:6–8 NKJV)

Here it is evident that accumulation will not bring us satisfaction. One must look for something larger to do with one's life because just accumulating will leave us empty. What should we do if we won the lottery today? What would we buy? How long would it be before we came up for air? How long would it be before we thought about our blessing considering someone else's need? The lottery is one way that some have gained fame and riches, but there are many other ways.

How Wealth and Fame Are Gained

It is amazing how some people will sell out on their morals for fame and fortune. Since this book is targeting those that want to be better Christians, let's start with some people who got their start singing in the church. Singers that start off in church singing gospel. They start off singing about the goodness of God and the power of God. They end up singing about sex, going to bed with whomever is close by, or some form of idolatry. Then we, who call ourselves Christians, smile, buy their recordings, and idolize them because they became rich and famous.

What would Jesus do (WWJD)? Would He condone making the fast money any way you can at the expense of the lives being impacted by the message being shared in the music? How can we enjoy, promote, and sustain morally wrong, unrighteous messages if we are supposed to love our fellow man or woman? Do we only care about using them to get rich like the drug dealer that does not care about his customers? The Bible says, "Therefore, whatever you want me to do to you, do also to them, for this is the Law and the Prophets" (Matthew 7:12). Don't get me wrong; many times good, uplifting, positive, encouraging songs are thrown in the mix with the "I am going to do my own thing" songs. How does one go from the nightclub to the church in just a few hours? The Holy Spirit does not condone everything going on in the nightclub. The truth is that a decision has been made to ignore what the Holy Spirit is saying internally so that fame and fortune can be had. The blessed voice gravitates to secular music because that leads to larger paychecks.

Many people make their living by acting. (Never mind Exodus 20:1–5, which talks about not making images of anything to be worshipped. This text was talking about other gods, but in reality, in our culture, there are many that worship actors and actresses because of how they are portrayed). The question for many of today's actors and actresses is, "Why do I have to see your nakedness for you to be a good actor?" If you are such a good actor or actress, "Why do I have to see your nakedness to appreciate your talent?" Is your acting ability that bad? Exactly what are you selling: soft porn or good acting? Should a person do whatever is necessary to grab attention, disregarding all Christian values, to become rich and famous? Many of our actors and actresses deserve the title of soft porn stars.

Perhaps someone has a job working in a corporate environment and feels untouched by the world of singers and porn stars. Well, what do corporations do to make people from the CEO to the assembly line worker rich and famous? Unfortunately, too often we have heard of unscrupulous stock manipulations, cooking the books, and Ponzi schemes. For the sake of being rich and famous, executive board members and those white-collar workers in management, high enough to be in the know, may do things that are designed to add to their own pockets even though it is horrendously devastating to the average worker and investor. Illegitimate annual report numbers like those used by Enron took the life savings of many people and left them devastated, all attempting to get rich quick. Unethical practices were in place. Somebody that knew about Christ should have spoken up and stopped this behavior.

Historically, several companies have demonstrated unrighteous behavior. Truthfully, it is not an unfeeling company but unrighteous, covetous people at the top that oversee these sinful deeds. Drug companies of any size, including (Purdue Pharma) which offered a $10 billion to $12 billion settlement for their part in the opioid epidemic are an example.

Bernie Madoff and Enron are other examples. Cigarette companies that hid scientific evidence that cigarettes were addictive and deadly for years before the public forced them to come clean. Until these companies were caught, it was all about the almighty dollar. It amounts to people using and murdering other people so they can drive fancy cars, take luxury vacations, and reside in fancy houses. That is getting rich at any cost.

Illegal drug dealers flash the fast money they are able to make and then justify their dealing by saying, "They came to buy it." Well, if an eight-year-old child came to buy a torch to set the house on fire, would you sell it to them and proclaim your innocence? The same detriment is present when you sell a drug to a child who is not old enough to understand the repercussions of what you are putting in his or her hands. What happens to a girl in junior high school when you turn her into a drug addict? What is the drug dealer setting her up for? Their easy money is killing people and communities.

This is not a complete list of sinful, evil ways people justify to get rich. Child traffickers belong on this list. Fly-by-night companies that take advantage of the poor and uneducated belong on this list. Companies that price gouge during a natural disaster belong on this list. Anytime human beings are taking excessive advantage of human beings to get rich, it is a sin.

> Now godliness with contentment is great gain. For we brought nothing into this world, and it is certain we can carry nothing out. And having food and clothing, with these we shall be content. But those who desire to be rich fall into temptation and a snare, and into many foolish and harmful lusts which drown men in destructions and perdition. For the love of money is a root of all kinds of evil, for which some have strayed from the faith in their greediness, and pierced themselves through with many sorrows. (1 Timothy 6:6–10 NKJV)

People do all kinds of evil things to gain fame and fortune. This text says just having the desire to be rich for the sake of being rich can get a person into a lot of arenas that are not good for their relationship with God. When the money and fame have you, instead of you having the money, a person may face choosing between fame and fortune or God.

> And, behold, one came and said unto him, Good Master, what good thing shall I do, that I may have eternal life? And he said unto him, Why callest thou me good? there is none good but one, that is, God: but if thou wilt enter into life, keep the commandments. He saith unto him, Which? Jesus said, Thou shalt do no murder, Thou shalt not commit adultery, Thou shalt not steal, Thou shalt not bear false witness, Honour thy father and thy mother: and, Thou shalt love thy neighbour as thyself. The young man saith unto him, All these things have I kept from my youth up: what lack I yet? Jesus said unto him, If thou wilt be perfect, go and sell that thou hast, and give to the poor, and thou shalt have treasure in heaven: and come and follow me. But when the young man heard that saying, he went away sorrowful: for he had great possessions. (Matthew 19:16–22 KJV)

This young man had lost control of his possessions. His possessions had him. His possessions had him willing to turn his back on Jesus. His possessions had him willing to turn his back on eternity. His possessions had him willing to turn his back on Almighty God. Everyone is not asked to sell all they have, but this man was because Jesus knew his heart.

Jesus knew that the pride this man had in his possessions was his stumbling block. Being rich and famous is not a sin. However, how a person achieves it and how a person carries it can be a sin.

> By pride comes nothing but strife, but with the well advised is wisdom. Wealth gained by dishonesty will be

diminished, but he who gathers by labor will increase. (Proverbs 13:10–11 NKJV)

Riches and Fame Can Come Easily

Patience, doing things God's way, and hard work can make a person wealthy. It may be overnight, or it may not be overnight, but it can happen.

> Whatever your hand finds to do, do it with your might; for there is no work or device or knowledge or wisdom in the grave where you are going. I returned and saw under the sun that the race is not to the swift, nor the battle to the strong, nor bread to the wise, nor riches to men of understanding, nor favor to men of skill; but time and chance happen to them all. (Ecclesiastes 9:10–11 NKJV)

Time holding on to a stock investment or the chance of winning the lottery can make us wealthy. It is a blessing from God. The riches and fame that a person achieves should be enjoyed if it is not to the detriment of others. Do not ever forget that in the middle of your fame or just when you have a million-dollar idea, God can allow it to continue to come to fruition or not. "The Lord makes poor and makes rich; He brings low and lifts up" (1 Samuel 2:7 NKJV).

Therefore, Lord, I repent for wanting to be rich and famous at all cost. Lord, please forgive me, and help me to do better.

Chapter 38

I REPENT FOR NOT GIVING LIKE I SHOULD

Oh my goodness. Every pastor's nightmare—the need to ask for money. They say, "Do I really have to ask for money?" Good, honest pastors feel guilty because even though they know they desperately need the money, they also know it causes distress to the congregation. People say, "Dishonest, unscrupulous pastors cannot seem to get enough." People in the pews are thinking, *He's just after money!* Widows are giving their last dime. Wealthy people are giving one half of 1 percent. Children give the same dollar until they graduate from high school. What if I love the Lord with all my heart, but I am homeless and do not have a dime to give? The trustees keep saying everybody must give fifty dollars for homecoming. I do not have it. Can I give my service? What a dilemma. What is really important about giving? What is it that keeps us from giving? Are there different ways to give?

Cheerful Giver

Giving can bring out the best in us and the worst in us because it reveals the heart in us. I once had a business associate that always bragged about how much money he gave to charity. We both had vending businesses, and he would frequently tell me that he gave a lot to charity as a tax write-off. Time passed, and this associate decided he wanted to sell his business. I was a potential buyer, so he shared his financial details with me. To my surprise, this man who had always bragged about his charitable giving, gave less than three hundred dollars a year to charity. He made around one hundred thousand dollars a year. When it comes to giving, that was the lesson that taught me that giving is in the eye of the beholder. The perception of the "value" of your giving is personal. It is always between you and God.

> Now Jesus sat opposite the treasury and saw how the people put money into the treasury, and many who were rich put in much. Then one poor widow came and threw in two mites, which make a quadrans. So He called His disciples to Himself and said to them, "Assuredly, I say to you that this poor widow has put in more than all those who have given to the treasury; for they all put in out of their abundance, but she out of her poverty put in all that she had, her whole livelihood." (Mark 12:41–44 NKJV)

It is clear here that money given can be looked at from several vantage points: (a) why it is given, (b) the actual amount given, and (c) the sacrifice of the giver to give it. Earlier in chapter 12 of the book of Mark, Jesus is admonishing the scribes for doing things for show. Giving to be seen is not pleasing to God. In some congregations, what people give is still reported, so the big givers can feel important. God is not interested in individual accolades.

> Take heed that ye do not your alms before men, to be seen of them: otherwise ye have no reward of your Father which is in heaven. Therefore when thou doest thine alms, do not sound a trumpet before thee, as the hypocrites do in the synagogues and in the streets, that they may have glory of men. Verily I say unto you, They have their reward. But when thou doest alms, let not thy left hand know what thy right hand doeth: That thine alms may be in secret: and thy Father which seeth in secret himself shall reward thee openly. (Matthew 6:1–4 KJV)

The amount given and the sacrifice it represents to the giver should not be disregarded in either case. If someone can give one million dollars to support the cause of Christ and they give it in the right spirit, then they are doing good, and God will recognize it. If someone gives just five dollars, and they have to miss a lunch next week because that is all the money they have, then they are doing good, and God sees it, God knows their heart, and He will reward it. All God wants is for us to give cheerfully (2 Corinthians 9:7) because we understand His purpose and support His cause. Give what you can, and you will be blessed. When it comes to money, attitude is more important than the amount. Jesus also points this same lesson out in His parable about a tither.

> And he spake this parable unto certain which trusted in themselves that they were righteous, and despised others: Two men went up into the temple to pray; the one a Pharisee, and the other a publican. The Pharisee stood and prayed thus with himself, God, I thank thee, that I am not as other men are, extortioners, unjust, adulterers, or even as this publican. I fast twice in the week, I give tithes of all that I possess. And the publican, standing afar off, would not lift up so much as his eyes unto heaven, but smote upon his breast, saying, God be merciful to me a sinner. I tell you, this man went down to his house justified rather than the other: for every one that exalteth himself shall be abased; and he that humbleth himself shall be exalted. (Luke 18:9–14 KJV)

What's Holding Us Back

> And Moses called Bezaleel and Aholiab, and every wise hearted man, in whose heart the LORD had put wisdom, even every one whose heart stirred him up to come unto the work to do it: And they received of Moses all the offering, which the children of Israel had brought for the work of the service of the sanctuary, to make it withal. And

they brought yet unto him free offerings every morning. And all the wise men, that wrought all the work of the sanctuary, came every man from his work which they made; And they spake unto Moses, saying, The people bring much more than enough for the service of the work, which the LORD commanded to make. And Moses gave commandment, and they caused it to be proclaimed throughout the camp, saying, Let neither man nor woman make any more work for the offering of the sanctuary. So the people were restrained from bringing. For the stuff they had was sufficient for all the work to make it, and too much. (Exodus 36:2–7 KJV)

Moses had led the Hebrews out of Egypt with the strong hand and stretched-out arm of God. Now, it was time to build the tabernacle. In this text the people gave enthusiastically. They gave and kept on giving. They were supporting the cause of the ministry. All ministry leaders would love to have such enthusiastic support. Sometimes people have the money to give, but they hesitate. There are various reasons some may hesitate.

A. The most pronounced reason people do not give is because they either do not believe or they do not trust God's ability to multiply the funds as He did in the Bible. Perhaps some people are still trying God out, or perhaps they are visiting the service just because their girlfriend goes to the church even though they are really not sold on Christ. Generally, people who do not believe in something will not support it. The real question is why give the change in your pocket or a dollar or five dollars. Be a truthful person.

B. Many that do not believe in the accuracy of the scripture believe that the 10 percent tithe is too much. The Bible calls for us to give 10 percent. Tithing is referenced in the Bible from Genesis to Hebrews. In the Exodus 36 text mentioned earlier, the people were giving a freewill offering. The Bible teaches both types of giving. Someone will have to take it up with God if they think it is too much.

C. Many may believe the people in charge of the ministry are a motley crew. The people in charge may seem shady, dishonest, or untrustworthy. This is not the givers' concern. God will handle the misuse of funds. We need to do our part.

> And he said unto them in his doctrine, beware of the scribes, which love to go in long clothing, and love salutations in the marketplaces, And the chief seats in the synagogues, and the uppermost rooms at feasts: Which devour widows' houses, and for a pretense make long prayers: these shall receive greater damnation. (Mark 12:38–40 NKJV)

D. There are many options for our giving. The United Way, Salvation Army, Saint Jude Children's Hospital, the Children's Miracle Network, and the Red Cross all are good charities. Good causes like the American Cancer Society, UNICEF, Habitat for Humanity, and your local hometown charities are all worthwhile. Many people may give to a cause instead of a Christian congregation. However, the Bible instructs us to bring our tithes into the storehouse.

> "Will a man rob God? Yet you have robbed Me! But you say, 'In what way have we robbed You?' In tithes and offerings. You are cursed with a curse, for you have robbed Me, even this whole nation. Bring all the tithes in to the storehouse, that there may be food in My house, and try Me now in this," says the Lord of hosts. "If I will not open for you the windows of heaven and pour out for you such blessing there will not be room enough to receive it." (Malachi 3:8–10 NKJV)

Giving is not an option. God commands His people to be givers. He tells His people where to pay their tithes. God says to try Him. That makes giving an act of faith. God always has a plan. There are benefits that most Christians cannot imagine if we all did our giving God's way.

Benefits of Trusting God and Doing It His Way

Small Congregation Tithing Example	
Congregation 40 members 30 adults 10 underage youth	30 adults
Individual income for 30 adults $2,000 / month	$2,000
Tithe amount per adult	$200
Total house of worship monthly income from tithers (30 x $200)	$6,000
Total house of worship annual income from tithers	$72,000

Larger Congregation Tithing Example	
Congregation 1,000 members 750 adults 250 underage youth	750 adults
Individual income for 750 adults $2,000 / month	$2,000
Tithe amount per adult	$200
Total house of worship monthly income from tithers	$150,000
Total house of worship annual income from tithers	$1,800,000

In the small congregation example, suppose a church has forty members, ten youth, (baby, toddler, or school-age children) and thirty working adults. Then, suppose each of the thirty working adults brings home just $2,000 per month ($24,000 per year). Of course, some will make less, but I believe they will be offset by several that make much more. Now, suppose all thirty of the working adults were tithers. Thirty adults x $200 per month x 12 months, (30 x $200 x 12 = $72,000 per year income for the church. This is a very conservative estimate. In most cases, the income is higher, and the percentage of working adults is higher than we have used in this example.

It is awesome to imagine all that could be done if those that say they love the Lord put their money where their mouth is and trust God. Each giver has an individual relationship with God, and God is keeping tabs on your faith in Him, individually.

> Honor the Lord with your possessions, and with the first fruits of all your increase; so your barns will be filled with plenty, and your vats will overflow with new wine. (Proverbs 3:9–10 NKJV)

Many of us have decided our own best way to handle giving, like other chapters in this book. And as with other chapters, many of us should repent. Something happens to us when money gets involved. Yes, discernment is wise, and it is listed as a gift from God in Ephesians 4. We can discern if a ministry is doing the will of God. However, God's Word does not allow us to choose to complain and restrain our giving as if we are withholding a ransom. Giving is good for the giver, the receiving Christian ministry, and the community surrounding the ministry.

Therefore, I repent for sometimes not giving as I should. Lord, please forgive me, and help me to do better.

Chapter 39

I REPENT FOR NOT FORGIVING PROPERLY

Forgiveness is very tricky. If you ask a person about people who are still holding grudges against them, they will quickly say that some people cannot put things behind them and let bygones be bygones. They not only want to be forgiven, but will make comments inferring that they deserve to be forgiven. However, if you ask that same person about ways or instances when somebody did them wrong, then the forgiveness they should hand out, it takes on a more self-righteous tone. "Do they deserve it? "Have they apologized?" "How long has it been?" "How many times have they done me wrong?" "I will never forget it." The attitude changes. In other words, many people's definition of forgiveness depends on whether they are the receiver or giver of the forgiveness. This should not be the case. The Bible is very clear about forgiveness. There are several great examples we can learn from.

Neutrality and Our Relationship with God

> And forgive us our debts, as we forgive our debtors. And do not lead us into temptation, but deliver us from the evil one. For Yours is the kingdom and the power and the glory forever, Amen. For if you forgive men their trespasses, your heavenly Father will also forgive you. But

> if you do not forgive men their trespasses, neither will your
> Father forgive your trespasses. (Matthew 6:12–15 NKJV)

In this model prayer, we are instructed to ask to be forgiven as we forgive others. In other words, we are counting on being a good forgiver, to receive good forgiveness. That puts the burden of the forgiveness you receive on you. It is based on the forgiveness you give to others. He does not say, forgive "as" they forgive you. That would put the burden on others. So, if a person wants to be forgiven without someone asking, if they deserve it, then that is the same way that person should forgive someone who does him or her wrong. Also, if a person wants to be forgiven without someone asking, how long has it been, then, that is the same way that person should forgive someone who does him or her wrong. If a person wants to be readily forgiven with no questions asked, then that is the way they should forgive. Our belief about forgiving should be neutral; whether we are receiving or giving, it should be handled the same way.

God also points out in this model prayer that a person's willingness to forgive will affect his or her relationship with Him. God created the person who does you wrong, just like He created you. Therefore, the person who does you wrong deserves to stand before God and be forgiven just like you do. We have all done wrong and made mistakes. The word here is saying plainly that a person will not be forgiven by God if he or she holds grudges and refuses to forgive others. Forgiveness is between you and God, just as much as it is between you and the person that wronged you. Jesus tells a parable about this in Matthew 18:23–35.

Forgiveness should also not be limited to times per day, times per month or times per lifetime. Our responsibility as mature Christians is to keep on forgiving. We are called to be long-suffering. We are called to be patient as Christians. If you get tired of forgiving someone after five times, suppose God had only given you five times to get it right. In fact, our spiritual maturity is and can be measured by our ability to forgive.

> Then Peter came to Him and said, "Lord, how often shall
> my brother sin against me, and I forgive him? Up to seven

times?" Jesus said to him, "I do not say to you, up to seven times, but up to seventy times seven." (Matthew 18:21–22 NKJV)

Forgiveness should come quickly when requested. Parents of young children are usually great at this. Young children make a lot of mistakes. Suppose a parent kept a list of all the mistakes a child makes between three years old and ten years old. Most often, loving parents do not keep this kind of list. Usually, one, "I'm sorry, Mommy." wipes the slate clean, and the parent-child relationship is restored. A person should not be put on hold when they ask for forgiveness.

Consider Jacob and Esau

A rift is made

> And when Esau heard the words of his father, he cried with a great and exceeding bitter cry, and said unto his father, Bless me, even me also, O my father. And he said, Thy brother came with subtilty, and hath taken away thy blessing. And he said, Is not he rightly named Jacob? for he hath supplanted me these two times: he took away my birthright; and, behold, now he hath taken away my blessing. And he said, Hast thou not reserved a blessing for me? And Isaac answered and said unto Esau, Behold, I have made him thy lord, and all his brethren have I given to him for servants; and with corn and wine have I sustained him: and what shall I do now unto thee, my son? And Esau said unto his father, Hast thou but one blessing, my father? bless me, even me also, O my father. And Esau lifted up his voice, and wept. And Isaac his father answered and said unto him, Behold, thy dwelling shall be the fatness of the earth, and of the dew of heaven from above; And by thy sword shalt thou live, and shalt serve thy brother; and it shall come to pass when thou shalt have the dominion, that thou shalt break his yoke from

off thy neck. And Esau hated Jacob because of the blessing wherewith his father blessed him: and Esau said in his heart, The days of mourning for my father are at hand; then will I slay my brother Jacob. (Genesis 27:34–41 KJV)

Twenty years later, pending meeting.

Then the messengers returned to Jacob, saying, "We came to your brother Esau, and he also is coming to meet you, and four hundred men are with him." So Jacob was greatly afraid and distressed; and he divided the people that were with him, and the flocks and herds and camels, into two companies. (Genesis 32:6–7 NKJV)

Jacob and Esau meet.

And he passed over before them, and bowed himself to the ground seven times, until he came near to his brother. And Esau ran to meet him, and embraced him, and fell on his neck, and kissed him: and they wept. And he lifted up his eyes, and saw the women and the children; and said, Who are those with thee? And he said, The children which God hath graciously given thy servant. Then the handmaidens came near, they and their children, and they bowed themselves. And Leah also with her children came near, and bowed themselves: and after came Joseph near and Rachel, and they bowed themselves. And he said, What meanest thou by all this drove which I met? And he said, These are to find grace in the sight of my lord. And Esau said, I have enough, my brother; keep that thou hast unto thyself. (Genesis 33:3–9 KJV)

The Jacob and Esau story in the Bible shows us a few clear things about forgiveness. First, it shows us that "time" is a true asset when someone has wronged another. Rebecca, (Jacob and Esau's mother), tells Jacob to leave home until his brother's hatred goes away. In time, God has blessed both brothers, and there is no need for the anger to persist. Sometimes, it may be best to distance ourselves for forgiveness to take place. Second, this text demonstrates to us that even time does not erase the memory of the wrong. An apology is still necessary. Forgiveness must still be given. It is not rational to believe that even though twenty years may have passed the relationship can be renewed without still addressing the wrong that occurred. Jacob openly demonstrates his desire to make amends as Esau approaches. He does not expect to meet Esau and act like nothing ever happened. Jacob shows us that when it comes to receiving forgiveness, a person should have a very repentant attitude. Jacob approaches his twenty year later meeting with Esau by bringing gifts and bowing before his brother whom he had done wrong. Esau, on the other hand, appears already prepared to forgive. An appropriate attitude by both parties makes forgiveness easier.

Consider Jesus and Peter

Peter denies his friend.

> Now Peter sat without in the palace: and a damsel came unto him, saying, Thou also wast with Jesus of Galilee. But he denied before them all, saying, I know not what thou sayest. And when he was gone out into the porch, another maid saw him, and said unto them that were there, This fellow was also with Jesus of Nazareth. And again he denied with an oath, I do not know the man. And after a while came unto him they that stood by, and said to Peter, Surely thou also art one of them; for thy speech betrayeth thee. Then began he to curse and to swear, saying, I know not the man. And immediately the cock crew. And Peter remembered the word of Jesus, which said unto him, Before the cock crow, thou shalt deny me thrice. And he went out, and wept bitterly. (Matthew 26:69–75 KJV)

God uses an angel to invite Peter back after the crucifixion.

> And entering the tomb, they saw a young man clothed in a long white robe sitting on the right side; and they were alarmed. But he said to them, "Do not be alarmed. You seek Jesus of Nazareth, who was crucified. He is risen! He is not here. See the place where they laid Him. But go, tell His disciples, and Peter that He is going before you into Galilee; there you will see Him, as He said to you." (Mark 16:5–7 NKJV)

Moving on, a conversation between Peter and Jesus.

> This is now the third time that Jesus shewed himself to his disciples, after that he was risen from the dead. So when they had dined, Jesus saith to Simon Peter, Simon, son of Jonas, lovest thou me more than these? He saith unto him, Yea, Lord; thou knowest that I love thee. He saith unto him, Feed my lambs. (John 21:14–15 KJV)

In the gospels, Jesus demonstrates the ultimate example of forgiveness. He does not even mention Peter's denial. Peter is welcomed back into his discipleship leadership position and has an opportunity to reaffirm his love for Jesus. Jesus, being the son of God, knows that all humanity sins and makes mistakes, so He does not dwell on Peter's denial as something abnormal. How often do some people blow a mistake or sin out of proportion and act like it is the worst thing that has ever been done in all human history? A person with a forgiving heart will have to be able to keep things in perspective. The old saying that "action speaks louder than words" is very true when it comes to forgiving. This is difficult to do. However, if someone has done you wrong, invite that person back into your life, like Jesus did for Peter.

Jesus and Peter's relationship also points out to us that love and purpose are more important than a sinful mistake. What Peter did to Jesus was horrible. Peter abandoned Him at His most crushing time of need. Everyone would have expected Peter to continue the brash, loyal attitude he demonstrated in the Garden of Gethsemane when he cut off the soldier's ear (Matthew

26:51–52). Peter, however, was just like us. Sometimes we stand up for God and do the right thing, and sometimes we do not. Jesus's forgiveness demonstrates that the love between Him and Peter is more important than Peter's sin. Jesus's forgiveness demonstrates that the purpose for Peter's life was not finished, and it was more important than Peter's sin. It is not a good thing when we let sin, of any magnitude, stop God's purpose.

Consider Stephen and His Stoners

> Ye stiffnecked and uncircumcised in heart and ears, ye do always resist the Holy Ghost: as your fathers did, so do ye. Which of the prophets have not your fathers persecuted? and they have slain them which shewed before of the coming of the Just One; of whom ye have been now the betrayers and murderers: Who have received the law by the disposition of angels, and have not kept it. When they heard these things, they were cut to the heart, and they gnashed on him with their teeth. But he, being full of the Holy Ghost, looked up stedfastly into heaven, and saw the glory of God, and Jesus standing on the right hand of God, And said, Behold, I see the heavens opened, and the Son of man standing on the right hand of God. Then they cried out with a loud voice, and stopped their ears, and ran upon him with one accord, And cast him out of the city, and stoned him: and the witnesses laid down their clothes at a young man's feet, whose name was Saul. And they stoned Stephen, calling upon God, and saying, Lord Jesus, receive my spirit. And he kneeled down, and cried with a loud voice, Lord, lay not this sin to their charge. And when he had said this, he fell asleep. (Acts 7:51–60 KJV)

A mature Christian is prepared to live and die for Christ. Stephen's death is chronicled in our Bible just as Jesus's death is. In both cases the person being killed does not resist. Some would say they expect that from Jesus because He was the Son of God. However, Stephen was just a mere mortal man like you and me. He was a deacon of a small, upstart religion. Yet, he believed in who Jesus was so much that he was willing to lay down his life for his beliefs. Not only that; he was strong enough to ask that his perpetrators be forgiven while they were in the very process of stoning him. It takes a very mature Christian to forgive someone while they are still talking about you, lying on you, stealing from you, or sticking a knife in you. The wrongdoers do not apologize to Stephen. The wrongdoers do not show any remorse to Stephen. Yet, at the very moment Stephen is feeling pain, he asks God to not hold the perpetrators accountable. This means whether a person has been wronged in the past or if the wrongdoing is occurring right now, the perpetrators deserve forgiveness. This is an example we all need to follow concerning forgiveness.

Therefore, Lord, I repent for not forgiving properly. Teach me to be mindful of my unforgiving attitude toward others. Lord, please forgive me, and help me to do better.

Chapter 40

I REPENT FOR CELEBRATING SEX APPEAL, SEXUALITY, AND SEXINESS OUTSIDE OF MARRIAGE

This is a weighty message to deliver on a subject that affects all of us. Nobody is immune. Sex and sexuality are on display so much in our culture that to consider it an issue now is like talking about metastasized cancer. It has spread everywhere. It is on billboards, television shows, television commercials, movies, cell phones, and everywhere we live and breathe. Our culture uses sex to sell everything. Our culture encourages us to feel and look sexy. What does it mean to be sexy? Human beings have been disrespecting their bodies (often referred to as "flesh," in the Bible) since time began. To be truthful, it is not a new issue. The Bible discusses sex, harlots, virgins, eunuchs, fornication, homosexuality, and adultery. Sex is not a new creation.

By definition, sexy means to be appealing or desirable sexually. It means the way a person looks is exciting or arousing in a physical way. The word implies that there is something about a person that might make one want to have sex with him or her. The implications are different from saying someone is pretty, beautiful, or handsome. Sexy is a word that has connotations underneath the clothes a person is wearing. The use of sex is very pervasive. It is so pervasive that most everyone alive today does not even realize the trap Satan has set for us.

We are all involved.

> And even as they did not like to retain God in their knowledge, God gave them over to a debased mind, to do those things which are not fitting; being filled with all unrighteousness, sexual immorality, wickedness, covetousness, maliciousness; full of envy, murder, strife, deceit, evil-mindedness; they are whisperers, backbiters, haters of God, violent, proud, boasters, inventors of evil things, disobedient to parents, undiscerning, untrustworthy, unloving, unforgiving, unmerciful, who, knowing the righteousness judgement of God, that those who practice such things are deserving of death, not only do the same but also approve of those who practice them. (Romans 1:28–32 NKJV)

This text explains why this is such a weighty issue. We are all involved. Verse 32 points out that we not only participate in sexual immorality, but we also encourage participation from others. This has helped to drive our culture in the direction it has taken. We have all rewarded the behavior. We are accomplices. Every time we buy a ticket to see more of the same, we are encouraging the behavior. Every time we turn on a television show and watch something sexually provocative, which increases the ratings, which increases profits for the show, we are encouraging the behavior. Every time we wear clothing too tight, or too short, or too high, or too low for the public to see, we are encouraging the behavior.

Has anybody ever wondered why Hollywood actors have become accustomed to showing more and more flesh? We have failed to ask some critical questions. If you are such a good actor or actress, why do I need to see your naked or skimpily clad body? A good question for all married men and women in the entertainment industry is why do you want to be sexy to someone else besides your spouse? To anybody anywhere, in any profession, do you want others to lust to have an affair with you? Why do I have to see skimpily clad cheerleaders at a football game? Does their half-nakedness make the football player play better? Is there a prize for who can show the most flesh? Is there a prize they will earn after the game is over? Where did this thinking come from? If I go to a high school volleyball game, "Why are the female players in outfits that look like panties?" What is on display, athletic ability or female flesh? Why is it customary today to send our teenage daughters out on prom night dressed more provocatively than some hookers on the street? From country music to R&B, any ten songs in a row will most likely include at least two or three that are sexually explicit, short-term sexual encounters, or one-night stands, outside of marriage. One magazine chooses what it says is the sexiest man every year and displays him on the front cover. What does that mean? Surely, every woman in America should not gaze at this man and desire to have sex with him. Is that the intent? Should wives compare their husbands to him? Another magazine changes its format every year and incorporates a swimsuit issue, which has nothing to do with its regular coverage. A television show makes a contest out of stars dancing in what should be bedroom outfits. Why is this okay?

For years, men took advantage of women by verbally and sexually abusing them in our culture. Now, it seems as if Hollywood is trying to make sure women get their equal share of misuse by portraying female actresses using men for cheap sex. One show portrayed a couple having sex, and then the female actress asked the man for his name, after it is over. Men were portrayed as dogs, and now many women are portrayed as having the same attitude. In the age of the "Me Too Movement," both men and women have been guilty of allowing a culture to exist that says, "That's just the way it is around here." Society has supported it by continuing with our ticket purchases, silence, and applause. We are all guilty, Christians included. Sexuality has metastasized into our culture so much that many of us do not even blush anymore when we see it.

Idol Worship

> Therefore God also gave them up to uncleanness, in the lusts of their hearts, to dishonor their bodies among themselves, who exchanged the truth of God for the lie,

> and worshiped and served the creature rather than the Creator, who is blessed forever. Amen. (Romans 1:24–25 NKJV)

Many people have made idols of their bodies. Today some people have spent more time in the mirror, spa, or shopping for the right outfit to give them the right sexy look, than they have spent trying to learn about their Creator. Many people are more concerned about their sex appeal than their appeal to attract someone to Christ. People are celebrating their own bodies more than they are worshipping the Creator that made the body. Even grandmothers and grandfathers today are still trying to be sexy to the world at sixty and seventy years old.

Nothing Is New Under the Sun

> That which has been is what will be, that which is done is what will be done, and there is nothing new under the sun. Is there anything of which it may be said, "See this is new"? It has already been in ancient times before us. (Ecclesiastes 1:9–10 NKJV)

So, what has changed over time? What has changed in our American culture concerning our celebration of sex, sexuality, and sexiness outside of marriage? What has changed is the acceptance, and overindulgence, of our sex-driven society. The behavior is deemed normal. God instructs us to be in the world but not of the world. God instructs us to be holy and set apart.

> Blessed be the God and Father of our Lord Jesus Christ, who has blessed us with every spiritual blessing in the heavenly places in Christ, just as He chose us in Him before the foundation of the world, that we should be holy and without blame before Him in love, having predestined us to adoption as sons by Jesus Christ to Himself, according to the good pleasure of His will. (Ephesians 1:3–5 NKJV)

The Bible Sets the Standard

Two slightly different words are used in two different texts in the Torah of the Old Testament of the Bible.

> You shall not covet your neighbor's wife; and you shall not desire your neighbor's house, his field, his male servant, his female servant, his ox, his donkey, or anything that is your neighbor's. (Deuteronomy 5:21 NKJV)

> You shall not covet your neighbor's house; you shall not covet your neighbor's wife, nor his male servant, nor his female servant, nor his ox, nor his donkey, nor anything that is your neighbor's. (Exodus 20:17 NKJV)

The Hebrew word for covet in Deuteronomy is *avah*[26]. It means to wish for, desire, lust for, or long for. The Hebrew word for covet in Exodus is *chamad*[27]. It means to delight in, desire, pleasant, beauty, or lust. Leviticus 18:20 talks about discovering the nakedness and having sex with my neighbor's wife. These texts point out that as a child of God, no one should be looking at a member of the opposite sex in a way that causes him or her to desire that person sexually unless they are married. Therefore, why is our culture so entrenched in showing it off? Does this desire to show it off come from the Holy Spirit inside of us, or does the desire to show it off and be sexy come from our sinful flesh?

> But as it is written: "Eye has not seen, nor ear heard, nor have entered into the heart of man the things which God has prepared for those who love Him." But God has revealed them to us through His Spirit. For the Spirit searches all things, yes, the deep things of God. For what man knows the things of a man except the spirit of the man which is in him? Even so no one knows the things of God except the Spirit of God. Now we have received, not the spirit of the world, but the Spirit who is from God, that we might know the things that have been freely given to us by God. These things we also speak, not in

words which man's wisdom teaches but which the Holy Spirit teaches, comparing spiritual things with spiritual. But the natural man does not receive the things of the Spirit of God, for they are foolishness to him; nor can he know them, because they are spiritually discerned. (1 Corinthians 2:9–14 NKJV)

Here we see a discussion between mankind driven by the Holy Spirit and the natural man, which ignores and dismisses the Holy Spirit of God. Everyone must determine the drive in their life to lust after and covet the flesh of someone other than their spouse.

How Did We Get Here: Progression of the Risqué Nature of Our Culture

- On the beach—full bathing suits → bikinis, G-strings
- Female attire—always wear dresses → pants, miniskirts, hotpants, leggings
- Female tops—button-up shirts → tube tops, halter tops, sheer fabric see-throughs, deep plunging cleavages, low cut breasts exposing blouses and dresses
- On television—*Lassie, Bonanza,* and *Leave it to Beaver* → *Three's Company,*

The Bachelor, The Bachelorette, Sex and the City, Victoria's Secret Fashion Show, etcetera

- Perfume and cologne advertisements—selling the scent → always with sexual connotations
- Celebrity events—How classy and modest can I be? → How much can I show?

- Pornography—Not available → Had to be seen going into a XXX-rated movie or buy *Playboy* or *Hustler* magazine → on our cell phones every moment, every day
- Television—watershed programming at 9:00 p.m. → streaming, relaxed rules on what is considered appropriate, cursing anytime, suggestive commercials all day Super Bowl practical nudity: twerking, and gyrating

Open Our Eyes

No other sin demonstrates our American moral debacle more than this one. Mainly because we have allowed our flesh nature to become so comfortable with it. This comfort has caused us problems in many ways. Please remember that all sin has a harvest. All sin (a deviation from the will, way, and word of God) leads mankind to destruction. Some sins lead to a quick physical death. Some sins lead to a slower physical death. America's fixation on sex, sexuality, and sexiness is a slow death. The tentacles of our fixation impact many aspects of our life. Think of what impact this sin might have on marriages, divorces, child abuse, sex trafficking, impotence, arguments, rape, isolation, loneliness, and depression. We do not get a free pass on this sin. It may seem like it is not a big deal, but this sin is eating away at the fabric of God and family.

Beauty comes from God. Hollywood has made us create idols to worship under false pretenses. The flesh we see in the mirror and fall in love with is a gift from God. We did not create ourselves. A human being is only temporarily caring for the body they are packaged in. The face was designed by God. The soul and spirit are designed by God also.

Therefore, I repent for celebrating sex appeal, sexuality, and sexiness outside of marriage. Lord, please forgive me, and help me to do better.

Chapter 41

I REPENT FOR NOT BELIEVING IN THE POWER OF PRAYER

Imagine getting behind the controls of a military tank, a 747 airplane, or an eighteen-wheel transfer truck for the first time. Looking around over the dashboard, most people would be in awe. There would be an appreciation for your own smallness. All the buttons, gauges, switches, and lights would seem dazzling and overwhelming at the same time. While gazing out of the front windshield, the ground would seem so far away. Knowing that all this power is in your hands would tend to be very unnerving. Am I ready for this? What if I forget something? If I mess up, there will be grave danger! The awesomeness of the power in one's hands is arresting. But then imagine the contrast if a three-year-old child sat in the driver's seat. It would be all playtime. Touch this or touch that would be the goal. Pull any lever in the cockpit and just see what happens. There would be total disregard for the power and/or danger at hand. This view of a three-year-old may be the way some people consider prayer. The power of the tank, airplane, or eighteen-wheeler remains the same, but the perception of what it could do makes all the difference. An adult and a three-year-old child see it differently. Do most Christians understand the power God has given us through prayer? Some mention prayer casually. Others say they do not know how to pray. Others say they will pray, and do not. A few know how to call on God through prayer, believe in Him, and trust His power to make it happen.

Casual Prayer

When events happen, people say, "Keep us in prayer." "I'll be praying for you." "Pray for them." "Keep them in your prayers." "Our hearts and prayers are with you." Sometimes I wonder if people realize what has come out of their mouths. Prayer is mentioned. I often wonder if these prayers are actually prayed. How often are these statements made and not followed up on? Some people spend more time talking about prayer than they do praying. In keeping with an analogy of the first paragraph, this is like telling a platoon of soldiers fighting a war against an enemy, "I will bring you a military tank tomorrow." Then, the next day you deliver a toy tank, or a blow-up tank. In other words, a worthless, empty, exaggerated promise is made without delivering anything real and powerful that could help the soldiers win the battle. A promise is made to deliver, but nothing of substance is delivered. The very powerful real tank is never delivered, which could help the soldiers be victorious in their battle. A casual promise is made, as if the promise itself can help the soldiers win. The word prayer is used like a pat on the back instead of an awesome weapon of defense that can work miracles.

> Is any among you afflicted? let him pray. Is any merry? let him sing psalms. Is any sick among you? let him call for the elders of the church; and let them pray over him, anointing him with oil in the name of the Lord: And the prayer of faith shall save the sick, and the Lord shall raise him up; and if he have committed sins, they shall be forgiven him. Confess your faults one to another, and pray one for another, that ye may be healed. The effectual fervent prayer of a righteous man availeth much. Elias was a man subject to like passions as we are, and he prayed earnestly that it might not rain: and it rained not on the earth by the space of three years and six months. And he prayed again, and the heaven gave rain, and the earth brought forth her fruit. (James 5:13–18 KJV)

Prayer should not be mentioned casually. It is powerful. It can change people's lives when the prayer's line up with the will of God. Prayer can determine whether or not it will rain on the earth. Surely, prayer can change anything going on in the world today if God chose to change it.

I Do Not Know How to Pray

Samuel did not know how to pray and talk with God when he was called. Eli had to tell him. Samuel did not even recognize who God was. However, he spoke with God in a most profound way that we all can mimic to talk with God.

> And it came to pass at that time, when Eli was laid down in his place, and his eyes began to wax dim, that he could not see; And ere the lamp of God went out in the temple of the LORD, where the ark of God was, and Samuel was laid down to sleep; That the LORD called Samuel: and he answered, Here am I. And he ran unto Eli, and said, Here am I; for thou calledst me. And he said, I called not; lie down again. And he went and lay down. And the LORD called yet again, Samuel. And Samuel arose and went to Eli, and said, Here am I; for thou didst call me. And he answered, I called not, my son; lie down again. Now Samuel did not yet know the LORD, neither was the word of the LORD yet revealed unto him. And the LORD called Samuel again the third time. And he arose and went to Eli, and said, Here am I; for thou didst call me. And Eli perceived that the LORD had called the child. Therefore Eli said unto Samuel, Go, lie down: and it shall be, if he call thee, that thou shalt say, Speak, LORD; for thy servant heareth. So Samuel went and lay down in his place. And the LORD came, and stood, and called as at other times, Samuel, Samuel. Then Samuel answered, Speak; for thy servant heareth. (1 Samuel 3:2–10 KJV)

This is an awesome first prayer to God. Samuel just acknowledged that he was present to hear from God. Prayer is a conversation. Like you would have with any friend. It is how we are instructed to communicate with Him. No one must pray as if he or she is a professional, expert at praying. The eloquence of a prayer does not dictate the answer from God. The words we use do not have to convince God we are worthy. God already knows that we are not worthy, and He knows our hearts. Jesus gives us instructions on praying.

> And when thou prayest, thou shalt not be as the hypocrites are: for they love to pray standing in the synagogues and in the corners of the streets, that they may be seen of men. Verily I say unto you, They have their reward. But thou, when thou prayest, enter into thy closet, and when thou hast shut thy door, pray to thy Father which is in secret; and thy Father which seeth in secret shall reward thee openly. But when ye pray, use not vain repetitions, as the heathen do: for they think that they shall be heard for their much speaking. Be not ye therefore like unto them: for your Father knoweth what things ye have need of, before ye ask him. (Matthew 6:5–8 KJV)

It is plain to see in this text that God does not require anyone to pray like someone else. He does not require people to use big words. We all have access to Him. That is something that happened when Jesus died on the cross, and the veil on the temple was torn. Mankind no longer must go through a priest to communicate with God. We do not have to say special words to converse with our Lord. We just must be willing to humble ourselves and say the words. He is waiting.

Unleashing the Power

Prayer is a method to unleash the power of God. If one believes in His promises, then one must trust His word.

And when they had come to the multitude, a man came to Him, kneeling down to Him and saying, "Lord, have mercy on my son, for he is an epileptic and suffers severely; for he often falls into the fire and often into the water. So I brought him to Your disciples, but they could not cure him." Then Jesus answered and said, "O faithless and perverse generation, how long shall I be with you? How long shall I bear with you? Bring him here to Me." And Jesus rebuked the demon, and it came out of him; and the child was cured from that very hour. Then the disciples came to Jesus privately and said, "Why could we not cast it out?" So Jesus said to them, "Because of your unbelief; for assuredly, I say to you, if you have faith as a mustard seed, you will say to this mountain, 'Move from here to there', and it will move; and nothing will be impossible for you. However, this kind does not go out except by prayer and fasting." (Matthew 17:14–21 NKJV)

The disciples could not do it. But Jesus tells them if they want to have that kind of power, they must do more praying and fasting. Communicating with God is important. We should pray all the time. Not just when there is a catastrophe. The Bible says it should be a part of our Christian armor. praying always with all prayer and supplication in the Spirit, being watchful to this end with all perseverance and supplication for all the saints (Ephesians 6:18 NKJV).

Powerful Biblical Prayer Results

Who Prayed	Occurrence
Abraham; **Genesis 20:17–18**	Abimelech, the King of Gerar, his wife and his maidservants are restored in their ability to have children after a near violation of Abraham's wife, Sarah.

Joshua; Joshua 10:5–16	Joshua speaks to the Lord and asks for the sun to stand still during a battle with the Amorites. God delivers, and the sun and the moon stand still.
Gideon; Judges 6:24–40	Gideon hears from God about building an altar. Then, Gideon petitions God when a skirmish is started after he tears down an altar of Baal. God answers and provides direction.
Hannah; 1 Samuel 1:9–20	Hannah is sorrowful because she has not had children. She prays to God so fervently that she is believed to be drunk. God allows her to have a son.
Elijah; 1Kings 17–18	The prophet Elijah communes with God while he duels with King Ahab and the prophets of Baal. A drought is started and ended, and fire is called down from heaven.
Hezekiah; 2 Kings 20:1–7	Hezekiah, a strong believer in the God of Abraham, Isaac, and Jacob, prays for healing. He is healed, and God grants him fifteen more years.
Solomon; 2 Chronicles 6:1–7:3	Solomon prays after building the temple. Fire came down from heaven, and the glory of the Lord filled the temple.
Jesus; Matthew 26:36–46	Passion week is drawing to a close. Jesus is sorrowful about what He is about to go through. God the Father does not rescue Him but gives Him the strength to get through it.

Prayer is powerful. Respect it. Use it. Practice it daily, weekly, monthly, and annually. Practice praying constantly. Sometimes, people have taken it for granted and used it like we use greetings and salutations. It makes sense to be more deliberate when we pray.

Therefore, Lord, I repent for not respecting and believing in the power of prayer. Lord, please forgive me, and help me to do better.

Chapter 42

CONCLUSION: I REPENT BECAUSE GOD SAID SO

Arriving at this last chapter and having gone through the specific lessons, the question looms large: What will you do with it? The Bible is the sola scriptura. It is the ultimate source of knowledge. The purpose of this book has been to summarize some thoughts about specific topics that will encourage the reader to question, pray, study, and come face-to-face with the Holy Spirit about each subject. The Bible has given us many reasons to consider the repentance theme. The love of God and the love of our fellow brothers and sisters should always be what guides us. We cannot blame the state of America, our states, neighborhoods, or our families on others or bad churches. Each one of us has our own charge from God to fulfill His desire for our lives.

Now That You Have Read

It is with great humbleness that I have written this book. Every time I think about the word of God, I am taken aback, because He must use such imperfect people to deliver His message, myself included, of course. We are all sinners, saved by grace. All our righteousness is as filthy rags compared to the awesome holiness of Almighty God.

> There were present at that season some who told Him about the Galileans whose blood Pilate had mingled with

> their sacrifices. And Jesus answered and said to them, "Do you suppose that these Galileans were worse sinners than all other Galileans, because they suffered such things? I tell you no; but unless you repent you will all likewise perish. Or those eighteen on whom the tower in Siloam fell and killed them, do you think that they were worse sinners than all other men who dwelt in Jerusalem? I tell you, no; but unless you repent you will all likewise perish. (Luke 13:1–5 NKJV)

Therefore, I can readily say that everyone that has read this book will have a chapter or two or four or fifteen that needs to be personally, seriously dealt with, before God. Do not ignore the Holy Spirit if you were convicted as you read a chapter. God intended for you to be convicted because He knows you are committed. Make the changes necessary and get closer to God. The alternative is to know something is wrong between your relationship with Him and let it continue to separate you from Him.

Repentance Reasoning

On behalf of God.—He loves us. God loves every human being on the planet. He would prefer that we follow His guidelines so that we can have a safe, healthy, and joy-filled life. In fact, an analogy is made in the Bible comparing ninety-nine saints to one person that repents and comes to Christ. In Luke 15:7, it appears that heaven and all of glory is more excited about the repentant sinner than all the ninety-nine that have already repented. Every parent would love to see their child graduate and be able to live a good, comfortable, and peaceful life. God wants His children to do the same. His advantage is that He knows what it takes to make that happen. It takes paying attention to His word.

Matthew—two masters. The problem in America is that we have been carrying on as if it we are living in an open marriage. We have been living as if we, God, and the devil can enjoy a three-way relationship wherein we can hang out with God one day (especially on Sunday between eleven o'clock and one o'clock), and have free time with the devil anytime we feel like it. Unfortunately, just like in our human courting relationships, one party is jealous. Yes, we serve a jealous God. Why? Because God knows the devil is not out for our good. Unlike God, he makes false promises about things that will ultimately lead us to death. We cannot have this three-way. We cannot hang out with two opposing views (Matthew 6:24). If we try to, we will find ourselves leaning one way or the other. That is what America has done. We have been courting the devil pretty hard lately. So much so that we are beginning to despise the word of God.

Hebrews—sin willfully. A little child about two or three that does not know any better might get their first box of crayons, go into their room, put the coloring book down, and commence to coloring all types of animated figures on their bedroom wall. They would be peacefully oblivious to the disciplinary action that is coming. This is so much different than a seventeen-year-old, who is aware of the world, deciding to draw on their bedroom wall. In one case there is innocent ignorance, and in the other case there is willful, deliberate disobedience from what is expected. At seventeen, ignorance about using a crayon or permanent marker on a wall would not be acceptable. God is the same way with our sin (Hebrews 10:26–27). If it is done deliberately, then there is no longer any excuse that can atone for the deliberate behavior. The only thing left is to wait for the certain punishment that is coming.

1 John—confession. Denial will not work against God. We all know what we know. We know when the Holy Spirit is telling us, do not do this, or do not do that. Our problem, if we try to get away with our sin, is that God knows too. He knows our thoughts, both spoken and unspoken. Therefore, we are only fooling ourselves if we think we are getting away with something (1 John 1:8–9). America needs to repent and come clean with God. It is time to stop acting like the spoiled child that does something and then tries sneak away and hide it. God knows. He will forgive us if we tell the truth, go back to His word, and turn away from our unhealthy, detrimental, non-Christian behavior. We can be brand new in the eyes of God.

Isaiah—while he may be found. We have all seen it. Sometimes pent-up anger between two people is like a powder keg. Neither person has been talking. Both have been pouting. They had an opportunity to keep a level head and discuss the situation, but because they refused to talk and handle it, it will now be blown out of proportion. A similar situation is when someone has a bill that they could pay but because of procrastination the bill lingers on for months, adding interest and late fees with each passing day. These are just two examples of how not taking care of something in a timely manner can exacerbate the situation. Isaiah 55:6–7 implies the same thing. In our case, we need to repent now. Waiting may not be an option because when God decides we have gone too far, there may be no turning back. Right now, God is listening, but we cannot act like we can continue in our sinful ways.

Timing is important. At some point even God has proven that He will allow great calamity to come among even His chosen people. In Numbers 21, the complaining children of God endured fiery serpents that killed them when bitten until Moses mounted a brass serpent, on a pole, for the people to get relief. God decided the Egyptians had gone too far after the tenth plague, and the firstborn of Egypt died. God decided that His chosen nation had gone too far, and both Israel and Judah went into captivity. We need to seek the mercy of the Lord now, while it is still available.

James—if you know. We need to repent in America because to not do so is a sign of our own arrogance. We are thumbing our nose at God. We are telling God outright that His creation, His love, and His commands do not matter. We Christians all know better. Of course, everybody in America does not go to church, but many people in America have been going to church all their lives. Some people have been going to church twenty, thirty, forty, or even fifty years or more. There are enough churchgoers that know the gospel. Therefore, there should be more uproar about some of the things going on in our country. Instead, we are either remaining silent or participating in the calamity. This is a sin for those that know (James 4:16). God is patient, but He will not be bullied. He is aware that we know better but are simply choosing to be hardheaded and arrogant.

Love

This book is written because of what I firmly believe Jesus made clear in the Bible about the most important commandment in all the world. In Matthew 22:35–40, Jesus puts love on a pedestal.

> Then one of them, a lawyer, asked Him a question, testing Him, and saying, "Teacher, which is the great commandment in the law?" Jesus said to him, "You shall love the Lord your God with all you heart, with all your soul, and with all your mind. This is the first and great commandment. And the second is like it. You shall love your neighbor as yourself. On these two commandments hang all the Law and the Prophets." (Matthew 22:35–40 NKJV)

In other words, Jesus said nothing is more important than love. So, what led me to write *Why America Needs to Repent*? Well, the short answer is that I love my children, grandchildren, family, friends and acquaintances. I grew up in an era when parents always wanted their children to have a better life than they did. Most people are still hoping this is true today.

Based on what is happening in America today, if people want their children to live better, it is time for all Christians to do the most powerful thing we can do to keep God on our side.

Repent! Repent! Repent!

If you love your family and want to leave a better world for your children, nieces, and nephews, then we must do what our ancestors did. We must stop suffering from "couch disease" and get up and stand up for Christianity. The Bible says:

> Therefore, submit to God. Resist the devil and he will flee from you. Draw near to God and He will draw near to you. Cleanse your hands, you sinners; and purify your

> hearts, you double-minded. Lament and mourn and weep! Let your laughter be turned to mourning and your joy to gloom. Humble yourselves in the sight of the Lord, and He will lift you up. (James 4:7–10 NKJV)

We have not been doing enough resisting, but we can start now. We can make the devil flee. We are not living according to God's design. Putting our hope in the knowledge, skills, and abilities of humanity is not going to work. The politicians will not be able to fix our society. Wars and bombs will only generate more hate. The war on drugs has failed, and the money from the drug trade is leading to all kinds of other maladies. Hollywood and television are getting more risqué. Single-parent homes have become too many people's reality. Divorce is too readily accepted, and "shacking up" or living together before marriage seems to be the norm. Parents are killing and abusing their own children. Racism in America is still a daily topic, more than 150 years after the Civil War. Homosexuality has become the law of the land. Mass random shootings and mass incarceration are deemed "realities." This is the work of the devil and our sins.

There are many things in our society that the Bible speaks specifically against that have become commonplace. We are not shocked by the headlines anymore. It seems that some people feel that if it does not affect our family or our neighborhood, we can dismiss the things happening today by saying, "That's life!" Well, as Christians that believe Christ rose with all power, we cannot sit around and accept this as life. In fact, it is not life. The Bible says the wages of sin is death (Romans 6:23). So, what many have accepted as life is really death. Should we accept death? The apostles in the Bible demonstrate to us that we should not accept it. Fast death or a slow death because of our lifestyle is still death. Christians today must fearlessly speak up.

To all Americans, the word for today is, "Repent!" Jonah said to Nineveh, "Repent!" John the Baptist said to Jerusalem, "Repent!" Jesus said, "except ye repent, ye shall all likewise perish" (Luke 13:5). So, here I am loving my children, my grandchildren, my family, my church family, and all my fellow Christians. I say to all of us, repent, repent, repent. We do not have to accept the ways of this world. God has promised in His word:

> If my people, which are called by my name, shall humble themselves, and pray, and seek my face, and turn from their wicked ways; then will I hear from heaven and will forgive their sin, and heal their land. (2 Chronicles 7:14 NKJV)

The *turning* is repentance. Let us repent together and perhaps God will have mercy on us and heal our land. Perhaps He will see fit to forgive us like He did Nineveh. We cannot expect God to continue to "Bless America" if we continue to ignore His word, His will, and His way. Doing so is like expecting any parent to reward a child, not for doing good, but for acting out and rebelling. Who would continue to do that? God will not and cannot continue to reward this behavior either. He is a righteous God.

Hypocrisy and Bad Congregations

There have been bad scandals in some churches, but any group of people can have bad apples. I know you may have found your pastor to have failures and inconsistencies, but Jesus died for him too. Deacons and church officials may have proven to be hypocrites and act like devils, but so did the religious scribes and Pharisees in the Bible. I know "those church folk" are always putting people down, but they too should not be expected to have reached perfection. All of us are products of the world we are living in, and we all have the same challenges to overcome. We all must stop looking at everyone else and consider ourselves. Are we answering the call Jesus has on our life? Using others as an excuse for sinful behavior is like breaking the law and then telling the judge, "I do not deserve a penalty because other people are breaking the law too."

Make a difference and stand up in your congregation. While standing up, we must keep in mind not to become another bad example. We must use the word of God to make points clear at church meetings. We must present views in such a way that people will find themselves arguing against God instead of us arguing against each other.

Charge

In so many areas, the culture says yes, but the Bible says no. Let us repent together and perhaps God will see fit to forgive us. Paul told Timothy that we have a charge to keep.

> Those who are sinning rebuke in the presence of all, that the rest also may fear. I charge you before God and the Lord Jesus Christ and the elect angels that you observe these things without prejudice, doing nothing with partiality. Do not lay hands on anyone hastily, nor share in other people's sins; keep yourself pure. (1 Timothy 5:20–22 NKJV)

My fellow Americans, my fellow Christians, you have been duly charged and commissioned to repent and spread the word about repentance. Somehow or another we must leave a better world for our children and grandchildren. The only way to do that is by turning back to God. This book is in no way an unabridged synopsis of everything we need to repent for in America. This book is just to start the conversation. I pray that you have that conversation, one lesson at a time.

Jeremiah 16—This Is Why We Must Repent Now; We Do Not Want to Get Here!

> The word of the Lord also came to me, saying, "You shall not take a wife, nor shall you have sons or daughters in this place." For thus says the Lord concerning the sons and daughters who are born in this place, and concerning their mothers who bore them and their fathers who begot them in this land: "They shall die gruesome deaths; they shall not be lamented nor shall they be buried, but they shall be like refuse on the face of the earth. They shall be consumed by the sword and by famine, and their corpses shall be meat for the birds of heaven and for the beasts of the earth."

For thus says the Lord: "Do not enter the house of mourning, nor go to lament or bemoan them; for I have taken away My peace from this people," says the Lord, "lovingkindness and mercies. Both the great and the small shall die in this land. They shall not be buried; neither shall men lament for them, cut themselves, nor make themselves bald for them. Nor shall men break bread in mourning for them, to comfort them for the dead; nor shall men give the cup of consolation to drink for their father or their mother. Also you shall not go into the house of feasting to sit with them, to eat and drink."

For thus says the Lord of hosts, the God of Israel: "Behold, I will cause to cease from this place, before your eyes and in your days, the voice of mirth and the voice of gladness, the voice of the bridegroom and the voice of the bride.

"And it shall be, who you show this people all these words, and they say to you, why has the Lord pronounced all this great disaster against us? Or, what is our iniquity? Or, what is our sin that we have committed against the Lord our God? Then you shall say to them, because your fathers have forsaken Me, says the Lord; they have walked after other gods and have served them and worshipped them, and have forsaken Me and not kept My law. And you have done worse than your fathers, for behold, each one follows the dictates of his own evil heart, so that no one listens to Me. Therefore I will cast you out of this land into a land that you do not know, neither you nor your fathers; and there you shall serve other gods day and night, where I will not show you favor." (Jeremiah 16:1–13 NKJV)

This is a horrible state to be in. Verse 4 sounds like being in the middle of a pandemic when people are dying so fast that they cannot be buried. In verse 5 God says not to even cry for this people. Verse 13 ends with being in a situation wherein God is forgotten and other gods of all types will be worshipped. Whoa to America if this happens to us.

Serious

This is how serious this book is. There are forty chapters about forty different topics. As the author, I have put together what the Spirit has revealed to me as logical biblically based analogies. Now, as the reader, your challenge is to look at each subject, agree with the text and scenario given or find other biblical text that supports a different theory. It needs to be that serious. It cannot be ignored, or the reader would be ignoring God. Once you look at each chapter, you as the reader have three choices: (1) repent; (2) look in the mirror and flatly tell God no, and tell God you do not believe the Bible, and tell God that you do not believe that He had the ability to direct what went into the Bible; or (3) call a time out to do more personal study on your own, seeking God and His understanding. You owe it to yourself to find out what God said and what He meant about each subject. Decipher the Bible for yourself. Otherwise, you might as well stop faking it and just throw your Bible away.

While we are studying, we must allow God some leeway. He is the Creator, not us. Anything He takes the time to explain is at His discretion and out of His love. Abba, Father.

> Repent America
> For
> The Kingdom of God is at Hand!

Epilogue

At first, I wanted to give equal weight to each topic, but in the end, as I was going through, I realized that some topics could not be given any justice in just five or six pages. Also, there are some topics that, frankly, I believe in the eyes of God have been more traumatic than others to our American culture. Many of these lessons are just scratching the surface. A lot more needs to be delved into.

So, what does it all mean? Did this book accomplish the purpose? I certainly hope so. The idea was not for you to agree with every point made. The idea was to open the conversation and send you back to the Bible, not as a literature book, but as the Word of God. To all Americans, it is the people who make the country. As fellow American citizens, I encourage us all to take a more serious look at a man named Jesus. Every time something bad happens, we spend our time asking why. "What was the motive?" "Why did it happen?" "How did this happen here?" How did we get here?" Well, the short answer is there are only two powers in this world: God and Satan. Christians already know, "Why?" If God and His love is "not" behind it, then He is allowing Satan and his attacks and his diversions to cause corruption in our lives. That is why evil persists. There is only one answer. Consider Jesus. He is the only answer. *Repent, America, for the kingdom of God is at hand.*

> Do you not know that friendship with the world is enmity with God? Whoever therefore wants to be a friend of the world makes himself and enemy of God. Or do you think that the scripture says in vain, "The Spirit who dwells in us yearns jealously"? But He gives more grace. Therefore,

He says: "God resists the proud, but gives grace to the humble." Therefore submit to God. Resist the devil and he will flee from you. Draw near to God and He will draw near to you. Cleanse your hands, you sinners; and purify your hearts, you double-minded. (James 4:4–8 NKJV)

Love has been perfected among us in this: that we may have boldness in the day of judgment; because as He is, so are we in this world. There is no fear in love; but perfect love casts out fear, because fear involves torment. But he who fears has not been made perfect in love. (1 John 4:17–18 NKJV)

Beloved, I pray that you may prosper in all things and be in health, just as your soul prospers. (3 John 2 NKJV)

I had many things to write, but I do not wish to write to you with pen and ink; but I hope to see you shortly, and we shall speak face to face. Peace to you. Our friends greet you. Greet the friends by name. (3 John 13–14 NKJV)

GOD BLESS AMERICA

Reader's Prayer - Conclusion

> Dear Lord,
>
> I realize that none of us are deserving. Personally, I pray that my pride and stubbornness do not get in the way of my relationship with You. I pray that as I have reviewed these chapters that I have been honest with my own soul and weighed the message of your Spirit in my heart. I pray for wisdom, strength, and courage to respond to all that Your Spirit continues to teach me. Please help us all to keep growing, Lord.
>
> Amen.

Endnotes

Bible References

Earl D. Radmacher, ThD, Ronald B. Allen, ThD, H. Wayne House, ThD, JD, *New King James Version,* (Thomas Nelson Publishers, Nashville, 1997.)

1. "Five Solae of the Protestant Reformation," Wikipedia, contributors, Wikipedia, the Free Encyclopedia, November 11, 2019; https://en.wikipedia.org/w/index.php?title=Five_solae&oldid=925658859.
2. Christians in America, Pew Forum, Pew Research Center, "Religion and Public Life," "Religious Landscape Study"; copyright 2020.
3. "The New Strong's Expanded Exhaustive Concordance of the Bible," Thomas Nelson Publishers, Copyright 2001, Hebrew, reference 5162; page 184.
4. "The New Strong's Expanded Exhaustive Concordance of the Bible," Thomas Nelson Publishers, Copyright 2001, Hebrew, reference 5162; page 184.
5. "The New Strong's Expanded Exhaustive Concordance of the Bible," Thomas Nelson Publishers, Copyright 2001, Greek, reference 3340; page 162.
6. "The New Strong's Expanded Exhaustive Concordance of the Bible," Thomas Nelson Publishers, Copyright 2001, Greek, reference 3340; page 162.
7. "The Histomap," Four Thousand Years of World History, The Relative Power of Contemporary States, Nations and Empires, John B. Sparks, Histomap Inc, Cartography Associates, David Rumsey Collection.
8. The Constitution of the United States of America
9. According to AARP Bulletin (January – February 2016 issue), "The New Face of Hunger" According to a 2014 Gallop survey.
10. "Bridges out of Poverty," Ruby K. Payne, PhD, Philip E. DeVol, Terie Dreussi Smith, 2001; Aha! Process, Inc., pages 39–48.
11. "The Long History of Racism Against Asian Americans in the U.S.," Adrian De Leon, PBS.org/Newshour, This article republished from The Conversation under a Creative Commons license. April 9, 2020.

12 "The Long History of Racism Against Asian Americans in the U.S.," Adrian De Leon, PBS.org/Newshour, This article republished from The Conversation under a Creative Commons license. April 9, 2020.
13 "The New Strong's Expanded Exhaustive Concordance of the Bible," Thomas Nelson Publishers, Copyright 2001, Greek, pages: 10, 11, 284,357, 694, 933, 934, 954 (Some words in this chart with sexual connotations have been translated from the King James version to the New King James version of the Bible).
14 "Homophobia." *Merriam-Webster.com Dictionary*, Merriam-Webster, https://www.merriam-webster.com/dictionary/homophobia. Accessed 5/13/2020.
15 "Heterosexism." *Merriam-Webster.com Dictionary*, Merriam-Webster, https://www.merriam-webster.com/dictionary/homophobia. Accessed 5/13/2020.
16 "The New Strong's Expanded Exhaustive Concordance of the Bible," Thomas Nelson Publishers, Copyright 2001, Greek, reference 8441; page 296.
17 Elie Wiesel, (2006) *Night*, narrated by George Guidall, Available from www.RECORDEDBOOKS.COM.
18 "The New Strong's Expanded Exhaustive Concordance of the Bible," Thomas Nelson Publishers, Copyright 2001, Greek, reference 2054; page 102.
19 "The New Strong's Expanded Exhaustive Concordance of the Bible," Thomas Nelson Publishers, Copyright 2001, Hebrew, reference 3198; page 113.
20 "The New Strong's Expanded Exhaustive Concordance of the Bible," Thomas Nelson Publishers, Copyright 2001, Greek, reference 1260; page 66.
21 Ted Talk; Dr. Nadine Burke Harris; "*How Childhood Trauma Affects Health Across a Lifetime*"; ted.com/talks/nadine_burke_harris_how_childhood_trauma_affects_health_across_a_lifetime?language=en#t-2726; TEDMED 2014.
22 "Psychology Today"; National Institutes of Health – National Library of Medicine; U.S. Department of Health and Human Services: Administration for Children and Families and Office of Child Abuse and Neglect; Acts of Omission: An Overview of Child Neglect, by the United States Children's Bureau; psychologytoday.com/us/conditions/child-neglect; 2/22/19.
23 TIME Magazine; "*How to Stay Married*"; Belinda Luscombe; June 13, 2016; page 40.
24 "*The Five Love Languages*"; Gary Chapman; Northfield Publishing, Chicago IL, page 35.
25 "The New Strong's Expanded Exhaustive Concordance of the Bible"; Thomas Nelson Publishers; Copyright 2001; Hebrew, reference 7676; page 271.
26 "The New Strong's Expanded Exhaustive Concordance of the Bible"; Thomas Nelson Publishers; Copyright 2001; Hebrew, reference 183; page 7.
27 "The New Strong's Expanded Exhaustive Concordance of the Bible"; Thomas Nelson Publishers; Copyright 2001; Hebrew, reference 2530; page 90.

This book is written for all those who would like an answer for what is happening in the world today. When we hear of a mass shooting, we ask, "Why?" When we hear about the opioid epidemic, we ask, "Why?" When little boys and little girls are trafficked for sex in our society, we ask, "Why?" When we hear about rumors of wars, white supremacy, homosexuality, racism, large companies gouging or otherwise taking advantage of the public, identity theft, college admissions cheating, divorce and adultery being commonplace, we wonder, "Why?" We want to know the cause. We want to know what inspired someone to commit such evil against someone else.

Well, one cannot discover the answer to all these societal catastrophes by looking at the symptom. The answer can only be found if we analyze the cause. We must peel the onion back far enough to see what is underneath. The answer is sin. Christianity is not just a religion; it is a solution. America is far away from the love and blessings God has for us because we are so far away from how God has told us to behave and live. We are far away from Him, and we need to repent and turn back to God.

> For if we sin willfully after we have received the knowledge of the truth, there no longer remains a sacrifice for sins, but a certain fearful expectation of judgment, and fiery indignation which will devour the adversaries. Anyone who has rejected Moses' law dies without mercy on the testimony of two or three witnesses. Of how much worse punishment, do you suppose, will he be thought worthy who has trampled the Son of God underfoot, counted the blood of the covenant by which he was sanctified a common thing, and insulted the Spirit of grace? (Hebrews 10:26–29 NKJV)

- This book is for Christians who want to grow. This book is for Christians who are ready for meat instead of milk.—Pastor Dwane Massenburg

1.
"Pastor Massenburg, a 21St Century Prophetic Trumpet delivers a powerful and bold Clarion Call to God's People in this book that echoes the Voice of God through John ... crying in the Wilderness! This is a Must Read; that will lead 'To an About Face!' REPENT!"

Rev. Dr. Penni Sweetenburg-Lee, BA, MDiv,
On Kingdom Business Ministries
Founder & Senior Pastor

2.
Dwane Massenburg's book *Why America Needs to REPENT* is BOLD, BIBLICAL, RELEVANT, AND INSIGHTFUL. It challenges, convicts and charges Christians to be Christian. Its truth speaks to the heart and the reality of our faith.

Pastor Darrell Thomas
Union Baptist Church, Lexington, NC
Senior Pastor

3.
Why America Needs to Repent is a book that promotes people to repent for the Kingdom of God is at hand. It is written in a simplified format that is easy to read and understand with biblical references. It is inspiring to read about the author's personal testimonies about love for his God and love for his country.

Rev. Margaret Minnicks, BA, MACE, MDiv.
The Way of Life Spiritual Development Center
Founder and Director

4.
Pastor Massenburg's insight challenges and reminds us of our responsibility to actively engage in ministry opportunities to potentially improve the lives of those who are poor, disenfranchised, socially outcast, and suffering, oftentimes, due to situations that are no fault of their own. His down to earth enlightenment of the Fruits of the Spirit provides us not only with an understanding of what they are, he also reminds us of the powerful character traits we possess as Christian Believers. He meticulously illuminates our failures, as Christians, to effectively and purposely practice the principles of discipleship, and as a result, we not only owe God a sincere apology, we must also repent of our sinful neglect because we have not lived up to our Christian responsibilities as followers of Christ.

Rev. Dr. Tyron D. Williams, BA, MPA, MDiv. and DMin
Mount Olive Baptist Church, Wicomico Church, VA
Senior Pastor

5.
The believer has been given the Christian responsibility of serving this present age, while trusting the Holy Spirit to lead us in and through this challenging and ever-changing 21st century society. As people of God, we must repent for our lack of response to the Holy Spirit as He compels us to make society better through service and ministry. Our repentance is the first step, "call to action," for those followers of Jesus Christ who desire to carry out the mandate of making Christ known to the world.

The author makes it clear that penitence becomes the direct result of walking out the Fruit of the Spirit, as it becomes the thrust of the believers walk and witness. This is clearly a call to action designed to restore the Kingdom of God throughout the land as we see our sins, and as a response turn from them.

Rev. Dr. Charles R. Whitfield
Virginia Baptist Convention, President
First Baptist Church, Martinsville, VA
Senior Pastor

CPSIA information can be obtained
at www.ICGtesting.com
Printed in the USA
LVHW030911190322
713646LV00003B/3